PARTNERING AND
COLLABORATIVE WORKING
LAW AND INDUSTRY PRACTICE

PRACTICAL CONSTRUCTION GUIDES

Design and Build: Uses and Abuses
by Jeremy Hackett
(1998)

Professional Negligence in the
Construction Industry
by Neil F. Jones & Co.
(1998)

Construction Adjudication
by John L. Riches and Christopher Dancaster
(1999)

Construction Claims:
Current Practice and Case Management
by Jeremy Hackett
(2000)

PARTNERING AND COLLABORATIVE WORKING
LAW AND INDUSTRY PRACTICE

EDITED BY

DAVID JONES, DAVID SAVAGE
AND
RONA WESTGATE

LONDON HONG KONG
2003

Informa Professional
(a trading division of Informa (UK) Ltd)
Informa House
30–32 Mortimer Street
London W1W 7RE
professional.enquiries@informa.com

EAST ASIA
Informa Professional Publishing Ltd
Suite 1802, The Centrium
60 Wyndham Street
Central
Hong Kong
informa.asia@informa.com

© David Jones, David Savage, Rona Westgate
and contributors 2003

First published 2003

British Library Cataloguing in Publication Data
A catalogue record for this
book is available from the
British Library

ISBN 1-84311-248-5

Text set in 10/12pt Postscript Plantin by Tony Lansbury,
Tonbridge, Kent
Printed in Great Britain by Cromwell Press,
Trowbridge, Wiltshire

FOREWORD

His Honour Judge Humphrey LLoyd QC

I was both pleased and honoured to be invited to contribute the Foreword to this innovative, timely, informative and stimulating work.

The basic elements of partnering have been in practice for a long time even if, as Don Ward says in the first contribution in this book, they may not have been recognised as such by those involved. They are present wherever client, contractor, sub-contractors, suppliers and professional advisers work together as a team, generally because they have all been on a previous project and have been brought in at very early stages. However, in the historic past opportunities for such collaborations tended to arise in the public sector where special features were present – perhaps wartime, perhaps because the project was of national importance or was technically novel or highly complex. Cost control was not normally of key importance; it probably could not really be implemented without prejudicing the success of the project (which also explained why such ventures were not popular in some quarters). Partnering was present before any contract was negotiated – indeed there might never be a contract. Partnering was not confined to the relationship created or recognised by contract; it was about the formation and development of the necessary relationships – which in law might or might not be recognised or be recognisable.

The same applied where it was imperative to build or modify new plant, a new factory or a new production line. Clients who are satisfied turn to those upon whom they can rely. The oil and petro-chemical industries are good examples. But such opportunities occurred infrequently in the normal work of the building and engineering sectors of the construction industry. Nevertheless at least one highly successful national contractor made its reputation by demonstrating that team work was not just a catchy selling point or logo. Even where they operated in conditions of competitive tendering those contractors recognised how important it was to avoid disputes and arbitration and litigation. Their management was adept at avoiding or controlling confrontation. At times they lost money rather than risk the adverse publicity that might affect their reputation.

* A Judge of the Technology and Construction Court, High Court of Justice, London. Editor-in-Chief of *The International Construction Law Review*.

v

However, traditional forms of procurement where little or no account was taken of the contribution that could be made by early collaboration, and the nature of competitive tendering itself, made it difficult for both clients to get the best out of providers (to use a neutral term). This was seen, for example, over 20 years ago in the United States when partnering was developed by the US Army Corps of Engineers. It has since been used extensively throughout the Corps and, like many other pioneering leads from the Corps, adopted by others. It is now a key feature of the way in which the Corps operates, aiming to reduce conflict and to resolve problems by discussion and ADR. Whilst originally the focus was improving relationships with contractors, it found that the principles of partnering could be applied to others and to every project.

Don Ward lists the many reports which for decades have pointed out faults in attitude and structure in the construction industry in Great Britain and which recommended measures such as partnering as agents for real change. They had their counterparts in other countries, notably the United States, where there is all too often a confrontational approach to the execution of some construction projects. The advent of the New Engineering Contract (now in its improved form, the Engineering and Construction Contract – with a partnership option) and the pioneering work of its proponents, notably Dr Martin Barnes, led to a real interest in how things could be done better if the relationships were right. In this country the value of partnering was thus formally recognised in 1994 in the Latham report. Sir Michael Latham noted however that it required "openness between the parties, ready acceptance of new ideas, trust and perceived mutual benefit...". Only in that way might "partnering bring significant benefits by improving quality and timeliness of completion whilst reducing costs".

At the beginning some in the US Army Corps of Engineers thought, somewhat naively, that if provision was made in the partnering arrangements for dispute resolution that dispute would surely arise. Yet acceptance of the principles of partnering should mean that differences of opinions do occur even in the best of situations and there will be additional trouble if the participants do not plan for them. That will probably mean not tacking on a standard dispute resolution provision, or even a sophisticated one (where part of the solution seems to be the challenge to find a way through the maze). I do not suppose that I am alone in wondering why in 1996 Parliament thought that parties who had endorsed partnering should not be exempted from the obligation to adopt "statutory" adjudication as the next (and virtually compulsory) stop after discussion. The ethos of partnering arrangements almost certainly points in another direction. But, as I and others have recognised (on more than one occasion), the list of exemptions shows how very carefully they were considered, even if we have yet to discern the principles that must presumably have underlain the decisions.

It is now accepted that participants can benefit if an intermediary or adviser is on hand, preferably as part of the team. That person's role is to guide the parties' discussions and to assist them in the process of making decisions, but not to advise on or make specific decisions. Thus, whilst knowledge of construction and of its techniques and the law applicable within it may be of value, these attributes are secondary; what is essential is experience in negotiation, team building, and group dynamics.

Yet to many lawyers, perhaps especially to those not fully versed in partnering, a focus on "team building" must be accompanied by a real understanding – of the expectations of the other parties, of the performance required of other parties, of the performance that is really deliverable by other parties, of the areas where problems could occur, of the contractual and other legal documents that create and delimit the relationships between the parties, and, perhaps, sadly, but necessarily from the point of a lawyer, of the dispute avoidance and resolution procedures. The role of the lawyer has to be seen in that context. Ideally, just as there may only be one insurer, there should be only one lawyer to advise and guide the partners, rather than many lawyers each advising a separate party. That stage (which is considered in Chapter 5) has yet to be reached, at least as a matter of course. In the United States the concept of a single project lawyer – the project counsel – remains more of an idea than a reality. However, the treatment of that topic by David Jones (a partner and Global Head of Construction, Engineering & Projects, Hammonds) and Alan Crane provides a very good illustration of the range and quality of this book.

Partnering creates a variety of opportunities and concerns for the participants. This book thus has two main parts, although they are not separate, nor should they be considered separately. The book should be read as a whole. The first part is mainly directed to those in the construction industry itself. This comprises Chapters 1 to 4. The second part is about the law and for lawyers (Chapters 6 onwards).

I have referred to the authors of the first chapter, which is entitled: "The Story So Far". The authors are exceptionally well qualified to tell that story and to provide an insight into partnering from the viewpoint of those who have had to practise what others may only preach. The first section comes from Don Ward, the Chief Executive of Collaborating for the Built Environment and formerly Chief Executive of the Construction Industry Board, 1996–2001. He sets out the background to and history of the evolution of partnering in this country. He provides two helpful illustrations from projects for GlaxoWelcome and the Ministry of Defence. Alan Crane CBE is the Chairman of Rethinking Construction, the government task force which was established to oversee the implementation of the Egan reforms. As acting Chief Executive he also set up Construction Excellence. In 2001 we were both appointed by the Government to be members of the Architects Registration Board so I know the authority that he brings to a subject such as partnering. In the second section of Chapter 1, Alan Crane covers extensively and comprehensively "The management challenges of partnering". This is an exceptionally important subject since the ordinary management approaches require reconsideration and modification if partnering is to work. He explains that, provided that the basic understandings required of the nature of partnering are present and can be realised, it is possible to do so, just as it is possible to work with standard forms of contract, suitably but not radically altered.

In line with the different opportunities and concerns that partnering faces, Chapter 2 is written by Paul Wilkinson who is Head of Corporate Communications, BIW Technologies. He examines the technological challenges that are present or should be anticipated by the adoption of partnering, concentrating on information and communication technology (ICT) – in particular, internet-based technology. In principle partnering should enjoy the best of ICT. However, as the author points out, the construction industry has been both reliant on slow, paper-based processes to transmit project information, and markedly reluctant to share accurate and timely information which is critical for all participants. Thus attitudes have to change as true partnering requires a more collaborative approach and ICT can serve it well. The author provides numerous instances where collaboration technology has succeeded and what can (and cannot) be achieved by application service providers. He also covers very fully the main legal implications so here, as elsewhere, readers of one part of the book must also read the other part.

Armed with what could be done, the book takes the readers to look into the future in Chapter 3 with two contrasting views from Alan Crane and Richard Saxon CBE, a Director of Building Design Partnership, and a Vice-President of the Royal Institute of British Architects. Alan Crane covers the possibility of the "virtual company". Chapter 4 sets out a number of case studies that chart the experience of collaborative working from one of the earliest examples in 1996 to more recent ones.

Chapter 5 discusses the role of lawyers in partnering projects, which, as already noted, is by David Jones and Alan Crane. It provides a snapshot of the current position of lawyers who specialise in construction law. It is needed in order to mark the changes that would be required for a lawyer to serve the interests of partnering.

Procurement through partnering presents problems in the public sector, at least, given the legal framework that has to be observed. Chapter 6 – Procurement and Competition Issues – is written by three members of Hammonds: Richard Cooke, a partner, with Brona Heenan and Corin Ramsden, both solicitors. They discuss the main published industry construction contracts intended for use for partnering, including the first multi-party partnering contract PPC 2000 and the Non-binding Charter produced by the Joint Contracts Tribunal. A particularly innovative approach, which at the time of writing, is still in the consultation phase, is the approach adopted by the Movement for Innovation, which proposes the vehicle of a "virtual company". In addition the authors cover the extent to which partnering can be implemented where the project is subject to the European Union rules relating to public procurement and other measures intended to promote competitiveness which form part of our law.

In Chapter 7 Marina Milner, a solicitor with Hammonds, writes about "Contracting for Good Faith". This is a subject which generates a good deal of speculation. In the construction industry the question can be academic. Some contracts specifically require "good faith" from each party in the performance of their respective obligations, e.g., GC/Works/1. Any contract resulting from or directed to a partnering arrangement would nowadays surely contain a similar express provision. Other contracts contain equivalent obligations or are to be read to achieve the objectives thought to be attained by such an obligation. It is usually quite difficult to see what can be achieved by the addition of some implied obligation of good faith which would not be achieved by the use of the existing provisions, supplemented by inferences which bring out the parties' presumed intentions. It is not necessary (or it should not be necessary) to have recourse to Lord Hoffmann's restatement in *Investors Compensation Scheme* v. *West Bromwich Building Society* [1998] 1 WLR 896. The intentions of the participants in partnering arrangements should be transparently plain if the openness and trust that are indispensable are present. There should be no room for misunderstanding, still less misrepresentations. The record (which will include the charter or the like) will be plain: "By their work you will know them." Of course the language used in it or in some of the contractual documentation may not be that which would be appropriate in a traditional legal relationship. Judged by the standards of the law, there may be ambiguity or a lack of clarity. Hence dispute resolution should be entrusted to people who understand partnering. That will include lawyers with requisite the knowledge and background; it ought even to include those judges and arbitrators who are attuned by experience to the world of partnering.

Some years ago I had to consider a somewhat rudimentary partnering arrangement in *Birse Construction Ltd* v. *St Davids Ltd* [1999] 4 BLR 194. I am sorry if I disappoint anybody who thought that I might take advantage of this occasion to debate further some of the points that arose in that case or in subsequent commentaries on it. However, a judge cannot discuss (outside court) any decision that the judge has made or the decisions of other judges. Even allowing for the downturn in arbitration and litigation (in the latter case partly due to the introduction of adjudication) the paucity of cases bearing on partnering is perhaps surprising, at least at first sight. The very nature of partnering must be the main factor, as Alan Crane points out in the course of his excellent contribution (in the second section of Chapter 1). As described to me by Lester Edelman, an American lawyer with long experience of partnering: "The partnering process does not change the contract terms – what it changes is the mind-set or the attitude of the participants so that the objective becomes one of co-operation, openness and trust." If those attributes are expressed as or can be found as contractual obligations then is there still a practical need for some super-added obligation of good faith?

Chapter 8 looks at three specific areas covered by innovative contractual arrangements. The authors are Jonathan Hosie, Tara Corcoran and Diana Harvey, of Hammonds. They look at a number of the standard forms that have been developed for partnering: *PPC 2000*; the *NHS LIFT Strategic Partnering Agreement*; the *Defence Estates' Prime Contract (Regional and Stand Alone Capital Projects)*; the *Be Collaborative Contract*; the *M4i Virtual Company Model Form*; the *ECC Partnering Option X12*; and *JCT Partnering Charter for a Single Project*. With the possible exception of the ECC Form, none can strictly be called a standard form as they are not established (one at least is still experimental) and experience is limited. The authors rightly point out that in examining any standard form for use in partnering the question should be asked: was it devised to regulate the parties' behaviour (like a familiar standard form) or is it there to support the parties' own partnering arrangements. This approach then permeates the authors' consideration of the three main issues of time, cost and quality management. These themes follow on from the first part of the book. Their thoughtful and detailed analysis of each of the forms selected is applicable to other forms of contract so this chapter, in common with many others, has considerable general value. The themes follow up the first part of the book by focusing on time, cost and quality management.

Chapter 9 is by Mike Butler, solicitor with Hammonds. It is an extensive examination of the impact of the many intellectual property laws on the allocation of rights resulting from collaborative design working. It covers many points which are not confined to the question of partnering.

Chapter 10 is by another member of Hammonds, Katie Graham. Its title "Insurance in a Changing Industry" shows that, like the previous chapter, the subject is of general interest. It could well have been included in the first part. Katie Graham rightly draws attention to the seminal article by Robert J. Smith on "Risk Identification and Allocation: Saving Money by Improving Contracts and Contracting Parties" [1995] ICLR 40 in which he argues that contractual misallocation of risk is the leading cause of construction disputes in the United States. Certainly misallocation leads to people attempting to avoid the consequences of their contract. It also leads to insurers of the risk trying to reallocate to the party whose insurers they consider to belong to those who should have borne the risk.

The final chapter, by Linda Grayson and Diana Harvey, both solicitors with Hammonds, is about "Resolution of Disputes". Second only to the allocation of risk, this is perhaps the most difficult area for someone to grasp who is not familiar with the methodology of partnering. The authors wisely approach it by looking at the customary methods of dispute resolution, which are based on an adversarial or confrontational approach that negates the essence of partnering and is an anathema to it. (Such approaches have to be provided for in contracts that presuppose their use.) By adroitly highlighting the deficiencies in such methods for use in partnering they fortify the case for really more suitable techniques which they have earlier identified in their thoughtful discussion of

PPC 2000, the *ECC Partnering Option X12*, the *Be Collaborative Contract*, the *M4i Virtual Company Model Form* and the *JCT Partnering Charter*. This chapter is a fitting culmination to an extraordinarily interesting book. Like every earlier contribution it is informed and thought provoking and, but for the common thread that weaves its way through and links each chapter, might have stood by itself as a paper worthy of publication.

I therefore found this book full and, in many places, fascinating, particularly in the first group of chapters. Readers should be very grateful to those at Hammonds and their principal collaborators in industry both for their remarkable work but also in securing so many knowledgeable people. The book combines the virtues of being a topical analysis of the practical issues that need to be resolved to make partnering work and a perceptive look into the future. It is of real value now and, I trust, will remain of value for the immediate future.

Humphrey LLoyd

PREFACE

The idea for this book came about one wet day last October when we were debating internally the structure of a seminar to be delivered on partnering in the construction industry. As lawyers in Hammonds' Construction, Engineering & Projects Department we were aware of the wide experience our team had of documenting new forms of construction procurement, from partnering agreements, strategic alliances, and prime contracts to framework agreements amongst others. We also had good relationships with a number of leading innovators within the construction industry, in particular with Alan Crane, who is our industry special adviser.

The idea behind producing this book was to try to bridge the gap between a purely legal view of issues raised by collaborative arrangements in the industry, and the practical implications and history of adopting such arrangements from an industry perspective, as expressed by those closely involved in such projects to-date.

Rather than attempting to be simply a comprehensive but academic legal treatise, the book seeks to identify particular key industry and legal issues from a practical point of view, addresses how these issues are dealt with in the existing partnering standard form contracts, and provides an industry and historic perspective on experience to date. The book is not therefore addressed exclusively to either lawyers or construction professionals, but to anyone interested in understanding the history and practicalities of working with partnering and collaborative contracts in the field of construction procurement.

As editors, we are greatly indebted to the many people who have helped make our original idea come alive in a relatively short period. In particular we wish to thank the busy and senior figures from within the industry who agreed so willingly to contribute to the book, the stimulating nature of their contributions, and for working to short writing deadlines. We also wish to thank all the contributing lawyers from Hammonds' Construction, Engineering & Projects Department for their enthusiastic participation, and our clients for instructing us on a number of partnering and collaborative arrangements over the years – without those instructions this book might never have been written.

Finally, although the basic elements of partnering can be said to have been in practice for many years within certain parts of the industry, there is also much of the industry for which it remains untested and novel. We hope that this book can make a small contribution to informing future developments, and that readers will find it both practical and a useful reference tool.

David Jones, David Savage & Rona Westgate
19 August 2003

CONTENTS

AUTHORS' BIOGRAPHIES

DAVID M JONES

David Jones is the global head of Hammonds' Construction, Engineering & Projects Department. He is based in Hammonds' London office. With over 65 specialist construction, engineering and project lawyers, Hammonds has one the largest and most experienced legal teams in the UK, with other offices throughout Europe and in Hong Kong.

David has extensive experience of all aspects of legal practice in the construction and engineering industries. He has undertaken substantial construction and engineering litigation/arbitration disputes both nationally and internationally. He has also drafted a number of specialist contracts including in particular the development of Prime Contracting for the Ministry of Defence with its integrated team approach and its collaborative working philosophy. He has also worked on a number of major projects around the world.

DAVID J SAVAGE

David Savage is a London based partner in the Hammonds' Construction, Engineering & Projects Department.

Formerly in practice at the Construction Bar, David joined Hammonds in 1997. He has extensive experience of major litigation and arbitration proceedings, and has dealt with disputes and differences arising out of some of the world's largest construction and engineering projects. He has a particular specialisation in the transport sector generally, and railways in particular.

In non-contentious matters, David prepares documentation for projects, including amending standard forms, drafting bespoke contracts, and reviews all forms of construction documentation including bonds, warranties and guarantees.

He is also a specialist on the legal implications of the use of internet technologies and E-business in the construction sector, and a contributing author to a leading textbook on law and E-commerce.

RONA WESTGATE

Rona Westgate is the senior Professional Support Lawyer for Hammonds' Construction, Engineering & Projects Department.

She was formerly in private practice as a specialist construction lawyer, and writes extensively on construction law matters, both for training of Hammonds' lawyers and for client and marketing publications.

JONATHAN HOSIE

Jonathan Hosie is a partner in Hammonds' Construction, Engineering & Projects Department and is Hammonds' main representative within Be. Since 1997 he has been actively involved in the development of partnering, and has chaired a number of working groups involved in mapping partnering processes and techniques onto a commercial framework. Jonathan also serves as an external tutor on the Masters' course in construction law and arbitration at King's College, London and is currently chairing a JCT working group on the drafting of a new form of professional appointment for use in the public sector. Jonathan led the team advising the integrated project team on the UK's first Prime Contract in 2000, the £23m logistics centre at Andover.

KATIE GRAHAM

Katie Graham is a solicitor in Hammonds' Construction, Engineering & Projects Department. She is an experienced practitioner in all areas of construction law. She has acted on large litigation and arbitration matters (both domestic and international) and has drafted and advised on contracts and methods of procurement for a number of substantial projects in the UK and overseas. She has a particular interest in insurance related issues having a background in insurance litigation and co-authored the insurance module of the IBC written course in construction law. Katie also contributes regularly to a number of construction industry publications.

MARINA MILNER

Marina Milner is a solicitor in Hammonds' Construction, Engineering & Projects Department. She has carried out work on projects sponsored under the PFI, as well as large and smaller scale developments. She is a non-contentious lawyer and has drafted construction contracts as well as consultants appointments and warranties. She also worked as a lecturer law at the University of East Anglia from 1994 to 2000, where she taught and published in a variety of subjects.

RICHARD COOKE

Richard Cooke is a London based partner of Hammonds' Construction, Engineering & Projects Department.

He specialises in construction and engineering and oil/gas with an emphasis on infrastructure, major projects and disputes. His practice covers contentious work, including disputes management, adjudication, ADR, mediation, expert determination, arbitration and litigation, as well as non-contentious drafting and project advice. His experience covers civil, structural, mechanical and electrical and process engineering; transport; energy; utility, mining, and petrochemical sectors as well as commercial building and construction products.

PAUL WILKINSON PhD BA MIPR DipPR (CAM)

Paul Wilkinson is head of corporate communications of BIW Technologies (BIW), Europe's leading provider of web-based collaboration technologies to the construction and property sectors.

He has extensive experience of the professional services sector of the UK construction industry, having joined the marketing department of consulting engineer Halcrow in 1987, while completing a PhD in criminology at the London School of Economics (1991). After seven years at Halcrow, Paul spent four years at Tarmac Professional Services (now part of Carillion) before establishing an independent consultancy. His clients included HBG Construction, the Construction Best Practice Programme, the Building Centre Trust and BIW - who he joined in 2000. At BIW he has written extensively on collaboration technologies and related e-business issues.

ALAN CRANE, CHAIRMAN OF RETHINKING CONSTRUCTION

Alan Crane is Hammonds' Industry Special Adviser.

He has 38 years' construction experience including posts as CEO of major contractors. He acts as a Construction Consultant and is non executive director to a number of companies.

He is also Chair of Rethinking Construction, and a member of the Strategic Forum for Construction. He was awarded a CBE in the New Years Honours list for services to the construction industry.

MIKE BUTLER

Mike Butler is a solicitor in the Hammonds' Commercial and Intellectual Property Department working out of Hammonds' London office.

Mike advises on a wide range of legal and commercial issues for both suppliers and users of information technology. He advises one of the world's leading hardware manufacturers together with numerous e-business suppliers and consultants. He also regularly acts for companies within the WPP Group, the world's leading advertising organisation, which is a client of Hammonds.

Prior to joining Hammonds, Mike was in-house counsel at Sun Microsystems in the UK. He speaks regularly at conferences (most recently on legal issues relating to internal communications) and is also a contributor to Hammonds legal textbook on E-commerce and Internet law.

LINDA GRAYSON

Linda Grayson is a solicitor in the Hammonds' Construction, Engineering & Projects Department working out of Hammonds' Leeds office. She specialises in dispute resolution.

DIANA HARVEY

Diana Harvey is a know-how lawyer working in the Construction, Engineering & Projects Department based in London.

Prior to joining Hammonds Diana worked as a research assistant for a member of the bar at a set of specialist construction chambers and in private practice. She writes and edits publications on a wide range of construction topics both for internal use at Hammonds and for marketing purposes.

CORIN RAMSDEN

Corin Ramsden is a solicitor in the Construction, Engineering & Projects Department at Hammonds based in Leeds. As a specialist construction lawyer Corin has advised on a number of disputes and on the use of standard from contracts within the construction and engineering industries.

Over the last few years Corin has been involved in advising both the public and private sector on infrastructure projects on various issues, including in particular issues relating to public procurement and state aid. Corin has also spent time working in the Hammonds' Brussels office.

BRONA HEENAN

Bróna Heenan joined Hammonds' Brussels office in January 1999. She graduated from Trinity College, Dublin with a law degree in 1989 and obtained an LLM in European Law at Kings College, London in 1998. Her areas of practice are competition law and public procurement. As regards the latter, she has advised a wide range of public sector bodies and utilities on the application of the procurement rules, particularly in the light of the UK's Private Finance Initiative and other Public Private Partnerships. She has also advised numerous private companies on the application of the remedies available under the procurement rules.

TARA CORCORAN

Tara Corcoran is a solicitor in the Construction, Engineering & Projects Department of Hammonds, based in London. Tara specialises in both non-contentious construction and projects work. In addition to advising clients on the use of the standard form construction contracts she has developed bespoke and innovative partnering arrangements involving the supply chain of a large public sector client. In her work in the field of PFI and PPP projects she has extensive experience of advising both the public and private sectors on all aspects of the project and is currently heavily involved in the developing NHS LIFT initiative.

DON WARD

Don Ward is Chief Executive of Collaborating for the Built Environment, known as Be, the leading UK supply chain body for property and construction, and a Director of CWC Ltd, the Collaborative Working Centre of Be.

He was formerly Chief Executive of the Construction Industry Board for its five-year life from 1996-2001.

RICHARD G. SAXON, CBE, B.ARCH, MCD, RIBA, MCIM, FRSA

Richard Saxon is a Director and former chairman of Building Design Partnership, Europe's largest architect/designer/engineer. He is also Chairman of Be, short for Collaborating for the Built Environment, a 100 firm body crossing the supply chain from clients to manufacturers. Be works to improve the benefit and decrease the cost of building, through research and training. As a vice-president of the RIBA, Richard leads the Institute's support for practices. He is also a founder and past-president of the British Council for Offices.

TONY BROWN

Tony Brown is the Partner responsible for Bucknall Austin's Prime Contracting division (Prime Solutions). Based at their Bristol office, Tony and his team established their innovative consultant led 'virtual company' approach, which has proven so successful on the Andover North Site Redevelopment Prime Contract for the Defence Logistics Organisation and Defence Estates.

Tony was the Project Director for this award-winning project, which was the first Prime Contract to be let by MOD and the first to be completed. The Project is held as an exemplar for Prime Contracting by Defence Estates and received the BIFM PFI/PPP Project of the Year Award in 2002.

CHARLES BRIEN

Charles Brien is the senior commercial lawyer with Scottish Water. He has been heavily involved with the innovative procurement strategy adopted by Scottish Water for the delivery of its capital investment programme.

Charles has been a solicitor in Scotland for more than twenty years, is qualified in England, a Fellow of the Chartered Institute of Arbitrators and a recently graduated LL.M. at the University of Strathclyde. He has gained extensive experience of the legal aspects of the construction and engineering industries while working for Livingston Development Corporation, both East and West of Scotland Water and Scottish Water.

TABLE OF CASES

TABLE OF LEGISLATION

TABLE OF STANDARD FORMS

TABLE OF INDUSTRY REPORTS

CHAPTER 1

THE STORY SO FAR

Don Ward and Alan Crane, CBE[1]

THE HISTORY OF PARTNERING

CONTRIBUTED BY DON WARD

"There is nothing new in partnering, it's how we have always done things in our firm."

This is a frequently expressed view amongst construction industry practitioners. There is one common variation on this theme: "it's how we always did things in our firm in the 1960s."

These statements are undoubtedly founded on some element of truth, as we shall see, but only because they reveal a fundamental problem – every person has a different understanding of what they mean by partnering. So this review of the history inevitably intertwines consideration of the definition of partnering with the history of the elements that contribute to that definition. It also focuses on key reports and guidance documents as the routemap to that history.

Partnering has long been advocated as a procurement strategy to help cure some of the problems of the construction industry. These problems have been well documented and include such matters as fragmentation by using a sequential procurement process, lack of integration, and its adversarial culture. The belief of those promoting partnering is and was that the adoption of a more joined-up and collaborative approach would result in the achievement of a continuous and sustained improvement in construction procurement, which in turn would result in cost savings and eliminate waste and poor quality.

1. This chapter provides insights into the partnering process by two individuals who have had a particularly close involvement in the promotion of partnering as one of the solutions to the construction industry's problems. In the first section of the chapter, Don Ward provides an overview on the history of partnering and will trace how this form of procurement has been brought across from other industries into construction.

  Don is the Chief Executive of Collaborating for the Built Environment, known as Be, the leading UK supply chain body for property and construction and a Director of CWC Ltd, the Collaborative Working Centre of Be. He was formerly Chief Executive of the Construction Industry Board for its five-year life from 1996-2001.

  In the second section of the chapter, Alan Crane, CBE looks at some of the challenges that are presented to contract management if the parties opt to take partnering on board. Alan is the Chair of Rethinking Construction and a member of the Strategic Forum for Construction.

2 Partnering and Collaborative Working

Although the main impetus for change in the UK context is considered to be the Latham Report (and that is also the main starting point for this chapter), that is not to ignore the numerous reports about partnering that pre-date Latham – Emmerson (1962), Bowley (1963), Banwell (1964), Higgins & Jessop (1965), Bishop (1972), NEDO (1978), Munday (1979), Ball (1980), Allen (1983), NEDO 1983.

Many of these reports which comment on the need to improve costs, time, quality and fitness for the end user are listed in Appendix 4 of the National Audit Office Report *Modernising Construction*, 11 January 2001, which is referred to below. These reports were driven by client concerns about the impact on their commercial performance by the inefficiencies and waste that were so prevalent in the construction industry.

Common themes running throughout these reports are the need to improve trust, foster a collaborative culture, and eliminate adversarial relationships. These aims provide many challenges to the management of organisations, not only in terms of developing trust between business organisations, but also at the level of individual behaviour on a project. Some of these are discussed in the second part of this chapter.

In terms of setting the background context, it is also important to understand that partnering, per se, is not construction, or construction industry, specific. Several other industries in the UK adopted partnering techniques before construction spotted the opportunity, notably the oil and gas sector (see the discussion about CRINE below), the car manufacturing industry (including Rover) and the retail industry (J. Sainsbury, Dixons, BAA). The experience in these other business sectors is not commented on in detail in this book, but these industries' experiences have influenced the adoption of partnering techniques in the construction industry, and have provided lessons for construction to learn so as to avoid some of the early pitfalls they experienced. These industries also played a key role in transferring partnering practices from their core businesses to the procurement of built facilities to enable and enhance those core businesses. For example, supermarket retailers were some of the earliest clients of the construction industry to adopt partnering techniques, and have been amongst the most successful in their implementation.

No particular distinction is made here between "project specific" partnering and "strategic" partnering (or "alliancing") in this historical section. Project specific partnering, as its name suggests, is about partnering on individual projects. Strategic partnering is about long-term relations between parties who are prepared to work together over long periods of time. Strategic partnering requires a more thorough and detailed knowledge and understanding of each parties' business, so maximising the effectiveness of each other's business. However, it should be noted that strategic partnering is the option preferred by the *Accelerating Change* Report referred to below, under the guise of supply chain integration.

Latham

The widespread growth of interest in partnering in the construction industry can be traced to the 1994 Latham Report *Constructing the Team*:

"Partnering includes the concepts of teamwork between supplier and client, and of total continuous improvement. It requires openness between the parties, ready acceptance of new ideas, trust and perceived mutual benefit .... We are confident that partnering can bring significant benefits by improving quality and timeliness of completion whilst reducing costs."

Sir Michael Latham, Constructing the Team, 1994, quoting
the Chartered Institute of Purchasing and Supply

"Partnering arrangements are also beneficial between firms... Such arrangements should have the principal objective of improving performance and reducing costs for clients. They should not become "cosy". The construction process exists to satisfy the client. Good relationships based on mutual trust benefit clients."

Sir Michael Latham, Constructing the Team, 1994.

Following the Latham Report, the Construction Industry Board ("CIB") was set up to oversee the implementation of Latham's 53 recommendations and to deliver his headline target that a 30% real cost saving ought to be achievable within five years. In July 1995 the Construction Industry Board set up a working group at the request of the then Construction Clients Forum, which a year later published a report seeking to develop and illustrate Latham's views of partnering whilst setting out to quash a few myths about the subject.

In 1996 the CIB Report *Partnering in the Team* defined partnering as follows (emphasis added):

"Partnering is a *structured* management approach to facilitate teamworking across contractual boundaries. Its fundamental components are *formalised* mutual objectives, *agreed problem* resolution methods, and an *active search* for continuous *measurable* improvements."

It is suggested that the emphasised principles distinguish true partnering from other forms of co-operative working practices. These involve levels of management rigour that have rarely, if ever, been evident in the construction industry – at least until the 1990s.

The CIB Report went on to explain that partnering:

"...should not be confused with other good project management practice, or with long-standing relationships, negotiated contracts or preferred supplier arrangements, all of which lack the structure and objective measures that must support a partnering relationship."

It is the history of these clear distinctions that are considered below.

It follows from the above that there is no need to go any further back than the late 1980s in tracing the history of partnering as a formalised approach in the UK construction industry. One could have chosen to quote Alfred

Bossom, a practising architect between the wars, as some have done. Equally, as Latham did in his interim Report *Trust and Money*, one could have quoted the plethora of government-led industry reports after the Second World War, such as Emmerson (1962) and Banwell (1964). But the explosion of interest in the application of partnering to the construction industry can be traced to the late 1980s / early 1990s, following major successes in other industries and other countries.

Lean thinking

Much of modern partnering can be traced to the revolution in manufacturing led by the Japanese which became evident once their products were allowed into Western markets. In 1990, Womack, Jones & Roos brilliantly chronicled the benefits of lean production in the automotive industry as epitomised by the Toyota Production System compared with the old (Western) mass production systems in their seminal work, *The Machine that Changed the World*. This described how Toyota spread lean production through its supply base in the 1970s and its distribution and sales operations in the 1980s.

Jones and Womack's second book on the subject, *Lean Thinking*, made generic the approach, whose starting point was to clearly define value from the end customer's perspective, to then target all the wasteful activities throughout the entire chain of firms involved in jointly delivering the product (the 'lean enterprise'), hence allowing better value to flow.

CRINE – Cost Reduction Initiative for the New Era

The first UK business sector, with major similarities to the construction sector, to embrace partnering was the offshore oil and gas sector. In the late 1980s this sector was faced with an industry threatening crisis – the UK continental shelf had become uneconomic to exploit unless major cost savings (30% or more) in the total cost of drilling could be delivered.

These pressures for the background to the evolution of the CRINE initiative in 1993. This was led by oil company project managers and concluded that changes needed to be made in the way the industry interacted on the broadest basis (across oil companies, government, contractors and suppliers) to increase mutual trust and confidence and move away from adversarial relationships. Amongst the most startling achievements was that of the BP Andrew oil field development and exploitation.

ACTIVE – Achieving Competitiveness through Innovation and Value Engineering

ACTIVE was launched in June 1996 and ran for five years with the support of the DTI and the European Construction Institute (ECI). It was driven by a desire by Government for the UK to be the preferred base for investment by international companies within the process plant industry where there is a choice of location within Europe. Partnering was once again seen as the key to success, and a target of reducing total project costs by 30% was set.

Reading Construction Forum

In 1995 the Reading Construction Forum (RCF) published *Trusting the Team – the Best Practice Guide to Partnering in Construction* by Professor John Bennett and Dr Sarah Jayes of Reading University. This remains arguably the best introductory text on the subject, and drew the key distinction between project partnering (as applied to one-off schemes or teams) and strategic partnering (as applied to a series of projects, and often also referred to as "alliancing" or "strategic alliancing"). RCF suggested typical cost savings from adoption of partnering principles of between 2 and 10%, and as much as 30% in some cases.

The case studies of successful strategic partnering, from both the UK and USA, were drawn mostly from the civil engineering, utilities or process plant sectors, where typically the risks were higher, or from the retail sector, where some repeat clients had begun to seek to transfer their knowledge of supply chain management in their core businesses to their construction functions.

In 1998 the RCF's follow-up Report *The Seven Pillars of Partnering* suggested the evolution of a third generation of partnering, in which rather than project or repeat-client focused,

"modernised construction firms will use co-operation throughout their supply chains to build up efficient 'virtual organisations' that respond to and shape rapidly changing markets."

Early research suggested cost savings of 50% or more could be achieved, and construction times could be reduced by 80% or more. Now the case studies began to feature buildings projects more frequently, and it was around this time that partnering began to mature as a technique amongst the leading edge firms and clients of the industry, rather than just the very large repeat procurers of construction (see Box 1).

BOX 1

GlaxoWellcome's "Fusion" Projects

In the mid-late 1990s Kevin Thomas of GlaxoWellcome pioneered Fusion, "an ethical and equitable approach to working that develops a rewarding environment; creating one team, where people can contribute to their full potential and individual and corporate needs are satisfied". Three projects with a total value of about £50m were delivered to the principles of Fairness, Unity, Seamless, Initiative, Openness, and No blame.

The Fusion website (*www.fusion-approach.com*) describes the process and these projects in some detail, and demonstrates an impressive list of business benefits. To quote from parts of the material on the site:
  • A £3 million reduction in the initial estimate of works.

- Flexible and adaptable facilities … which completely met the needs of the users and have continued to meet their changing needs.
- No claims or contractual correspondence were produced.
- The project resulted in about one twentieth of the normal level of paperwork.
- Getting it "right first time" saved some 15,000 man-hours and associated materials.
- An estimated £3-4m was saved in variations and claims.
- Final accounts were agreed before project completion.
- All team partners made a profit.
- Business needs were met on time and to budget.
- The facilities provided met the users' needs at the end of the project - not just at the outset.
- Work started seven months earlier than it would have done using traditional methods, with a further six months reduction on the time to completion.
- This saved £2.25m on time alone.
- Lean Design and Right First Time construction methods resulted in a 550 man months reduction in resources. This equated to a 20% saving in manpower worth £1.5 million; a further £750K being saved by minimising reworking.
- Flexible approach to scope allowing significant development of client needs with no consequential delay to completion.
- Extremely high end-user satisfaction with excellent quality product.
- Excellent team working culture created - no claims, no contractual issues, no correspondence.
- Minimal paperwork – shared electronic filing with access for all.
- On-line creation of operations and maintenance manuals.
- Compared to traditional methods – significant additional costs mitigated by partner philosophy – plus £250,000 real cash returned to business for reinvesting elsewhere.

Egan and Rethinking Construction

The CIB's *Partnering in the Team* sought to promote the uptake of good practice in partnering between client and supplier at any point in the supply chain. However it acknowledged that the extension of partnering down through the supply chain was then (1996) in its infancy. It was this slowness of uptake, amongst other factors, which persuaded the incoming Labour government to ask Sir John Egan, former Chief Executive of Jaguar Cars and widely credited with achieving the turn-around of that company's fortunes, not least through the application of lean thinking, to undertake a new and more radical review of the industry in late 1997.

The Construction Task Force was asked

"To advise the Deputy Prime Minister from the clients' perspective on the opportunities to improve the efficiency and quality of delivery of UK construction, to reinforce the impetus for change and to make the industry more responsive to customer needs."

The membership of the Task Force was drawn largely from manufacturing and larger clients of the industry. Professor Dan Jones, the Director of the Lean Enterprise Reseach Unit, Cardiff Business School was also in the team.

This straight away gave an insight into the likely thrust of the report – lean thinking. And so it proved.

In a parallel development, in February 1998 the DETR and CIB jointly announced a framework for the new Construction Best Practice Programme. Backed by around £2m per year from DETR, the Programme's services initially comprised a major website to signpost users to relevant guidance material; company networks and visits; advice on benchmarking tools; an advisory service; and details of case study exemplars and demonstration projects. By the time the Construction Task Force Report *Rethinking Construction* was published in the summer of 1998, the Programme was ready to launch, and a breakthrough in the ease of access to guidance and role models was at hand. Partnering was one of its 14 improvement themes and prominent in several others, including supply chain management and lean thinking.

Movement for Innovation

Rethinking Construction was published in October 1998. It identified five drivers for change, and four process improvements, one of which was partnering the supply chain. The report also called for a movement for change as a group of people, possibly supported by a secretariat, committed to improving the delivery of their projects and the performance of their companies by applying the ideas that the Task Force had set out. In particular it would oversee a series of demonstration projects to be put forward by the industry. At the launch conference Alan Crane was invited to chair the movement, which called itself the Movement for Innovation. The acronym M4i was preferred over the alternative option, MFI .

Over the next year or two M4i spawned sister organisations focused on housing (The Housing Forum), local government (Local Government Task Force), and central government (Central Government Task Force).

Arguably M4i's most significant achievement (along with the sister organisations) was to inspire over four hundred demonstration projects to the value of more than six billion pounds (Egan's target had been half a billion pounds) involving more than 1,000 firms. It also established a network of 10 regional clusters to exchange lessons learnt from these projects. Well over half these projects claimed to be demonstrating partnering. It is arguable what proportion actually adopted the formalised methods by now widely promulgated by the M4i and the Construction Best Practice Programme, but the size of the movement was impressive and undoubtedly took the language and many of the principles to new parts of the industry.

Construction Clients' Charter

A further example of the moves within the industry towards improved performance was the launch of the Construction Clients' Charter by the

Confederation of Construction Clients in 2001. This had been called for by Deputy Prime Minister John Prescott when speaking at the M4i's first annual conference in 1999, identifying the need to bring together several strands of work aimed at empowering clients and encouraging them to show leadership to their supply chains. The Charter sets out a commitment in four key areas of client leadership, integrated team working, a quality agenda and people. One of the Charter's key tenets of client leadership is to "adopt a partnering approach wherever possible" and promote a "team-based, non-adversarial approach amongst clients, advisers and the supply chain".

The Charter is essentially a tool that enables clients to develop their working culture through achieving a better understanding of their role, improving communication, team working and staff development. Two years on, and notwithstanding the demise of the body that gave birth to it (the Confederation of Construction Clients folded in 2002), Brian Wilson, MP, the then Minister for Construction, said of the Charter:

"The adoption of the Charter principles helps clients gain maximum value from construction procurement. It is central to the industry's improvement agenda...." (January 2003)

The social housing sector in particular has responded well to this initiative, and over 400 mainly public sector clients remain signed up to the Charter.

Public sector partnering

Accounting for around 40% of the construction industry, the public sector is a key driver of behaviour in the industry. It is the client from whom the industry appears to learn most of its tricks.

Government's traditional approach of awarding contracts to the lowest bidder in the name of value-for-money, and then reaping the harvest of claims and overspend, began to be seriously questioned by senior civil servants almost as soon as the Latham Report was published. In 1996 the Levene Report, *Efficiency Scrutiny into Construction Procurement by Government* concluded that government bodies were partly to blame for the poor performance of the industry and made recommendations which led to the establishment of the Government Construction Clients Panel (GCCP) as a mechanism for implementing change across government.

The key barrier appeared to be the public sector procurement rules. An early attempt to address this had been the European Construction Institute's 1997 *Toolkit for Partnering in the Public Sector*, endorsed by HM Treasury, the National Audit Office and the Audit Commission. This provided a significant demonstration of how partnering should be applied to projects after the award of contract – hence complying with all the EU and UK regulations for public sector procurement. However, given that it was produced by an essentially supply side body from a different sector, the report carried little weight.

Nevertheless, the first Treasury and GCCP guidance on partnering soon appeared, as did the first central government clients prepared to go down this new route, most notably the Ministry of Defence with its Building Down Barriers projects (see Box 2).

BOX 2

MoD's Building Down Barriers projects

In 1997, the Ministry of Defence, Defence Estates combined with the Construction Directorate of the then Department of the Environment, Transport and the Regions to sponsor an initiative christened "Building Down Barriers". Involving Amec and Laing, the initiative set up a learning mechanism for establishing the working principles of supply chain integration in construction. It had three overall objectives:

- To develop a process for integrating the supply chain within a construction project;
- To test this and refine it on two Pilot Projects for Army Land Command, establishing the benefits in terms of improved value delivered to the client and profitability for the supply chain;
- To assess the wider relevance of the new approach to UK construction and disseminate this understanding.

On the two pilot projects, Amec and Laing each acted as Prime Contractor in the provision of an indoor sports and training centre, including a swimming pool, for the Army garrisons at Aldershot and Wattisham respectively. The role of the Prime Contractor involved leading a supply team of designers, specialist contractors, and materials suppliers and components manufacturers. This team worked collaboratively with the client Project Sponsor to develop a design, and then delivered the building and managed its maintenance and cleaning during a compliance monitoring period. During this period the Prime Contractor was to demonstrate that the building performs according to a predicted model for its through-life costs, including maintenance, cleaning and utilities consumption.

Laing handed over the Wattisham facility in February 2000, and managed its maintenance and cleaning for a 15 month compliance monitoring period. Amec handed over the Aldershot Garrison Sports Centre in June 2000, and retained responsibility for a two-year compliance period.

Working in close collaboration with the supply teams on each project, a research and development group developed and evaluated the supply chain process with supporting tools and techniques. The Tavistock Institute led this strand, working with Warwick Manufacturing Group, British Aerospace Systems, and Building Performance Group, as well as staff from Defence Estates, Amec and Laing.

A number of reports and a handbook are available on the lessons learnt from the projects, the performance gains achieved and what can be expected in the future. The toolkit and training manuals developed as part of the project has now been taken on by CWC, the Collaborative Working Centre of Be.

From 1999 Achieving Excellence sought to promote the change agenda across government by reference to a series of targets for improved performance. Targets included the use of partnering teamwork and the development of long-term relationships, amongst others. Achieving Excellence achieved such success that in 2001 the National Audit Office was able to draw on the practical achievements of four Departments (MoD, NHS Estates, Highways Agency and Environment Agency) in its Report *Modernising Construction* and to dedicate four pages to the subject of partnering or collaborative working on the basis that:

"partnering offers good potential to improve the value for money of construction".

The recent Office of Government Commerce publication, *Building on Success* (February 2003) builds on the success of Achieving Excellence and seeks to take it forward and embed its best practice principles.

Away from central government, local government procurement had also been changing. The 1980s policies of compulsory competitive tendering, which had transferred many local government activities to the private sector on the basis of lowest-price, had been replaced by the policy of best value. The Egan messages reinforced and pointed the way to easier and better procurement under best value. As a result it is interesting to note that about half the total number of M4i demonstration projects came from this sector.

Partnering contracts

In the early days (RCF, CIB etc), talk of "partnering contracts" seemed a contradiction in terms. CIB wrote that:

"partnering is not … a new form of construction contract".

Latham had advocated the New Engineering Contract (NEC, later the Engineering and Construction Contract, ECC) as the best and most collaborative form of contract. The CIB's view was that

"Partnering can be applied with any of the procurement methods in use in the industry today, e.g., traditional, design and construct, design and manage, management contracting, or construction management. It does not however remove the need to use a competent recognised modern form of contract, the choice of which requires that the usual consideration should be given to the choice of appropriate contract form. It is of course the hope and the aim expected that the spirit in which the works are carried out under a partnering agreement will minimise the need to resort to the contract."

The Egan Report itself commented that:

"Effective partnering does not rest on contracts. Contracts can add significantly to the cost of a project and often add no value to the client. If the relationship between the constructor and employer is soundly based and the parties recognise their mutual interdependence, then formal contract documents should gradually become obsolete."

In 1999 the Construction Industry Council (CIC) published the first edition of its document *A Guide to Project Team Partnering*. This contained suggested heads of terms for a partnering contract. Soon afterwards, the first multi-party Project Partnering Contract (PPC 2000) was published. The NEC soon followed suit with its X12 Partnering option. These contracts and others are examined in detail elsewhere in this book, but the jury is probably still out on whether a specific partnering contract is required for effective partnering. Logic suggests that, if old-fashioned behaviour is truly to be left behind, the contract must offer no excuse for retaining old habits "just in case" a problem arises.

The Reading Construction Forum also rose to Egan's challenge, and a working group set about developing a new Collaborative Construction Contract, eventually launched by Be in September 2003. The preamble states:

"The example of other industries more advanced in the adoption of collaborative arrangements and supply chain management suggests that contracts will not disappear – but they are likely to become much simpler with greater reliance placed on non-contractual relationships and processes (see, for example, the contractual arrangements between vehicle assemblers and their key parts suppliers in the motor industry).

Over the past 50 years, the traditional standard forms of construction contract have all been based on an underlying relationship of master and servant: the client knows what he wants and directs the contractor to provide it. This relationship also underpins most professional appointments and subcontract arrangements. It is an arrangement that does not sit happily with the emphasis placed on collaboration and team working, particularly given the usual absence of any express direction to work together and share information with other project participants.

The inherent nature of traditional construction contracts, allied to the unhappy experiences of cut-price tendering in the late 1980s and early 1990s has encouraged the adoption of protective drafting in construction contracts: from the client/purchaser side, the emphasis has been on passing risk under contracts and, from the supply side, the emphasis has been placed upon defining maximum (rather than minimum) levels of commitment. It is therefore little wonder that contracts should remain in the proverbial "drawer" during the initial stages of a project when relationships are being developed and why they produce such fertile ground for conflict when they are eventually taken out of the proverbial drawer when problems arise."

Finally, the JCT has now announced its intention to develop a collaborative form of contract in association with Be for the local authority sector (JCT, June 2003).

The Strategic Forum and Accelerating Change

In September 2002 the Strategic Forum, which succeeded the CIB in July 2001, published *Accelerating Change*, a manifesto for the next phase of change in the industry. It set a headline target for 20% of projects to be undertaken by integrated teams and supply chains by the end of 2004 and 50% by the end of 2007. The rationale for this target was as follows:

"The major long-term benefit from integrated team working is the potential for relationship continuity. Integrated teams should be based, wherever possible, on strategic partnering. Knowledge and expertise can then be transferred more effectively from one project to the next. Whilst this is clearly of benefit to repeat clients, the benefits to one-off clients should not be ignored, as such teams will be better placed to offer them an improved service based on past experience, the ability to innovate, and through the development of a culture of continuous improvement."

The target distinguished between two types of integration: Project team integration, and Supply chain integration:

"An *Integrated Project Team* includes the client and those designers, contractors, manufacturers and specialists that are pivotal to providing solutions that will meet the client's requirements. All members of an integrated team should have the opportunity to make an input to the design of the project.

An *Integrated Supply Chain* brings together all the parties responsible for a key element or elements of the project. Supply chains can extend from the designers and main contractor, through to those manufacturers and specialists that are not part of the integrated project team. Integrated supply chains are long-term standing arrangements, independent of a particular project."

Essentially this was the same distinction as drawn in the much earlier RCF reports between project partnering and strategic partnering. The future vision of *Accelerating Change* was essentially for the distinction to become academic as all project teams would comprise long-standing supply chains – RCF's third generation of partnering.

Collaborative working

To bring this version of history up to date, reference needs to be made to the work of Be and its Collaborative Working Centre, CWC, an arms-length training and consultancy business. As mentioned above its principles and supporting services derive from the MoD's Building Down Barriers projects, and are entirely consistent with the Strategic Forum's view of integration.

The name "collaborative working" emerged because leading practitioners became concerned at the widespread misuse of the term partnering. Because the new phrase does not carry with it any previous meaning or (mis)understanding of the principles, people have to learn afresh about the concepts. These go far beyond mere teamwork to critical success factors such as early involvement of suppliers in design, selection of all parties by value, performance measurement and continuous improvement, common team processes, and most importantly of all, supporting commercial arrangements that align risk and reward for all parties on demand and supply side – strategic partnering (or supply chain integration) rather than project partnering. But how long will it be before someone recognises enough in the description to say "there is nothing new in that, it's how we have always done things in our firm"?

THE MANAGEMENT CHALLENGES OF PARTNERING

CONTRIBUTED BY ALAN CRANE, CBE

Introduction

The history of partnering covered in the previous section to this chapter identifies that the roots of partnering in the UK construction industry reach back many years.

However, in this section the focus is on more recent developments. There is inevitably a degree of overlap with some of the reports referred to earlier but reference to them is necessary in order to set the scene. UK construction in recent years has enjoyed the benefits of two widely supported reports, namely the Latham Report, *Constructing the Team* and the Egan Report *Rethinking Construction*. Whilst they both have the shared objective of improving industry performance, their recommendations differed somewhat in their approach.

The Latham Report clearly linked the industry's poor performance relative to cost, time and quality to the prevalent adversarial attitudes. It made detailed recommendations for the industry to improve its traditional project based approach, but to do so by adoption of a new family of modern conditions of contract based upon the concept of partnering. It was rather circumspect in its terms because at the time there was little recorded experience of using partnering in UK construction.

The challenge of putting "meat on the bones" was picked up by the Reading Construction Forum and The University of Reading who produced in June 1995 their Report *Trusting the Team – the Best Practice Guide to Partnering in Construction*. In the foreword Sir Michael Latham welcomes "...guidance aimed at replacing the adversarial attitudes which proliferate with a new approach ..." based on practical actions encouraging team working.

The same team further developed the partnering research, particularly looking for case studies worldwide, and published in 1998 their Report, *The Seven Pillars of Partnering*. In its foreword Sir Nigel Mobbs, Chairman of one of the industry's largest clients Slough Estates, states:

"Partnering enables the industry to understand more clearly its clients needs and objectives. It gives clients direct access to the hard-won knowledge and expertise of suppliers, constructors and designers ... partnering is hard work because it makes all of us accountable to each other for improving our performance. It encourages us to work together to solve problems and drive out waste in our processes."

At this stage there is the start of convergence with the Egan Report, published that same year. Egan clearly stated in his recommendations that industry should use partnering, but as the basis of establishing long term relationships, rather than be single project based as suggested by Latham. In so doing, it should aim for continuous performance improvement, the benefits of which should be shared on an openly fair basis so that all parties have a real incentive and motivation to find different and better solutions. These project teams should include from day one all the design, manufacturing and construction skills working together in fully integrated teams.

This was essentially the same message that had been contained in the description of Second and Third Generation Partnering set out in *The Seven Pillars of Partnering*. However, Latham really only dealt with First Generation partnering. Egan also made clear that even long term partnering by integrated teams, based upon experiences from other industries, would not achieve the sustainable improvement needed unless the very processes of the industry were changed. The Egan Report set out five key drivers for this change programme to tackle four crucial process areas, and concluded with seven significant targets for annual improvement. Whilst the very thrust was partnering using integrated teams, Egan made clear that he did not share Latham's view regarding the need for a new family of construction contracts. His view was that the industry should end its reliance on formal contracts because these did nothing more than add significantly to the cost of projects without adding value for the customer.

Perhaps more significantly, since the Report's publication and establishment of the Rethinking Construction movement there has been absolute silence on this last point, even by Sir John Egan himself.

John Bennett of Reading University, co-author of both *Trusting the Team – the Best Practice Guide to Partnering in Construction* and *The Seven Pillars of Partnering*, in 2001 co-authored a further Report *NEC and Partnering – The Guide to Building Winning Teams*. This report further developed his earlier works, using Latham and Egan as reference points, and perhaps obviously taking the Latham contract approach in that it sets out arguments for using the NEC family of contracts and particularly Partnering Option X12. This report also draws upon the Construction Industry Council (CIC) Report, *A Guide To Project Team Partnering*, which is now generally accepted as the lay person's "practical and down to earth guide to partnering in construction" to quote Sir Michael Latham from its Foreword. The author of this section, Alan Crane, in his Foreword to the Report, said

"*Rethinking Construction* in its recommendations identified seven key drivers for the radical cultural change that the construction industry needed in order for it to deliver the improved performance so desperately needed. Of these, it has always been my view that the most fundamental was that of working in truly integrated teams; removing the barriers that we had erected in the past between the contributors to the construction process, in particular the separation of design from execution, and the resultant waste of skills held throughout the supply chain.

Partnering, working together to achieve a clearly defined and agreed set of mutual goals, not only demands integrated working but also encompasses the other six drivers identified in the Task Force Report."

From the outset, CIC worked closely with the *Rethinking Construction* organisations such as M4i and took the lead in developing simple, practical advice on what might be called the "What and Why" of partnering, in this first edition. This important template not only predated the development of forms of partnering contract, but gave many clients and construction teams the confidence to adopt a radical approach to procurement and project working.

The second edition builds on that advice based upon the ensuing two years of real, live practical experience of not only a variety of M4i demonstration projects but a significant group of clients, designers and contractors who have developed their own approaches. It provides advice on the "how", that is the practical implementation of partnering. It incorporates the tried, tested and proven application of Rethinking Construction principles, and will enable the industry to really take forward partnering as the norm, rather than the exception for the enlightened few.

This section of the chapter uses the CIC Guide as its major reference point for these reasons.

Cultural change

The central theme of the Latham and Egan Reports is that substantial improvements can be achieved in the procurement of projects through the early integration of the team and the procurement process. These are the main means identified to eliminate the deeply embedded adversarial attitude and culture of the industry; a culture of blame, which so often and so easily triggers construction disputes. The CIC Guide expressed the point in the following terms:

"For too long the construction industry has been divided by factionalism and conflict, which has contributed to poor performance, dangerously low profit margins and poor morale among consultants, constructors, specialists and suppliers ... what clients receive is too often of poor quality, late and overpriced, provided by a process seldom offering best value."

The Egan Report recommendations were based upon the conviction that an integrated project process will deliver, not just to the client and indeed the user, but to the whole team seven incremental commercial benefits:

- reduced costs
- reduced time
- reduced defects
- reduced accidents
- increased predictability
- increased productivity
- increased turnover and profit.

These benefits can only be secured if the talents of each member of the team are recognised and respected by every other team member, and then combined in the whole team, who should be engaged as early as possible. This team needs to contribute from concept to completion. The project partnering team must include the client together with designers, consultants, legal advisers, constructor, and key specialist constructors, sub consultants and suppliers and manufacturers.

Integrated team working was a key theme in the *Accelerating Change* Report. As the report put it, part of the vision for the UK construction industry is for:

"integrated teams made up of existing integrated supply chains, which once successfully formed are kept together and move from one project to the next taking their experience and a culture of continuous improvement with them."

However, assembling the team on this basis is unlikely to be enough. The members must organise and integrate their roles and responsibilities so as to act co-operatively and to make decisions in a blame free and trusting environment. There is a need to identify and focus on agreed common goals, those issues which unite rather than divide; a need for openness, a commitment to problem solving, to continuous improvement, to sharing of risk and reward.

All of this describes, indeed demands, a fundamental change in culture. A culture which eliminates the barriers which have developed between designers, constructors, specialists and other advisers; which encourages the sharing of knowledge, learning and experience to the benefit of all parties; a culture which embraces trust rather than blame.

The Strategic Forum for Construction has developed a toolkit which contains guidance on the techniques for integrating whole life activities, echoing this approach. In developing the changing culture and values, it advocates the empowering of people through training and education so that they have the skills to make decisions, to share and nurture continuous learning, to ensure open communication at all times, to engender trust by believing first that everyone is doing their best in the interests of everyone else and to encourage a no-blame culture so that the focus is on the solution to a problem rather than fault.

Defining the project objectives and aims

All clients, irrespective of the procurement route or methodology they may employ or be advised to use, will by definition have an underlying business need to invest in a new or extended or refurbished building or facility. As soon as the client, with appropriate and objective advice, has developed this business case in terms of budget, programme and facility requirements, it is time to commence building the partnering team. For the majority of clients, teams will be being built for the first time and in instances where the client is inexperienced, it may be that advisers who will later become members of the partnering team are brought in to assist in compiling this outline project brief.

From this brief, the client can develop and identify the detailed aims and objectives for the project. The client's advisory team, which should include wherever possible end users and operators of the building or facility, should identify the project objectives in terms of the product itself, its delivery processes, operational performance criteria, and of course cost and time for delivery to match the business case. All possible expectations and objectives must be considered, because it is the complete identification of these that will determine the success or otherwise of the project.

The CIC Guide describes this as:

"a process whereby the client identifies all the project objectives and allots a weighting to each according to their worth to the overall project. These weighted objectives are then used to determine project partner selection criteria. Candidates are scored on each of the criteria...."

Through this methodology, the client can seek to ensure that all members of the team can be united around common aims and objectives.

Selection of partners and advisers

The first thing to recognise is that the principles of partnering apply irrespective of project size, and this is equally true of team selection in terms of the principles. It is just the complexity and probably numbers of team members that differs with project size. It is equally clear that project partnering offers opportunity and frequently the requirement for significant change in the traditional roles of all team members. For example careful thought should be given to the benefit of incorporating within the team advisers such as planning supervisors, lawyers, chartered surveyors and others. However, it should be recognised that professional codes, insurance etc may prevent certain key disciplines from participating.

Perhaps the first appointment may be a partnering adviser. He or she can come from any suitable profession, but of course must have a full awareness of partnering practice and experience relevant to the scope and scale of the project. The partnering adviser must not be the client representative; it is imperative that he/she is seen by all team members to be independent. Neither should he/she be a party to the partnering agreement or contract.

The partnering adviser's role will include:

- facilitating the creation and development of the partnering team;
- assistance in team building;
- documenting team inter-relationships, commitments and expectations;
- providing a first point of advice in the event of partnering team disagreements or misunderstanding, and;
- guidance in the team selection process.

It is important to select team members on the basis of attitude to integrated team and process working, to provide positive solutions, to be innovative. Clients should of course look closely at past experience and track record. The ethos of collaborative working at senior management level is important, but perhaps more important are the skills, knowledge and culture of the people within the company or firm.

The nature and extent of each party's contribution should depend on the added value that they offer rather than on their assumed position in an industry hierarchy. The best team available should be the one appointed. Cost should not be the determinant – these costs represent a very small percentage of the overall project cost, and the best teams will secure the best value for money. So the selection process should be based on quality and it should of course reflect the size and complexity of the project.

Partnering team members may be selected on a negotiated basis, particularly if they have worked together successfully before and if the client is not

subject to legal or regulatory obligations to go through a competitive procedure. However, where negotiation is not the appropriate or permitted approach,
the client will need to draw up selection documents, the first of which should
be a questionnaire based on the criteria established from the detailed aims and
objectives described in the previous section. This will be sent to potential partnering team candidates, who should be requested to ensure it is completed by
those people who are likely to form the team for the project.

It is also advisable to obtain from candidates other elements of information
to inform the evaluation process. These could include detailed method statements for critical, complex elements; the CIC recommend that candidates
submit focused statements of quality which address capabilities, suitability as
project team members and their overall alignment to the project objectives, as
distinct from the detailed criteria in the questionnaire.

From the responses the client's advisory team using the previously
described criteria will select a shortlist, and the aim should be for a maximum
of three for each team member required. One of the major areas of waste identified in both the Latham and Egan Reports was that associated with over-
large pre-qualification lists and shortlists.

The evaluation process should, provided the criteria have been clearly identified in advance, be swift and efficient. If statements of quality have been
invited then an acceptance threshold level in respect of these elements should
have been established.

Each and every member of the advisory team should separately assess each
candidate using printed forms, which include the weightings and scores
against each of the criteria. All the scores should be collated to determine
those selected for the shortlist; and it is important that selection is determined
by consensus, bearing in mind the on going ethos sought for the whole team.

Normally they will be asked at this stage to provide information on their
required profit, overhead and fees. The shortlisted candidates should then be
interviewed by a selection panel drawn from the advisory team.

The panel should visit previous projects, contact past and current clients
and possibly visit the offices of the candidate team members.

The interview is crucial. The process must be standardised and rigorously
scored against previously determined criteria. But above all it must establish
that there is clear potential for the essential rapport between the client and
potential team members; a common understanding of the project objectives
and how these will be achieved; and a total commitment to project team partnering.

Provided that preparations have been carried out efficiently, then the final
selection should be able to be made on the day of interview. This will then
enable final negotiations on fee and terms of contract (covered elsewhere) to
be rapidly concluded.

A more detailed and definitive description of the appropriate selection
process can be found in the CIC Guide under *Selecting the Team*.

Commitment and teamwork

As described above, the construction industry is facing a period of significant culture change; and certainly the traditional culture does not permit the assumption that just because the client has decided to procure on a partnering basis, and has appointed team members also on this assumption, that the team will now simply move forward.

As referred to earlier, partnering is hard work and that hard work starts with building the team. This team building process is needed to enable the partnering team members not only to get to know each other, but to help them to set to one side their natural commercial prejudices and learn to work together in real determined pursuit of their common project goals.

This is best undertaken by means of a workshop, held away from the actual project and indeed any team member's premises. The workshop should be run by an experienced facilitator, attended by all appointed team members with no substitutes, and should include the partnering adviser. Whilst it is imperative that the senior staff who have given the commitments during the selection process attend, it is equally essential that those who will be working on the project full time are also in attendance. However, numbers have to be manageable and it may be advisable for a series of tiered workshops to be held, with overlapping attendance, for large projects and teams.

Real success comes by way of fully integrated supply teams working with integrated supply chains, and team members should be actively encouraged to extend the partnering principles through their supply chains including operating parallel workshops.

The workshop content is clearly set out in page 11 of the CIC Guide and must include the identification of members' fears and concerns as well as each individual's project objectives but related to the mutually agreed overall project objectives.

And the workshop process is not a one-off at commencement. They should be repeated through the life of the project in order to sustain the one team culture and environment; and also to take account of members joining the project team at later stages. At relevant times, they should also include participants from the building operations members and facility management.

If possible, the same facilitator should be retained through the life of the project.

Partnering principles and processes bring together all the members of supply teams and supply chains and seek to unite them around a set of common goals and objectives. Teamwork, properly established, brings key individuals together, committed to make decisions related to those common objectives by discussion and consensus.

Performance measurement: incentives and benchmarking

Apart from commitment and changes in culture a further principle to be adopted to allow for effective partnering is a commitment to processes and tools which enable performance to be measured and evaluated. Such an approach will not only encourage the continuous improvements that the industry is striving for, but also enable performance measurement to be used to ensure that over the life of the partnering arrangement improvement is being secured. These performance measurement criteria need to be agreed at the outset.

A basic management technique, adopted across all industries as the means by which to realise identified common objectives is the establishment of a project specific incentive scheme under which an individual or a team is provided with a reward based encouragement to achieve beyond that which would be otherwise contractually acceptable. Any incentive scheme must therefore define the means by which performance over and above that set by the contract can be measured and the specific benefit that this will attract. Equally, for an incentive scheme to carry any weight, the level of the potential reward, or the downside which may be levied in the event of failure to reach any given target, must be sufficient, albeit realistically set, otherwise, the parties may slip into indifference as to whether or not the objective is achieved. The following is a brief overview of how incentivisation and benchmarking has come to be applied across the construction industry.

Incentives

In 1991, HM Treasury, Central Unit on Procurement, published its guidance note (No. 58) headed *Incentivisation*, which was one of a series of guidances prepared by the CUP on purchasing and supply procedures and practices to assist compliance with the EC public procurement directives. The guidance note provided the following definition of incentivisation:

"A process by which a provider is motivated to achieve extra 'value added' services over those specified originally and which are of material benefit to the user. These should be assessable against pre-defined criteria. The process should benefit both parties."

The guidance note expressed the view that whilst incentivisation should always be considered, it is more likely to be of relevance to contracts that are of a sufficient scope and size to justify the investment in applying the technique such that the potential benefits have the capacity to be substantial. It is also suggested an incentive strategy should be used where improvements in performance and the achievement of value for money would otherwise be unlikely to take place at a rate to match the business need.

The challenges that this therefore sets for those responsible for the management of the contract are in both assessing whether the particular contract is suitable for an incentivisation strategy, and if so what should be set as realistic targets and disincentives that will not prove to be so burdensome as to have a demoralising effect on the team. The analysis that this is likely to involve includes:

- The identification of the project-specific benefits that the successful implementation of such a strategy could bring to both parties. For the client, these are likely to encompass lower cost, the speedier delivery of the completed project without having compromised the standard of quality; an improved functionality of the completed project. For the industry professional, the benefits are likely to relate to the potential for an on going source of business from that particular client and the experience that can be carried forward to other projects.
- The setting of performance standards that are realistic and capable of delivery, i.e., the performance targets are sufficiently defined so as to be both measurable and quantifiable. The analysis of what is achievable will involve a suitably in-depth assessment of the risks that might affect the project, both in terms of those that are project-specific and those that are equally applicable to all construction projects. This exercise will also focus the parties' minds on one of the central objectives advocated by Latham and Egan – the allocation of those risks to the parties best able to carry them.

What are the different incentive schemes that could be employed by the parties? In the *MoD/Industry Commercial Policy Group Guidelines, Number 2: Incentivisation of Contractor Performance*, the suggested different schemes include the following:

"Examples of Positive Incentivisation are:
- Target Cost Incentive Fee arrangements. (By way of explanation this process involves the calculation of a fixed target cost, based on given factors. If the final cost either exceeds or falls short of the fixed target, the outcome is split between the parties. The allocation of extra payments or savings as between the parties will by reference to an agreed share ratio formula, usually set at the start of the contract.)
- Variable Performance Incentive Contracting in which the contractor can earn higher profits in return for achieving performance above a guaranteed level (technical or otherwise), or improved quality, for which the MoD benefit is increased capability.
- Time Based Bonuses in which the contractor can earn improved profits for early delivery ... for which MoD benefit is lower risk to the achievement of In Service Dates.
- Increased Scope, in which the range or scope of equipment/services can be increased, thereby increasing the income, income generation and/or potential return for the contractor. MoD's benefit is either reduced costs through increased utilisation or sharing of improved returns."

Devising a workable incentive scheme is only half the story. In circumstances where the parties are looking to incentivise a team, this necessarily involves acceptance and commitment to the culture change that is discussed above, namely the shift away from the traditional, adversarial approach to contracting. It cannot happen without a mutual willingness to exchange information on cost and performance. As underlined by the CUP guidance note:

"incentivisation creates a more proactive, cooperative relationship between the supplier and the department. It is part of the wider agenda for developing suppliers and the market thereby achieving real benefits ... Incentivisation requires ... greater attention to performance and contract management than for traditional contracts generally. The higher investment in using this technique needs to be balanced against the additional benefits and savings to be achieved."

Benchmarking and key performance indicators

An incentive scheme must be linked to an effective method of performance measurement. *Rethinking Construction* sought to encourage the industry to establish a strategy that could effectively measure performance against objectives and targets. In a client-centred environment, there must be some means for the client to "differentiate between the best and the rest, providing a rational basis for selection and to reward excellence". In so doing, the report dismissed the myth that construction cannot be compared with other sectors such as manufacturing because every product is supposedly unique.

The report argued that many buildings are, in essence:

"repeat products which can be continually improved ... more importantly, the process of construction is itself repeated in its essentials from project to project. Indeed, research suggests that up to 80% of inputs into buildings are repeated ... The parallel is not with building cars on the production line; it is with designing and planning the production of a new car model."

The Task Force therefore called for:

- the production of a structure of objective performance measures agreed with clients;
- the preparation of comparative performance data that should be shared with clients and other industry participants. By reference to the experience of other industries, the Task Force believed that this could be achieved without compromising legitimate needs for confidentiality;
- a system of independently monitored company "scorecards", measuring companies' progress towards objectives and targets, instead of simple benchmarking. The names of the best performers would be made public and every company would be privately informed of where it stood in relation to its competitors
- the development of a knowledge centre providing details about good practices, innovations and the performance of companies and projects. Access to the information should be made available to both the industry and clients.

In 1998 Construction Industry Key Performance Indicators (KPIs) were developed by the Movement for Innovation (M4i) and launched as part of the Construction Best Practice Programme (CBPP) to assist in monitoring progress towards the targets set by Sir John Egan's Task Force. KPIs are a compilation of national data which focus on those aspects of construction operations critical to the success of construction projects from both the client perspective and the industry participants. Within a number of defined areas, the data addresses issues such as time/cost predictability, productivity, client satisfaction over a number of subjects, defects and heath and safety matters. KPIs have been used to measure the improvements made in the Movement for Innovation (M4i) demonstration projects. It is intended that these be updated on an annual basis.

The main areas in which the CBPP publishes KPI Wallcharts each year are:

- All construction, incorporating data on issues such as productivity, profitability, safety, time, defects, and client satisfaction with the finished product.
- Respect for people, incorporating data on issues such as qualifications and skills, safety, number of training days recorded and remuneration.
- Environment, incorporating data on issues such as carbon dioxide emissions, waste in the construction process, the amount of water used during day-to-day operations.
- Construction consultants, incorporating data on issues such as client satisfaction with quality, timely delivery, health and safety awareness and value for money.
- M&E Contractors, incorporating data on issues such as defects, predictability (time), productivity and client satisfaction with design, installation, operation and maintenance manuals and service.
- Construction Products Industry, incorporating data on issues such as client satisfaction with sales advice, delivery reliability and product quality.

Each wall-chart contains KPI graphs, to be used by organisations to benchmark their performance against the rest of the industry or their particular sector. The KPIs therefore provide a comprehensive, up to date source of information against which performance can be measured, and targets can be set for future attainment.

At the time of the launch of the 2002 KPIs, the available trend analysis from the previous four years demonstrated that the industry is improving over a range of areas, most notably in the accuracy of construction cost and time delivery predictability. Comparative exercises between the performance of the Rethinking Construction Demonstration Projects and the rest of industry shows how major improvements can be achieved by embracing innovation. The author of this section of the chapter summarised the 2002 launch as

"another significant step towards a comprehensive performance measurement system to embrace the whole sustainable construction agenda. Furthermore, it demonstrates clearly that the application of *Rethinking Construction* principles delivers business benefits to customers and the supply side, and most important of all significantly safer construction."

For ease of access to the information contained in the KPIs, there is the *www.KPIZone.com* website, which contains links to all published KPIs and provides details of all performance measurement and benchmarking activity. Amongst the general information provided on this website, there is guidance as to the management skills involved in the benchmarking process, i.e. the capacity to analyse in a systematic and logical manner the level of performance that has actually been achieved, and the establishment of targets for improvement. To quote from the website:

- "Benchmarking focuses improvement efforts on issues critical to success.
- It ensures that improvement targets are based on what has been achieved in practice, which removes the temptation to say 'it can't be done'.
- Benchmarking provides confidence that your organisation's performance compares favourably with best practice.
- For organisations in the public sector, benchmarking provides an assurance that 'Best Value' is being achieved."

The site also identifies the central management issues as being:

- "A clear understanding of what needs to be improved, and why. This analysis is usually the senior managers' responsibility. Benchmarking must align with the organisation's objectives if it is to be successful.
- Careful selection of who to benchmark against.
- Clear understanding of the reasons for any difference in performance.
- Establishment of goals and targets that are both challenging and achievable with effort.
- A willingness to change and adapt based on the benchmarking findings.
- Persistence! Results will not necessarily come quickly and easily."

In February 2003, the CBPP published its *Fact Sheet on Partnering* which emphasised that, once the areas targeted for improvement have been identified, performance should be measured on a regular basis in the workshop, with the results fed back to the project team. The document acknowledged that:

"This is not necessarily easy, but is essential. Simple measures can be used as a staring point, developing and refining them as the project proceeds."

As with most strands of partnering, the benefits of benchmarking and KPIs can only be realised by the team's commitment to open exchanges of information and by the adaptation to the cultural change that is described above. This is succinctly put by the CBPP in its Fact Sheet as follows "To achieve continuous improvement requires individuals and teams who do not quiescently accept the status quo, but constantly look for opportunities for improvement."

Dispute resolution

Even under a partnering arrangement, with all the inherent processes described in this book, the very nature of the design and construction process determines that disagreement and dispute will arise. However, what partnering should seek to overcome is the confrontational and un-cooperative stance between the contracting parties where each party looks at its own commercial interests ahead of the interests of the project. Nevertheless the success of this will ultimately depend very much on the individual party's commitment to a problem solving culture.

It can be said that there is nowhere to hide in a fully integrated partnering team. This should by definition make dispute resolution much simpler and quicker. It should also provide sufficient incentive for avoiding dispute in the first place. Also, because roles are clearly defined, risk allocation normally open and shared, and all parties are working to common agreement terms it will normally be simpler to identify where and why things have gone wrong.

The partnering concept works on the basis that it is better to put in place at the outset an effective system of problem resolution, which focuses on the management of the dispute before it escalates to the issue of formal proceedings. Dispute resolution is covered in more detail in the final chapter of this book but a key feature of the dispute resolution processes in partnering arrangements is the hierarchical approach to resolution of the dispute by a series of steps, each one progressively more formal. These would include mechanisms to monitor performance and early efforts to improve performance where it falls below an agreed standard, followed by discussion to resolve potential disputes at project level, management level and then core group level before the more formal mechanisms for resolving disputes come into play. As with many construction contracts if the project starts to slip it is often the early stages of managing the difficulty that play a crucial role. The partnering ethos is aimed at ensuring that the issue can be managed at an early stage in such a way that formal legal proceedings and traditional adversarial approaches are a thing of the past. Whether this is true in practice will depend on how successful that management is and how committed the parties are to the partnering process and ethos.

Based upon the authors' own direct experience and awareness of activities throughout the industry, and the record of the Rethinking Construction Demonstration Projects, there appear to have been remarkably few disputes thus far, but it is conceded that this is in a procurement and contractual arrangement where people are still feeling their way and developing practice.

There are no accurate data available, but in 2002–2003 it is generally accepted that some 15% of the industry workload is being undertaken with some form of partnering, yet there have been no disputes which have reached the level of public, or perhaps more significantly, industry journalist awareness. However, there is some evidence of the use of statutory or contractual adjudication in particular to settle payment issues, although this is largely anecdotal.

Of the current approximately 430 Rethinking Construction Demonstration Projects, partnering in some form is in operation on approximately 70% of the projects. Of these, there have been serious disputes on only three schemes.

In the case of two projects, the disputes arose where major design changes occurred resulting in significant additional costs directly. On one of these projects the cost of delay featured as well. Although at earlier stages in the projects the client had been happy to accept the shared benefit of cost savings and value engineering improvements, when the problems actually arose there was a refusal to share in the penalty. At this stage it appears the traditional industry approach of seeking to apportion blame took hold and the partnering approach ceased. It may have been significant that, in both projects case, standard forms were being used (in one case ICE 6th and in the other IChemE) albeit amended to include a Partnering Charter.

The third project had been procured traditionally using ICE 6th edition form of contract. All tenders had been quite seriously over budget, but one tenderer had provided an outline alternative design which it believed could be achieved at a cost closer to the client budget. Time was short and it was proposed to proceed on a partnering basis, based upon a charter, in order to avoid delay to the project. This went forward, the programme was achieved, and costs were in line with the contractor's alternative design cost indication. The project also received a design award. However, the client body was a special purpose vehicle set up solely for the scheme with two public sector bodies and a charitable trust as the funders on a fixed contribution basis with joint and several liability specifically excluded from the funding agreement.

In the event, one of the funders (contributing 49% of the cost) refused to accept the costs over the original budget, and held that they had not agreed to and were not signatories to the partnering agreement, which had been signed only by the funding party who were charged with acting as client representative. Full payment was not made to the contractor, who in turn withheld sums pro rata from two major subcontractors. The disputes continue some 30 months later, complicated further by the subsequent liquidation of one of the subcontractors and the administration of the contractor.

It is probable, although not provable, that in all three cases similar problems and disputes would have arisen had the projects been procured and executed under traditional forms of contract. There is clear indication in at least two of the cases that not all parties were fully committed to partnering from the outset. The resultant difficulties were also more difficult to resolve given that partnering forms of agreement had not been fully put in place.

However, notwithstanding these difficulties, the general experience from the demonstration projects has been that problems which traditionally could lead to dispute have indeed arisen, but have been overcome or avoided by a combination of the ethos of the partnering agreements and the dispute avoidance processes contained within the agreements.

Ultimately, it is only time and wider adoption of the principles, that will provide the evidence of success on a quantifiable basis.

CHAPTER 2

THE ROLE OF TECHNOLOGY

Paul Wilkinson[1]

In parallel with the development of partnering approaches in the UK construction industry, information and communication technology (ICT) – in particular, internet-based technology – has also begun to make an impact on how projects are delivered. These two drivers would appear to complement each other well, but the adoption of partnering by the industry has been slow (organisations have needed to make time-consuming changes to their internal attitudes, practices and procedures) and the pace of technological change has been hampered by industry resistance to – or scepticism about – new ICT.

Successful collaborative working is built on a combination of people, processes and technology, which means addressing some of the concerns voiced by potential ICT users. These have included: the credentials of the technology providers (sometimes referred to as application service providers, or ASPs); system reliability and security; compliance with information standards; and the legal standing of electronic communications, to name but a few.

Naturally, the ASPs have had to respond to these issues, often by devising new legal agreements, and this chapter details an ASP's responses on legal issues, drawing on the experiences of BIW, one of Europe's most intensively used web-based collaboration system for the construction and property sector. It concludes by looking ahead: will technology become an integral part of partnering? If so, will ASPs become a key part of project teams and other long-term supply chain relationships, or will they simply become just another ICT provider?

Partnering and internet technology

Key aspects of the inefficiency that provoked Latham (1994), Egan (1998, 2002) and similar calls for change (e.g., the Confederation of Construction Clients 2000, CABE/Treasury 2000, National Audit Office 2001, Cain 2001) were, first, the architectural, engineering and construction (AEC) industry's reliance on slow, paper-based processes to share project information, and, second, the lack of integration between the design and construction processes. Documents, drawings and correspondence, with all their ongoing amend-

1. Head of Corporate Communications, BIW Technologies.

ments – many out-of-date before they reached recipients by conventional means of delivery – remained the main communication media. During even very modest projects, project teams created, copied, distributed and stored huge volumes of information. Moreover, they rarely (if ever) shared information with the rest of their supply chains. Specialised suppliers were thus unable to contribute to design development from the outset.

In such an information-dependent industry, sharing accurate and timely information is critical for all participants. Wasted time and cost can almost always be traced back to poor co-ordination caused by late, inaccurate, inadequate or inconsistent information – sometimes a combination of all four.

Even as some innovative organisations began to adopt partnering approaches, communication between team members in the vast majority of AEC projects was still achieved through traditional means: namely, face-to-face meetings, telephone calls and paper-based communications. Postal services and couriers were being supplemented electronically by faxes and then email, but the core medium remained paper.

This is perhaps no surprise, as it reflects an industry that often lags behind in embracing new ICT. When the Latham Report was published in 1994, few construction businesses had websites and even fewer were investigating other uses of the information superhighway. Four years later (Egan 1998), websites were almost old hat, and, during the dot.com boom, we saw an explosion of interest in using the internet as a means of transacting business, with major contractors competing to launch online construction marketplaces (such as Arrideo, AECVenture, Mercadium and EU-supply) against existing AEC ICT vendors (Causeway Technologies, for instance, launched *buildingwork.com* and Ramesys launched Xchange) and newly-formed businesses such as BuildOnline. However, by the time *Accelerating Change* was published (Egan 2002), the dot.com bubble had burst and the heady optimism of the late 1990s had evaporated, as had many of the budding e-commerce ventures.

Despite technology market fluctuations, by the late 1990s almost all AEC professionals had become computer users, particularly for word-processing, spreadsheet work and computer-aided drafting (CAD), with high rates of email use and internet access. But for many users, the technology was not yet used to its full potential and capacity; training, lack of investment and a preference for paper were users' key concerns (Building Centre Trust 1999).

This gradual, practical adoption of new technology reflects a conservative, risk-averse industry in which projects frequently take months or even years to move from inception to completion. Quite justifiably, ICT advances would not usually be introduced partway through a project; and even if a project was still at inception stage, clients and team members would normally want reassurance that the new technology was already tried, tested and proven elsewhere, ideally on a project of a similar type and scale.

Similarly, the concept of supply chain management – already prevalent within manufacturing sectors such as the automotive and aerospace industries –

did not immediately appeal to the traditional AEC industry. True, some clients were beginning to develop longer-term, open-book supply chain relationships, and even to involve second and third tier suppliers in design development processes, but they were very much in the minority.

What most of the AEC industry lacked was a means both to reduce its reliance on paper and promote such instant and continuous supply chain involvement in key design and construction processes. Fortunately, Egan's manufacturing experience perhaps indicated where the AEC industry should begin to look for a possible solution.

During the 1990s, electronic document management systems (EDMSs) were becoming increasingly common in manufacturing. Users normally accessed these server-based systems via local or wide-area networks. As such, EDMSs were largely unsuitable in the geographically-dispersed teams found in most AEC projects. Moreover, being expensive to purchase, implement and support, they were unlikely to be attractive in an industry where profit margins were already thin. However, the rapid development of web-based technology during the late 1990s created a new breed of business applications: internet-based collaboration – or c-commerce – technologies. These did not tie users to particular networks and, being provided by application service providers (ASPs), did not require any major investment by customers or other end-users in new hardware or software (an important factor, perhaps, when partnering with smaller suppliers and other project participants).

What is collaboration technology?

For the purposes of this chapter, collaboration technology refers to systems that allow users to share information with other users via computers connected to the internet. Broadly, all such systems are accessed through a standard computer browser such as Microsoft Internet Explorer and perform the same basic functions. Authorised users, no matter where they are located or when they use the system, can get immediate access to a central repository of project data that grows as information about the built asset – a building, a road, a bridge, for instance – develops. Feasibility studies, budgets, sketches, drawings, approvals, schedules, minutes, photographs, specifications, standards, procedures and other relevant items can all be viewed; team members can then add comments, make amendments or requests, or issue new instructions, drawings and documents. Everyone works on the most up-to-date, accurate and relevant information, backed by all the archive material.

The partnering objectives of trust, openness and co-operation are, of course, promoted through the use of such technology, and Murphy (2001) found early adoption was certainly greater among organisations that had a "more progressive [approach,] actively integrating partnering, supply chain management and other such core developments into their management process" (Murphy, p. 3).

In such a transparent environment, everyone knows who did what and when. It is easy to see who is responsible for a delay or problem; peer pressure encourages team members to work harder to achieve targets and settle disputes before they result in litigation. Better information flow means that design changes have less impact and that decision-making is quicker, resulting in less delay, fewer attendant costs and a better chance of a project being completed on time, on budget and without defects.

Browsing through the websites and literature of the various ASPs, the main benefits claimed for both team members and clients include:

- faster communications, resulting in more timely involvement in key decisions;
- 24/7 access to latest information; and
- more open discussion of design issues, leading to
  - improved understanding (resulting in, for instance, better design, less duplication and re-work, fewer delays and fewer drawing revisions)
  - a more transparent audit trail encouraging accountability and ownership, cutting down the scope for disputes and claims
  - faster projects (resulting in lower on-site costs and earlier revenues to owner/developers through, for instance, use, rental or lease).
  - cost savings in document production, reproduction, distribution, storage, management and fewer site meetings.

The starting point for this chapter is the use of the technology by project teams employed on single projects. However, the technology can equally be used on multi-project programmes, for example by teams employed under five-year framework agreements. References to "project teams" in this chapter include such arrangements.

Early adoption of collaboration technology

By the late 1990s, websites, email and intranets were already improving communications. The challenge was to extend those benefits up and down the supply chain – a challenge taken up by both established names and new start-up businesses.

Some US-based EDMS vendors (for example, Documentum and OpenText) adapted their technology to try and get a foothold in the AEC market in the UK. Other AEC ICT vendors tried to enter the market (for instance, Bentley created ProjectWise, then Viecon; Autodesk backed – and later took over – Buzzsaw). Established industry names such as UK contractor Bovis and multidisciplinary practice Arup created their own project document handling systems (Hummingbird and Integration, respectively – the latter acquired by Causeway Technologies in 2001 and managed alongside its OpenText-based system) or developed solutions based on third-party software (for example, Atkins' iProNet was based on UK-based Business Collaborator, and Gibb – now JacobsGibb – used ActiveProject from US-based Framework Technologies). Newer businesses also began to emerge, including US-backed Cephren and Bidcom, and home-grown BIW Technologies (BIW), Cadweb, 4Projects, I-Scraper and Sarcophagus.

No single business model dominated. Some of the ASPs (such as BIW and Cadweb) originated before the dot.com boom. Others were heavily backed by venture capitalists and launched during the boom (for instance, BuildOnline and I-Scraper). Some – such as Sarcophagus – were ICT spin-offs of existing AEC businesses whereas others (like 4Projects, which is part of the Leighton publishing group) were e-business subsidiaries of larger companies or (in the case of Causeway Collaboration, for example) offerings from existing vendors of other ICT systems. Similarly, the products or services differed greatly in their origins, technical structure and capabilities, but most of the ASPs began to market them as web-delivered "project extranets" or "collaboration systems".

As mentioned, extranet technology emerged during a period of dot.com hysteria to which the construction industry was not immune (at the peak of the hysteria, it was estimated that over 100 providers were targeting the UK market). But when the dot.com bubble burst, the number of online transaction hubs and other would-be dot.com businesses quickly dwindled. Mercadium disappeared into Causeway Technologies; BuildOnline switched from online trading to collaboration services; Cephren and Bidcom merged to become Citadon (trading through Bidcom Ltd in the UK); and I-Scraper folded in early 2001, its UK and German operations being taken over by BIW and BuildOnline respectively.

Coupled with the proliferation of business models and different software applications, the dot.com implosion also fuelled uncertainty about the financial stability and long-term prospects of some e-businesses. But project extranets had already begun to achieve some credibility with a few leading AEC clients, particularly those who were already adopting partnering approaches, or even moving on to embrace approaches such as prime contracting (see Holti and others, 2000). Innovative organisations such as BAA and Sainsbury's justified building more long-lasting, strategic relationships with clusters of key suppliers on the grounds that they were also capturing information, experience and best practice.

Collaboration technology was a logical next step, and some clients began experiments despite its lack of track record. For example, in 1999, after testing the system on a store project in Clapham, south London, Sainsbury's – one of the UK's largest building clients – adopted BIW Information Channel as its corporate system, heralding a dramatic increase in the use of collaboration technology by its supply chains and, in due course, by those of other client organisations, such as BAA, Marks & Spencer and Stanhope.

Heeding the message of Egan and others, many clients (particularly those with large portfolios of property or other assets, such as retailers, transport operators and utilities) increasingly recognised that information created during project delivery was a valuable "whole life" asset that could be used to enable better planning, continuous performance improvement and risk reduction across their current and future property portfolios. This realisation was also shared by many within the AEC industry, particularly those focused on delivering private finance initiative (PFI) and public-private partnership (PPP) projects. The PFI/PPP project team – often a specially created consortium – is additionally responsible for raising the funding for the project and, post-construction, for operating and maintaining the completed facility to the end of a concession period which may be 25 or 30 years long. Like partnering-type arrangements, such projects place a high premium on long-lasting, strategic relationships with fellow project team members, including the ASP.

The early years of the twenty-first century saw rapid growth in the adoption of collaboration technology. For example, from 3,400 users in 570 companies at the end of 2000, usage of BIW's system grew to over 20,000 from 2,500 companies by the end of 2002. Such growth was projected to continue across the UK market. A *New Civil Engineer* survey (Hansford 2002) said that, on schemes worth over £5m, 55% of teams would be using collaboration systems in 2003, up from 25% in 2001 and 35% in 2002.

Culture issues – what the technology won't do

However, despite the new ground trodden by innovator and early adopter clients, there was, in early 2003, still some way to go before such technology became the AEC industry norm on a wide range of schemes (including the great majority of projects worth under £5m). This partly reflected the inertia within some organisations when it came to contemplating more open, collaborative approaches. Concerns about the technology often disguised deeper issues relating to the whole idea of working in a more integrated and transparent way.

This is hardly surprising. Experience in other industries (for example, ICT, retail and manufacturing) suggests that failure to understand and adapt human behaviour, rather than technology, is the biggest impediment to successful collaborative working. Business people have traditionally been resistant to the notion that they should share information. Key functions – such as sales, ICT, procurement, human resources and accounts – have all sat in "silos", with their own agendas and systems. Culture, people and psychology issues are even more important in the conservative AEC industry. Individual advancement frequently depends upon gaining time-consuming professional qualifications and years of project experience, using familiar, traditional, tried and trusted techniques. True partnering requires a more collaborative approach, and so AEC staff will need to adopt a different mindset and behave differently. New technology could add to the challenge – so it needs to be relatively straightforward and intuitive to use.

Once organisations have resolved internal issues about partnering, collaboration and/or ICT, they can then start to focus on breaking down the interorganisational fear and mistrust that often exists when businesses start to form external relationships with clients, consultants, contractors and suppliers. Collaboration technology can support both internal and external integration processes. It delivers a more transparent environment for the sharing and exchange of information between all project partners, and enables the monitoring and measurement of key activities reflecting collaborative practices.

Practical issues in choosing and using collaboration technology

While resistance to using collaborative technology may reflect concerns about working in a more transparent partnering-type environment, it may also evidence more specific concerns about selecting and using a new technology (and an internet-based system at that) to handle mission-critical information.

The basis for such fears can begin to be addressed, however, if clients and/ or their project team members regard their prospective ASP as another member of the team, delivering a service as opposed to a shrink-wrapped software product. This places obligations on the ASP. In keeping with the partnering ethos, it should be expected to adopt the same basic principles of trust, openness and honesty as all other team members. However, while the roles of traditional AEC team members will usually be easily understood, the ASP will need to overcome comparative ignorance about web-delivered software. Once team members have a better generic understanding of the technology, the ASP can then begin to address questions about its own software, its infrastructure and, perhaps most importantly, about its business and the people behind it.

While some clients and/or project team members may have previous experience of dealing with an ASP, in many cases a team may need to select from, at first sight, a confusing array of different companies and software systems. This section expands on the key issues identified by Construct IT (2003):

(1) the quality of the ASP's technology, its service features and the potential fit with the client's future needs (including connectivity, hardware and/or software requirements, and compliance with industry standards);

(2) the training, support and day-to-day liaison between end-users and the ASP;

(3) the track record and evidence of the benefits of using collaboration technology;

(4) the financial standing, strength and stability of the ASP, including the calibre and experience of its managers, the sophistication of its business model and pricing; and

(5) the service infrastructure (covering security, availability, performance, reliability and resilience issues), together with information about any third party organisation providing the ASP's infrastructure.

Quality of the ASP software

The ASP must show that its software has the necessary functionality to manage all information according to the current and – as far as they can be defined – future needs of the client and/or the project team, including its requirement for transparency and openness.

No application will be absolutely right for every project. For example, a relatively small project may not require all the sophisticated functions of a more advanced software package, but the latter may be perfect for managing interaction within a large multidisciplinary team working on a complex scheme or programme. In a partnering context, the client and team should seek a technology that will support their key processes and information requirements in the long-term. As mentioned, more and more teams are concerned about managing "whole life" costs (e.g., PFI/PPP consortia), and are looking for systems to collate information so that the technology can be used efficiently for future operation and maintenance purposes.

The project team should also look at how the software – and the team's needs – might develop over time, so the ASP's flexibility and responsiveness are also important. Much will depend on where and how the software has been developed to date, as this can be critical in adding new functionality or ensuring continuing support for the current system. Issues include:

- Geographic origin – some ASPs' systems were developed expressly for UK projects, others were initially developed in, say, the USA and have had to be adapted to suit UK project processes and telecommunications systems.
- Technical foundation – some systems are pure web services, developed from the outset for delivery via the web, while others are derived from EDMS client/server applications and then customised to suit AEC industry processes.
- Platform compatibility – not all applications work on both PCs and Apple Macintosh computers (many designers still prefer the Apple Mac platform over the PC-based systems employed in most AEC organisations).
- IPR and location of development team – it may, for instance, be easier to request new developments direct from a UK-based ASP that owns the intellectual property rights to its software than to deal indirectly with a US-based provider of an underlying proprietary application.
- Interoperability – to what extent has an ASP adopted ICT and/or AEC industry standards allowing information to be exchanged and reused by other applications both now and in the future?

For partnering, a key issue is the extent to which a system actually enables collaborative working. A system that simply replicates traditional AEC processes electronically may initially be attractive to someone taking their first steps online, but may not be flexible enough to genuinely promote genuine collaboration, defined by Schrage (1990) as: "the process of shared creation: two or more individuals with complementary skills interacting to create a shared understanding that none had previously possessed or could have come to on their own."

As this suggests, collaboration is a process of value creation that cannot be achieved through traditional communication and teamwork structures. The key requirement is an environment – ie an extranet – to which authorised collaborators have equal access, and which they can use to interact in real-time towards the achievement of an agreed objective.

Training, support and liaison with the ASP

Where collaboration is to be encouraged, new ICT is not a standalone solution. User support and specialised training is crucial as, without good back-up and support for the software, its use would fail. A partnering team should ensure that there is a mutual understanding between the ASP and fellow team members of all the relevant technology, people and process issues, as Confederation of Construction Clients' chief executive Zara Lamont (2002) wrote:

"What [clients] really want to see is IT adding value to their own operations ... If they [business processes] are the wrong processes, it will mean we are doing the wrong thing more efficiently. As a cash-rich, time-poor society, what really makes the difference is communication and collaboration....

We don't need e-commerce to do this. We need teams, chains and clusters that are prepared to work together over time in an open and honest way to develop the right processes.

... It will take considerable investment by all parties to sort out the right business processes, software interfaces and protocols. Having done that, you will then need to review and improve them in operation....

... the more you put into getting the processes right and changing the culture, the quicker the payback. But you don't want to be climbing the same learning curve on every project – hence the need to work as integrated teams over a series of projects."

In practice, this might involve an ASP (directly or indirectly) in:
- working with the client and the team to understand their process requirements, and to identify risks, key objectives and desired benefits;
- the configuration of the collaboration environment so that it is specific to the process needs of the project and the team;
- helping to identify and resolve any technical issues (eg auditing existing hardware and software, or advising team members on effective internet connectivity);
- training team members in the most appropriate use of the system for their specific roles, responsibilities and requirements;
- providing ongoing face-to-face user support, plus technical support via a helpdesk service, throughout the project/programme;
- undertaking regular reviews of actual project user activity; and

- particularly in strategic partnering arrangements, involving the customer and/or key team members in discussions on future software development to support changing or new business needs

Whether working directly with the ASP or through a third party, the project team should treat the relevant person(s) as another project partner. For instance, the ASP representative might attend initial project workshops and help develop partnering charters and other protocols. This ensures the ASP is clear about, for instance, the partnership's objectives, success criteria and risks so that it can play its full part in delivering services that optimise the team's overall performance.

Taking care to select the right technology to support long-term strategic partnerships will also cut the training and support requirements over time. Once undertaken for an initial project, many of the above tasks (eg system configuration, ICT audits or initial training) need not be repeated or, at least, not quite so extensively. Instead, existing users can focus on using more of the service's functionality, perhaps even working with the ASP to develop new functionality to reflect the team's evolving communication needs.

Track record and evidence of the benefits of using collaboration technology

Track record is, rightly, highly valued in the AEC industry. The technology may look good, the support service appears sound, but has the combination worked successfully elsewhere? In the early days, it required something of a leap of faith by innovator clients to entrust their projects to unproven systems (even now, new customers still tend to be cautious and deploy an ASP's technology on test or pilot projects first, before adopting – or rejecting – it for further projects). However, all the main ASPs in the UK can now provide details of clients and projects that have used their services, allowing prospective clients/partners to seek references. If the intention is to use the technology to support a partnering approach, then client references and case study information relating to previous or ongoing partnering projects should be sought.

Assessing the benefits of using collaboration technology, however, is more difficult. Apart from anecdotal evidence, there is – as American analyst Joel Orr (2002, pp. 11–12, see below) noted – little (if any) independent research confirming the benefits in terms of overall productivity improvements:

"We believe there are several reasons for this:
- To speak of 'productivity increases' requires careful measurement of productivity prior to implementation of the new technology. This is difficult to do in the project-oriented world of construction, and companies do not seem motivated to do it.
- Some issues are self-evident, and construction professionals do not want to invest time in proving them – for example, the fact that electronic transmission of documents … is much faster and cheaper, and more auditable, than using courier services….

- For many of the parties to a construction project, productivity is not a clearly defined concept. To put it bluntly, if one is being paid by the hour, reducing the number of hours required to get a job done is not an attractive proposition.... Only the owner is clearly motivated to do more with less....
- Most ... vendors underestimate the extent of computer-illiteracy in the construction community, and thus underestimate the amount of training required for successful project implementation.
- Construction projects are not highly disciplined affairs. Unless the use of a new tool can be tied to payment, subcontractors will tend to do things 'the old familiar way,' despite any benefits they might gain from the new tool."

In the absence of independent empirical research, potential customers have therefore tended to rely on vendor's surveys in which users give what Orr describes as "their (invariably favourable) experiences". Otherwise, benefits statements have often focused on tangible savings – often savings in the costs of producing and handling paperwork. For example:

- over £58,000 savings on printing, copying and postage during a £5m, 30-week retail project (BIW);
- a £50,000 saving on printing, information distribution and general administration on a £60m development (BuildOnline);
- a £12,316 saving on a £1m project (Cadweb); and
- a potential £27,250 net saving on a £10m, two-year project (Causeway).

By their very nature, it is more difficult to quantify the intangible benefits of using a collaboration system. For example:

- reductions in mistakes and reworking, and avoiding unnecessary project delays (consultant Gleeds estimated, for BIW, the potential savings during a £5m, 30-week retail project would be around £300,000 or six % of the project value)
- fewer claims for incorrect or out-of-date information;
- faster evaluation and resolution of claims;
- earlier completion dates due to time savings in transferring key information
- more efficient future operation and maintenance through having a repository of as-built data; and
- reuse of standard information across a series of projects.

Quantifying the benefits of using an extranet in a partnering project can be doubly difficult. For instance, team members may experience a dramatic reduction in the volume of paperwork produced, distributed and stored. This may partly reflect the use of an extranet to manage information flows, but the reduction may also be due to the partnering ethos (for instance, the non-adversarial culture removes the need for the many contract letters often found on traditional projects). One determinant might be the extent to which a technology actually encourages openness, communication and collaboration, rather than just replicating traditional industry processes electronically. If the technology genuinely enables collaborative working, then benefits delivered by a partnering approach are likely to be enhanced still further.

Strength and stability of the ASP

The importance of the ASP's financial stability reflects the key element of trust. In the short-term, of course, the client is going to be reliant on the ASP's system to manage all key project information. But the system could also become a key resource for subsequent projects. Partnering-oriented clients and their project teams will therefore be considering a long-term commitment to a business-critical relationship with the ASP, and should seek detailed information about the background, track record, structure, management, funding, financial performance (current and forecast) and revenue model of their prospective service provider before entering into a contract. The Construction Industry Computing Association (CICA, 2002) said: "the selection process should include an assessment of the technical, organisational and financial standing of the vendor organisation as the day-to-day provider of a central service" (p. 3). In short, partners need to know that the ASP will be around long enough to deliver all services associated with the project(s).

In some cases, the ASP may be part of a bigger organisation, so it is vital to understand whether information (relating, for example, to funding, financial performance, numbers of staff, customers or users) relates to the whole business or just the ASP operation. Similarly, if an ASP provides more than one product or service, serves more than one major industry sector or is active in several regions, again, it is vital to understand what proportion of revenues and resources are associated with the particular collaboration technology, the AEC market and/or the UK.

The ASPs may also offer different revenue models. For example:

- a fixed monthly subscription, usually paid by the ultimate client or a team member, to license the software's use for the duration of a project or programme of work (regardless of the number of users or drawings, for instance);
- as above, but advance payment of part or all of the subscription (when assessing the ASPs' financial performance, such large initial payments may mean little further revenue, something not revealed in balance sheet "snapshots");
- payment by end-user companies – ie members of the project team or supply chain, not the client – for system access; or
- payment by end-user or client according to, for example, the number of users or the volume of storage.

From a partnering point of view, the first options are perhaps more likely to encourage adoption of the technology down the supply chain. In some situations, an agent such as a construction manager may be the de facto client, managing the ASP relationship as part of its services to the ultimate client (reflecting the single point of contact between the client and an integrated design and construction supply chain recommended by, among others, the National Audit Office 2001 and Cain 2001). End-user charging – particularly in an industry working on thin margins – may deter some users, resulting in only partial take-up of the technology (and thus fragmented and inefficient communication processes). Similarly, payment according to the volume of communications or storage requirements may deter some making full use of the systems.

Perhaps reflecting that the industry still has some way to go before integrated teams become the norm, teams often debate whether the costs of a collaboration system should be born by the client or shared across the end-user companies. In a partnering context, this issue should, however, be quickly cleared up. If the ASP (or, say, a project manager including the extranet as part of its services) is to be an integral part of the partnership, then by virtue of the open-book approach, all team members will be able to weigh the costs of the system against the anticipated benefits and account for its use through the gain/pain-sharing ethos characteristic of partnering relationships.

Quality of service infrastructure

For mission-critical web services, particularly those involved in delivering multimillion pound capital projects or managing information over multiple projects procured through a long-term partnering arrangement, clients and their teams need a lowest-risk solution. With information entrusted to a central repository, users need assurance that the application and the data will always be available, 24 hours a day, 365 days a year.

They will also want consistently high levels of performance (for instance, when it comes to speed of access to data), and a high degree of reliability and resilience, so that the system will not crash due to the failure of any single infrastructure component (do all primary network system components, such as servers, power sources and telecommunication links, have secondary back-ups in case they fail?).

Given the business-critical nature of project information, clients and users will in addition expect high levels of infrastructure security (safeguarding against unauthorised access to servers, stopping hackers and protecting against viruses, for instance). Responsive, timely support and guaranteed uptime on all hardware, software and network functionalities is typically addressed by a service level agreement (SLA) (See Technology, partnering and law (Service level schedules/ service level agreements) below) with either the ASP or a third party organisation providing the ASP with hosting services.

Again, different ASPs offer different approaches. The servers and other infrastructure used to manage applications and their underlying data may be:

- housed in the office of the project client or other member(s) of the project team;

- managed in the ASP's own facility;
- located in an ISP's data centre; or
- managed at a specialised hosting/data centre.

Space precludes a detailed examination of the relative risks of the different options. However, the team might reasonably ask some searching questions. For example:

- Does an in-house ICT department have the technical facilities, resources, skills and experience needed to deliver the required high levels of service?
- Has creating and managing a service delivery infrastructure diluted the ASP's focus on developing, implementing and supporting its software?
- To what extent is an ISP or host focused on supporting application services as opposed to the different demands of website and email hosting?

Needless to say, if the ASP does outsource its hosting to a third party, then the client and project team should seek similar information to that sought about the ASP to satisfy themselves about, for instance, the host's financial stability, track record and depth of resources.

Technology, partnering and law

Many thought partnering might reduce the role of lawyers in the construction process, but the AEC industry is notoriously risk-averse, and experience suggests few (if any) UK organisations are yet prepared to procure work on trust alone. This probably applies doubly when clients and their project teams are considering using new ICT and forming partnerships with, as yet, still relatively unknown ASP businesses. Clients and end-user businesses have, accordingly, sought to protect themselves and base their working relationships with ASPs on contracts and other documents.

This is no easy task given that collaboration technology is relatively new to the AEC industry in the UK. Most construction and technology lawyers have only slowly begun to tackle a number of the key points (notwithstanding some of the cultural and practical questions surrounding the use of the technology, concern about legal issues could have delayed wider introduction of such ICT systems within the AEC industry (see Goodwin 2002), leaving the ASPs and their legal advisers to pick their way carefully through a still-evolving legal landscape. Legal articles in AEC industry publications (e.g., Hampton 2001 and Birkby & Nugent 2002) highlighted a few areas of particular legal concern, including:

- the legal status of electronic communications;
- legal relationships with the ASP; and
- service interruption or unforeseen termination of the service.

This next section looks at each of these areas.

Legal status of electronic communications

Broadly, the same legal principles apply whether parties communicate on paper or electronically. Paper-based records such as documents and drawings are simply records kept in a particular medium, and electronic media is no less valid. But it is important to ensure that records are authentic, accurate and accessible.

Contract provisions regarding electronic communications

Although the use of electronic media to exchange information within the AEC industry has become progressively more widespread, concerns about the legal status of electronic communications did cause some AEC professionals to delay decisions about using collaboration systems. This uncertainty was compounded by the absence of appropriate provisions in many standard contract forms. Few made explicit reference to the possible use of ICT; important communications were assumed to be delivered 'in writing' in a tangible, paper-based form, such as by letter or by the issue of drawings.

For example, many construction contracts require participants to issue formal notices, but are not always clear about how they shall be given and whether electronic communications will suffice. In a presentation to industry professionals at the ICE in London in December 2001, solicitor Ed White highlighted relevant clauses of several standard contracts; in his view, for example, FIDIC was adequate, but the JCT and Engineering and Construction Contract forms needed amendment for projects where an online collaboration system is employed. He cited with approval some sample clauses from a retailer's contracts:

"1.1 'Writing' includes e-mail, facsimile transmission and/or communication in another durable medium that is available and accessible
2.1 Any communication sent electronically by e-mail or otherwise:
  2.1.1 Will be deemed to have been sent once it enters an information system outside the control of the originator of the message;
  2.1.2 Will be deemed to have been received by the intended recipient at the time that in a readable form it enters an information system that is capable of access by the intended recipient."

A paper "The role of electronic information in construction contracts" written for BIW by solicitors Hammond Suddards Edge, outlined standards that can be applied to facilitate the use of electronic communications, including the UK Standard Interchange Agreement: a standard protocol for use by parties who wish to communicate electronically. It mainly concerns authenticity and integrity of data, when it was received and how data logs should be stored and maintained. The JCT provides, as an option, for the provisions of the Standard Interchange Agreement to be incorporated into construction contracts based upon its standard form, meaning that any communication that must be in writing will be validly exchanged when sent electronically.

Legal admissibility of electronic communications

White addressed the issue of legal admissibility by reference to the Civil Evidence Act 1995: "Where a statement contained in a document is admissible as evidence in civil proceedings, it may be proved: (a) by the production of that document, or (b) whether or not that document is still in existence, by the production of a copy of that document or the material part of it, authenticated in such a manner as the court may approve."

It is therefore important that a party using electronic information in the courtroom has a rigorous audit trail reliably logging when a drawing or document was created, every instance when it is sent or received, and if it has been amended (and if so, when and by whom). The court may need to understand how the original was turned into an electronic version stored in the system, then sent and received without alteration, up to and including its production in court. Arguments over admissibility of evidence can lead to investigations into the system that produced the paper, the method of storage, operation and access control, and even to the computer programs and source code. It may also be necessary to satisfy the court that the information is stored in a "proper" manner.

Both Masons and Hammond Suddards Edge agree that the ability to show that an electronic information system is managed in accordance with internationally recognised and audited codes of practice or standards – such as ISO 17799 – will be persuasive to a court of law. BSI codes of practice such as PD0008: 1999 (Code of Practice for Legal Admissibility and Evidential Weight of Information Stored Electronically), PD5000: 1999 (Electronic Documents and E-Commerce Transactions as Legally Admissible Evidence) and PD0010: 1997 (The Principles of Good Practice for Information Management) also provide guidance.

Legal relationships with the ASP

Entrusting mission-critical information created by a client's project team to a collaboration system places some strong obligations on the ASP and it is vital that appropriate legal arrangements are put in place to support the relationships:

- Between an ASP and a client (this and subsequent references to the client also include the client's agent – for example, a construction manager); this may involve a master licence agreement (also known as an ASP agreement).
- Between an ASP and end-users (ie supply chain members) of the ASP's technology; typically, this involves an end-user licence agreement or some form of standard terms and conditions, sometimes viewed on-screen when the application is first used.

Complementary information to these agreements may be contained in separate documents (forming part of the contract), for example schedules outlining agreed levels of service delivery. Sometimes described as the bedrock of contractual relationships with ASPs, service level agreements (SLAs) specify how the service will be delivered.

It may also be useful to specify relationships between individual supply chain members stipulating use of the ASP's technology to communicate with each other. This may require amendments to consultant agreements and/or contracts with the main contractor and subcontractors (see above), or may be covered in specific project protocol documents (see below).

Master licence agreement (MLA)

Describing the relationship between the ASP and the ultimate client, an MLA should cover:
- The grant of a non-transferable non-exclusive client licence to access and use the collaboration service in relation to its project(s)/business;
- restrictions on the use of the collaboration system (in relation to, for example, spreading software viruses, spamming or posting information that is illegal, defamatory or indecent);
- the parameters governing the use of project data by authorised project participants only;
- the terms whereby nominated participants will enter into an appropriate end-user licence agreement with the ASP;
- payment terms;
- copyright of the ASP's collaboration technology;
- ASP use of the client's branding and data;
- indemnification of the ASP against misuse or unauthorised use of the collaboration system;
- confidentiality, including security precautions with respect to user names and passwords;
- termination provisions (including what may happen to the data once the project is complete);
- jurisdiction; and
- the extent of ASP liabilities.

End-user licence agreement (EULA)

An EULA describes the contractual relationship between a project's participants and the ASP. In many key respects, it will reflect conditions imposed in the MLA, but at a level specific to participants. For example, it will cover:
- the participants' licence to access and use the collaboration system in relation to their role on particular project(s) and/or for particular client(s);
- the terms whereby this licence might be terminated (for instance, if the client relationship with the participant is discontinued); and
- the grant of a licence to the ASP to store and, subject to access privileges, to access and view project-related information where the participant owns the intellectual property rights.

Client contracts with designers usually include provisions about copyright in the designer's designs. Typically, the designer retains the copyright but grants a licence to the client and other team members to use the design in relation to the specific project. The EULA should reflect this principle, extending the licence to include viewing rights for the ASP.

The MLA and/or the EULA will normally seek to limit the ASP's liabilities for direct and indirect/consequential damages. Clients and/or end-users should check such agreements are well-drafted and that the ASP is not avoiding liability unreasonably. For example, it may omit liability for loss of data due to its own negligence, non-deliberate action, system non-availability, under-performance, or inaction, or it may limit liability to a small sum of money out of all proportion to the actual impact of any loss (the validity of such clauses in an ASP's standard terms is controlled by the Unfair Contract Terms Act 1977 – see also, for example, *St Albans City and District Council v International Computers Ltd* [1996] 4 All ER 481).

Clients should also be careful to ascertain that an ASP is adequately insured: can the ASP meet its liabilities if sued by the client? If an ASP is a subsidiary of a larger group, should the client seek guarantees from the parent company?

Service level schedules/service level agreements (SLAs)

If the ASP outsources its hosting infrastructure, the specified service delivery levels will typically reflect the service level agreements between the ASP and its hosting infrastructure provider; otherwise, the ASP may specify a SLA direct with the customer reflecting its own capabilities. SLAs (covered in ISO 17799) should include specifications covering:

- security provisions (including firewalls, and intruder and virus protection);
- the provision of appropriate back-up systems;
- compliance with the stated functionality;
- the integrity of data processed and stored on the system;
- the creation of, and provision of useful access to, a full audit trail of the project;
- each user's identity (for example, by entry of a password and username, although users should remain responsible for keeping their individual details secure);
- the provision of appropriate user access rights to access and view particular documents;
- sufficient levels of processor, system memory, disk space and telecoms bandwidth availability to allow adequate performance;
- levels of system availability (e.g., 99.5% during working hours but allowing for occasional planned downtime for equipment or software upgrades);

- the provision of upgrades to latest software versions, and a guarantee of continued compatibility of existing data with new functionality;
- clearly specified levels of customer support, perhaps defining elements such as response times and severity levels; and
- the extent and quality of end-user training, deployment and related services.

What is covered in a SLA is open to negotiation between a client and the ASP, and different ASPs will, of course, have different capabilities. Within a project team, users may already have some experience of working with different ASPs and clients might consider user preferences when it comes to assessing SLA specifications.

For example, an ASP might stipulate: "The system is not available between 4.00am and 6.00am daily, or as notified from time to time." What if it is unclear: (1) how much advance notification will be given, (2) how the notification will be delivered to the customer and/or end-users, and (3) how long such periods of non-availability might typically last? Prolonged or frequent periods of non-availability can prevent efficient use of the system. For example, a project may have a multinational team, or have stakeholders who travel to different time zones; limitations on system availability could impact on them.

Project protocol documents

Part of the standard implementation service offered by an ASP should cover the provision and tailored development of a project protocol document setting out the standards or rules of operation for user companies working on the collaboration system. Typically, it will:

- provide common protocols describing how users publish, retrieve and manage information quickly and efficiently;
- be modified by the client to suit its processes;
- need to be read in conjunction with non-project-specific guides (for instance, general user guides) on the use of the collaboration system; and
- detail the pragmatic working procedures to be followed by participants during any temporary suspension of service (see below).

Service interruption or unforeseen termination

Managing service interruptions

As already mentioned, an ASP can take great steps to ensure its service infrastructure is as robust as possible (for example, it can ensure high levels of redundancy: the availability of secondary, standby or back-up systems that take over if a primary system develops a fault). But no technology is infallible. Birkby and Nugent (2002) suggest customers and users need to be clear about what happens if and when a system crashes:

"... there must be a back-up system that enables each of the participants – designer, contractor, subcontractor, client – to carry on working with minimal delay to design or progress on site. This may mean that whenever a document is uploaded onto the network, the person who has created or amended the document keeps a copy in their own electronic file, so it is available if needed. Everyone will, of course, revert to emails and faxes and circulation of hard-copy drawings until the system is back up and running, but there must be a procedure for updating the extranet as soon as it is back online, so that everyone can have confidence in continuing to use it, and not resort to their own back-up system.

This is normally achieved by devising a series of rules for the operation of the extranet, sometimes called a protocol, which becomes one of the contract documents for each of the organisations working on the project."

Clearly, if the integrity of the single central repository for all data is not to be compromised, some back-up processes need to be specified. For example, BIW nominates a team member to act as project information co-ordinator (PIC), who assumes additional responsibilities should the service be interrupted. All emails and relevant attachments are sent to the PIC and, once the collaboration system is reinstated, it is his or her task to input drawings, documents, comments, requests, instructions and other relevant elements (a process simplified by the availability of batch processes for otherwise repetitive uploads).

Managing ASP termination

Given the relative immaturity of the UK collaboration service market and the number of ASPs competing for AEC market share, lawyers have understandably warned customers to take steps in case a chosen ASP becomes insolvent. Birkby and Nugent suggest that the contract with the ASP should provide:

"• A right to terminate a contract and transfer to an alternative service provider in the event of any doubts about the ASP's ability to continue providing services;
• An obligation on the ASP to provide assistance on transfer of the service to an alternative ASP, by providing access to all necessary records and data. Assistance in the form of consultancy services may also be required; and
• An obligation to make records available in specified formats that can be accessed by the ASP's customer."

Birkby and Nugent urge prospective ASP customers to monitor the financial status of their service providers so that they get early warning of any problems: "... insolvency of the ASP would be likely to cause serious problems and realistically, many provisions will become impossible to enforce in the actual event. So you may also wish to require the ASP to provide regular financial information, to try to detect early signs of any problems."

Of course, prevention is better than cure. As discussed, clients contemplating a lengthy commitment to a business-critical relationship should seek detailed information about the financial status (for example, audited accounts, management accounts, shareholder details and insurance cover) of their preferred provider(s) before entering into a contract. They will probably draw their own conclusions if an ASP appears reluctant to divulge detailed information about its financial position, either initially or at some later stage.

Should transfer of data become necessary, the ASP could offer consultancy services for which the client may be charged additional fees; clients should specify that any transferred records are to be delivered in an industry standard format (e.g., XML). Birkby and Nugent also urge prospective ASP clients to consider safeguards to ensure they can still access the extranet and the information it holds: "If use of the extranet or the records it generates requires any proprietary software, then it will be necessary to obtain the source code for this (which most software providers will resist) or to provide for the code to be placed with a third-party escrow agent under an agreement that provides for it to be made available in the event that the software provider or ASP becomes insolvent."

Such contingency arrangements may also extend to ASP agreements with third parties such as hosting partners to provide continuity of service regardless of the ASP's status. (BIW, for example, has an escrow agreement with National Computing Centre that, if the company ceased operations, would allow customers to use alternative hosting arrangements. It also has a contingency agreement with its hosting provider, Attenda, which would maintain access to the service for at least two months.) Clients may also want to consider whether third party expertise in the ASP's technology is available, through, perhaps, existing AEC consultants.

Aware that they needed to reassure clients about long-term access to their information, the main UK ASPs (Bidcom, BIW, BuildOnline, Cadweb, Causeway, 4Projects and Sarcophagus) formed the Association of Construction Collaboration Technology Providers in early 2003. Its objectives include "increasing interoperability between the different systems and engendering easy transfer of data through definition and adoption of standards", making it easier to migrate data from one system to another in the event of an ASP business folding.

This and the previous section have been devoted to understanding the key characteristics of collaboration technology providers and the related legal issues so that readers can begin to appreciate how an ASP's technology might be adopted by a project team. The remainder of this chapter considers ICT and partnering in the context of *Accelerating Change* (Egan 2002).

A faster rate of change

The AEC industry in the UK is about to enter a period of considerable change brought about by the convergence of two previously separate but complementary strands of development. Throughout the late 1990s, as this chapter has shown, the gradual cultural shift of the UK construction industry – post-Latham – towards partnering-type approaches has generally proceeded in parallel with the development of, and equally gradual adoption by the AEC industry of, new ICT capabilities (including email, websites and broadband communications). In the early years of the 21st century these movements have begun to converge and become intertwined, and, as the title to *Accelerating Change* (Egan 2002) suggests, the time has come to increase the pace of this convergence.

Accelerating Change puts integration of both the entire team and its ICT at the heart of its vision, envisaging an industry characterised by: "integrated teams, created at the optimal time in the process and using an integrated IT approach, that fully release the contribution each can make and equitably share risk and reward in a non-adversarial way" (Egan 2002, p. 10).

In short, collaboration technology and partnering are now irrevocably intertwined. In the early days, the individual ASPs expended considerable efforts in raising awareness and educating the market about collaboration technology, and partnering certainly helped to create some demand. If the AEC industry moves down the path advocated by *Accelerating Change*, changes already underway within existing partnering-oriented sections of the industry could well occur across much of the rest of the sector.

For example, some construction businesses, particularly those with responsibility for delivery of a scheme on behalf of their client (for example, construction managers and design-and-build contractors) have moved beyond simply being ICT-literate and now offer a complete solution, complementing their traditional strengths with expertise in implementing and supporting the underpinning collaboration technology (BIW, for example, works with consultants Mace, Gleeds, Citex and Woolf, and contractors Kajima and ISG).

A new breed of construction ICT specialists has also begun to develop. For example, Sainsbury's use of the BIW system is managed by Info-Matrix, construction manager PCM has a consultancy subsidiary called Knowledge-Online, and Asite worked with several technology businesses (including BIW and Bidcom) to provide collaboration, purchasing and tendering technology, supported by training, technical support and consultancy services. Existing mainstream ICT and telecommunications businesses such as BT and Logica could also move into this role.

Forming relationships with such businesses will also reduce some demands previously made directly on the ASP. Many marketing, implementation and support tasks can now be effectively outsourced to organisations working directly with each client's supply chain (similarly, hosting infrastructure might also be outsourced to clients' ICT services suppliers). The ASP can then focus on core activities such as software development, devising improvements and new features based on the collective experiences of both construction ICT partners and direct customers.

We should expect wider adoption of *Accelerating Change* working practices to be supported by an increased use of collaboration technology. At the time of writing, several UK organisations had reached a point where they felt confident enough to adopt one or other system as their corporate standard, and began to establish long-term strategic partnerships with their chosen ASP (in May 2002, for example, BIW announced a three-year deal with industry client Sainsbury's, and the following month a four-year deal with contractor Kajima). Particularly as other organisations follow suit, such strategic deals will cement the market position of any ASP with a strong business model and a good combination of technology and scalable infrastructure, hastening some consolidation in the marketplace; some ASPs will probably be squeezed out of the market or forced to become niche specialists as competitors grow their market share.

In the partnering context, ASPs entering into such relationships should be expected to fully release the contribution they can make, by responding positively to new or changing team requirements. For example, BIW worked with Sainsbury's supply chains to develop new functionality that produced an electronic health and safety file upon the completion of each project; this was rolled-out for all new Sainsbury's projects from January 2003 (a major step towards extending the use of information throughout the "whole life" of the retailer's assets). Such strategic relationships might also extend to the development of interfaces between the ASP's collaboration technology and other systems used by the client or other supply chain members (ranging from a client's enterprise resource planning (ERP) or asset management systems to, say, an architect's drawing register), increasing transparency and smoothing out and speeding up the flows of data between different applications and devices up and down the supply chain.

This is perhaps not an altogether surprising development as it reflects a fundamental difference between traditional vendors of ICT packages and the new generation of ASPs. Many AEC-specific packages focus on supporting particular professionals in discrete areas of work (for example, computer-aided drafting, structural calculations, estimating, site management, financials and drawing office management) and are delivered as traditional software. Collaboration technology, by contrast, has been designed for use by all project team members, regardless of their professional background, and the market is being led by service providers who have developed their applications from the ground up for internet-hosted delivery without any local software downloads. The web services approach will increasingly help to glue together different elements of key AEC business processes by enforcing definable and consistent rules, interfaces and procedures.

Two powerful movements – collaborative working and collaboration technology – have been converging for some years. *Accelerating Change* is a landmark insofar as it explicitly links team integration with integration of ICT systems. The experiences of what have been described as "more progressive" organisations (see Murphy 2001) are therefore set to become more widespread, heralding a much wider adoption of collaboration technology across the whole UK AEC industry.

Importantly, the changes will extend beyond the initial personnel involved in design and construction of facilities and increasingly begin to affect those responsible for ongoing operation and maintenance. Information built up during planning, design, construction and operation will become an intrinsic part of the built asset, and will help owners and operators – with the full knowledge, involvement and support of their supply chains – to make more informed decisions about future investment in both existing and new assets.

Following this through, perhaps collaboration technology might one day be regarded as a traditional part of the AEC landscape? In a reformed world-class industry of the kind envisaged by *Accelerating Change*, perhaps collaboration technology will become just another part of the plumbing needed to support AEC projects throughout their working lives. Given the rapid pace of change in recent years, we may not have to wait too long to find out.

Bibliography

Birkby, G., and Nugent, J. (2002) "The ASP with a sting in its tail", *Building*, 8 June, pp. 50–51.

Building Centre Trust (1999) *IT Usage in the Construction Team* (London).

CABE/Treasury (2000) *Better Public Buildings* (London, Dept. of Culture, Media & Sport).

Cain, C. (2001) *A Guide to Best Practice in Construction Procurement* (Watford, Construction Best Practice Programme).

Confederation of Construction Clients (2000) *Charter Handbook* (London, CCC).

Construct IT (2003) *How to manage e-project information* (Salford, Construct IT/ITCBP).

Construction Industry Computing Association (2002) *Guidance Note on Project Collaboration Extranets for Construction* (Cambridge, CICA).

Egan, J. (1998) *Rethinking Construction*, Report of the Construction Task Force (London, HMSO).

Egan, J. (2002) *Accelerating Change*, Consultation Paper by Strategic Forum for Construction (London, HMSO).

Goodwin, P. (2001) *Effective integration of IT in construction: final report* (London, Building Centre Trust).

Hampton, J. (2001) "Stung", *Construction Manager*, September, pp. 8–10.

Hansford, M. (2002) "Virtual Togetherness", *New Civil Engineer*, 5 December, pp. 22–23.

Holti, R., Nicolini, D., and Smalley, M. (2000) *The Handbook of Supply Chain Management* (London, CIRIA).

Lamont, Z. (2002), "IT is not the answer", *Building*, 19 April, p. 33.

Latham, M. (1994) *Constructing the Team* (London, HMSO).

Murphy, L. (2001) "Does the use of construction project extranets add value to the procurement process?" (London, South Bank University Faculty of the Built Environment), summary report available on *www.itcbp.org.uk*

National Audit Office (2001) *Modernising Construction: a report by the Comptroller and Auditor General of the NAO* (London, HMSO).

Orr, J. (2002) *Keys to success in web-based project management: Lessons learned from the Chicago Transit Authority Capital Improvement Program* (Bethesda, Cyon Research).

Schrage, M. (1990) *Shared Minds: the New Technologies of Collaboration* (New York, Random House).

CHAPTER 3

THE FUTURE

Alan Crane, CBE[1] *and Richard Saxon, CBE*[2]

EDITOR'S INTRODUCTION

In this Chapter two leading industry figures give their assessment of what the future is likely to hold for partnering and collaborative working in the construction industry.

In the first section, Alan Crane describes the various stages and levels of partnering, starting with fully integrated terms leading to higher levels of partnering with alliancing and finally what he calls "mature" partnering. He argues this third stage of development is required, leading to a level of development in partnering that builds on what has been accomplished already, but supplements it with new thinking from other industries, a better utilisation of standardised components, and further maturing of supply teams and chains.

Alan Crane also describes the "virtual" company model and its role in relation to partnering. It is in the editors' view important to distinguish between strategic alliancing and the virtual company model. The former is the development of a long-term strategy where a series of projects by the integrated team is delivered to one customer. The latter is where a group of companies, experienced in partnering, form a virtual company on a partnering rather than a partnership basis with a commitment to develop the relationship of the long-term.

In section 2, Richard Saxon looks at the external challenge to partnering in the construction industry, based upon a broad notion of "the built environment" and the potential for the industry to better address the issue of client satisfaction in the context of the total physical and economic context of any given building. He argues that the industry must rediscover its sense of identity and purpose, and not allow itself to be defined reactively by a short-sighted and narrow perspective of what it can achieve.

Richard Saxon also argues that there needs to be a move away from focus on pure cost to proper and wide consideration of the customer's real need, namely the use of the built environment as a performance-enhancing facility. Partnering, in Richard's view, lends itself to this delivery goal but he goes fur-

1. Alan Crane is Chair of Rethinking Construction and a member of the Strategic Forum for Construction.
2. Richard Saxon is a Director and former chairman of Building Design Partnership, Chairman of Be and Vice-President of the Royal Institute of British Architects.

51

ther by suggesting that the integrated solution provider would finance, design, build and operate the facility. This would ultimately enable the integrated solution provider to live on stable, long-term income streams whilst learning to improve the product and service it provides on a constant and ongoing basis.

THE NEXT STEP FOR PARTNERING

Contributed by Alan Crane, CBE

In order to address what the future holds for partnering in the construction industry, the current position first needs to be considered in the light of the progress that has been made in recent years. In short, what has been achieved in the nine years since the publication of the landmark 1994 Report of Sir Michael Latham, *Constructing the Team,* which promoted partnering as the way forward for the construction industry?

The answer would appear to be "quite a lot". On any view a considerable amount of research has been carried out, a number of reports have been issued, and a whole cultural change movement has been established across the industry on the recommendation of the Egan Report *Rethinking Construction.*

Crucially, partnering has been endorsed by both central and local government as a preferred procurement method for securing value based performance from construction projects and infrastructure investment. This appeared to have resulted in dramatic change. For example, a survey by the Office of Government Commerce in Spring 2003 into current procurement methods by central government departments reported that 60% of their projects were being procured on a partnering basis.

However, this figure caused expressions of disbelief within the industry. Informal surveys by Rethinking Construction, Construction Best Practice Programme and others have indicated that perhaps industry wide the figure is around fifteen percent of industry output, amounting to approximately £10 billion per annum. In an industry widely seen as being outdated in terms of its industrial practices, this more limited figure could still be seen as a measure of success and a good portent for the future.

In addition to the debate of the scale of impact achieved to date, debate and research in this area suffers from a lack of definition of what actually constitutes partnering, despite the many authoritative reports covering the subject.

Many companies, including construction clients for whom buildings are constructed, purport to have been partnering for many years prior to Latham. They claim that working together for many years with a significant element of repeat business and a generally high level of client satisfaction with performance is itself sufficient evidence of successful partnering.

Their argument is attractive at one level, but since they often cannot cite particular measures of improved performance over those years in terms of cost, time or quality, the assertion of success has less significance than might otherwise be supposed. In addition, such contentions seldom include within their definition of successful partnering an involvement, or even a mention, of the supply chain behind the project, save in respect of certain well documented examples such as the relationship between Bovis and Marks & Spencer, and the lesser known but successful relationship between Amec and Astra Zeneca which goes back over 15 years.

It is also true that the great majority of "first generation" partnering agreements in existence (i.e., those that resulted from the initial call for such working in Latham) do not extend partnering principles and arrangement beyond the first tier of participants, namely the client, the contractor and (sometimes) the principal designer. For example, whilst some 70% of the Rethinking Construction demonstration projects have partnering arrangements, less than 15% of these extended, to any real degree, to include even specialist contractors and suppliers. Similarly, very few current arrangements are other than single project agreements. However, this latter fact should cause no surprise given that the Latham Report was very much focused on this basis.

Despite these somewhat ad hoc approaches, there are now many clear examples of clients fully participating in project teams; of designers and contractors working together (sometimes with specialists) to produce improved, "right first time" designs. There are some, but rather fewer, examples where the issues related to the whole life of a building are addressed prospectively in the context of better integration of the design and construction process.

Despite the limitations of some "first generation" partnering arrangements, it is fair to say that there is a clear, and often not insignificant, reduction in cost and time of performance, and some improvement in quality if these arrangements are adopted. The annual Construction Key Performance Indicator results from CBP and Rethinking Construction have provided clear business case evidence in this regard.

However, if the construction industry truly is to secure a sustainable future, it needs to embrace more fully the process of partnering. If partnering is to be one of the keystones of that sustainable future, current practice needs to be further developed through at least three additional stages or options, leading to a more sophisticated strategic style of partnering. As *The Seven Pillars of Partnering* document put it, this would involve partnering being defined in the following terms:

"Partnering is a set of strategic actions which embody the mutual objectives of a number of firms achieved by co-operative decision making aimed at using feedback to continuously improve their joint performance."

If such an approach of pro-actively seeking critical feedback and acting upon it were to be adopted, the construction industry would evolve into a modernised industry where construction companies more fully understood their client's business and could provide truly innovative, comprehensive solutions and options to their client's requirements.

There are three key steps that need to be taken to guide partnering arrangements into this new arena:

(1) fully and better integrating of teams;

(2) appreciating the importance of "strategic" partnering (sometimes called alliancing), and

(3) implementing principles of "mature partnering", by developing industry practice in a way which is consistently informed with new thinking from other industries, for example by better utilisation of standardised components, and further maturing of supply teams and chains.

Each of these steps is consider further below.

Stage one: fully integrated teams

Every client, whether experienced or not, is entitled to delivery of construction products and services which provide value in terms of cost, time, and quality. In addition, the performance of the constructed asset should match the client's business needs over its whole life. True value will only be achieved where the supply side of the industry responds collaboratively to deliver against these objectives.

The structure of the supply side of the industry, separated as it is into multiple tiers of designers, contractors, specialist and other subcontractors, and product and component suppliers, by definition mitigates against these objectives.

Successful delivery of value to clients will only therefore be achieved by the creation, at the optimal time in the design and construction process, of fully integrated teams. These integrated teams will then be able to release their contribution in terms of best practice and modern and innovative working methods. In turn, this will allow the added value of their expertise to be delivered to the client. This process can only be fully realised in a non-adversarial contractual framework where all parties equitably share in the risks and in the rewards of their endeavour.

Such teams need to agree formally on how they can satisfy the client's project objectives, whilst simultaneously agreeing their own mutual objectives. For their part, clients must recognise the need to pay fair prices (and that means fair profits) in order to receive value for money solutions.

Such objectives will also need to be translated into clearly defined performance measures and targets forming part of the partnering agreement. The achievement of the objectives needs to be closely monitored and measured and formally linked to the reward mechanism.

All of this requires a significant commitment and investment in terms of money and time by the industry. It requires the input of people who are well educated and trained in modern business culture and process techniques, not just merely technically competent.

These individuals also need to be able to recognise their own lack of knowledge and accordingly respect the contribution of others. They need to have been specifically trained in collaborative working methods and behaviours. Without such skills, background and training, the attempt to create integrated teams is doomed to failure. With such a commitment, the prospect of integrated teams working proactively together to drive out the inherent waste in the design and construction process, who can recognise that initial capital cost is only a small percentage of the cost of a built asset over its whole life, who can ensure a quality of design that provides the function and flexibility needed by the user whilst enhancing the environment, and who can minimise risks to health and safety to all, becomes realistic.

This is the essence of real partnering, and the key to secure the benefits which were targeted in the Latham report.

Stage 2: Strategic partnering/alliancing

Whilst first generation partnering, on a properly integrated basis as described above, will undoubtedly yield significant performance improvement, Sir John Egan's *Rethinking Construction* report made clear that, based upon the experience of other industries, significant improvement in performance in terms of cost, time, quality, productivity, safety and profits could be achieved year on year. These year-on-year improvements can only be achieved if the industry adopts and implements integrated processes by partnering the whole supply chain with organisations which have long-term relationships with each other and are based on clear measurement of performance.

Strategic partnering therefore, in its simplest definition, is intended to enable long-term strategies to be employed to deliver a series of individual projects to one customer. Moving away from the more common pattern of total emphasis on a single project towards a series of individual projects allows for the establishment of a strategic team who can explore systematically better ways of working in design and construction. This strategic team is established on an integrated basis and seeks to identify specific improvements in performance over a series of projects, alongside the process and product changes necessary to achieve these. Members of the strategic team should include a senior representative of each organisation involved, each of whom need to have the authority to commit their own organisation to the agreed actions.

These specific improvements should reflect and secure the agreed long-term objectives of the client and the supply side companies forming the strategic team. Strategic partnering (or alliancing, as they are sometimes known) arrangements can and do include more than one participant in each role or trade, and thus the mutuality of objectives can be extensive and in certain cases variable.

How the specific objectives are determined and how the specific processes involved are established will be a matter for the strategic teams. There will need to be open communication with the other members of the partnering organisations to ensure that the individuals responsible for delivery of projects at the project level (i.e., the project teams) fully understand what is required and what the objectives are so that they can buy-in to the "one-team" approach. There will also need to be regular meetings at the strategic level to ensure continuing commitment.

Systems of performance measurement and benchmarking will also be needed. These should correlate with the areas where performance is to be improved and with the long-term team objectives. The proposed method changes could then be tried on a chosen project, the effect measured against the relevant benchmarks, and, if successful, the new methods would then become the base standard practice for future projects.

The benchmark system should allow for progressive targets to be set and measured over a series of projects in terms which are easily understood. It should also provide for periodic testing and comparison with similar facilities for other clients. This is important in terms of strategic partnering teams being able to demonstrate that they are competitive with the market and that the client is getting good value for money. It can also be used to measure "best in world" performance, the results of which can inform the target areas for improvement.

The strategic partnering agreement should also contain a clear definition of the cost and price mechanisms to be used. These should be directly related to the client's business case budget which establishes the customer value. Fixed overhead and profit agreements are set out together with the procedures for direct cost reimbursement and audit process. There will need to be agreement on how pain/gain sharing is to be dealt with amongst all the parties. Collectively these arrangements will enable and facilitate concentration on finding best practice within the overall client value budget.

The time investment of the strategic team should be dealt with in the agreed fixed profit agreed.

One of the major benefits often overlooked, or not properly valued, is the ability, through strategic partnering, to develop really effective and efficient integrated project team processes to an extent not usually affordable in cost and time terms of a one-off project. This also applies to procedures, standards, methods and even cultures; taken in the round these themselves can yield significant time and cost improvement through driving out waste.

Another area which yields benefits to performance is the ability to establish a formal post project evaluation process feeding back into the strategic team for required solutions, or to the planning teams for upcoming projects.

The various Egan targets of 10 to 20% year-on-year improvements are firmly based upon this model of partnering. The fact that the demonstration projects have achieved the Egan targets in each of the last four years on the basis of "incomplete" partnering as described in the opening remarks to this section of this chapter supports the statements in *The Seven Pillars of Partnering* that a 40 to 50% reduction in time and cost could be achieved over the life of a strategic partnering agreement.

There are emerging examples of successful strategic partnering arrangements over the past several years such as Taylor Woodrow with both Tesco and Shell, the BP/Bovis Alliance, Mace with Cannon Healthcare, and HBG with Argent Properties; all of which report improvements in line with if not better than the Egan targets.

Stage 3: Mature partnering

Mature partnering takes the concept of partnering to the next level. It reflects fully the calls of the Construction Task Force in *Rethinking Construction* to learn from other industries and to offer quality but innovative products to customers based upon proven, standardised components delivered by established supply teams and chains. In addition, the industry is asked to offer and deliver this quality product to one-off or occasional clients who make up the majority of industry's workload.

The principle is that groups of supply-side companies, experienced in collaborative, integrated team working with each other, form a virtual company on a partnering rather than partnership basis with a commitment to a long-term relationship. By working long-term on a collaborative basis these supply-side firms can achieve continuous but significant improvement in performance with the aim of delivering the higher levels of profitability needed to invest in innovation. This high level of profitability which determines the ability to invest in new technologies and innovation is unlikely to be achieved by the individual firms working on their own.

The theory is therefore that together the individual supply side organisations become expert at developing products or services aimed at specific sectors within the industry and that together they can provide the expertise to make innovative improvements.

Consequently, the supply-side firms need to identify specific sectors or categories of clients and work together to develop and produce products and services specific to those needs. Offering standardised, proven and developed products and services provides surety of performance to clients. Providing these on an almost automatic basis releases time and resources for researching new designs, processes and innovative techniques and technologies. These can then be employed to provide "bespoke" variations, and also to produce progressively improved standard offerings.

The benchmarking process described above will provide the participants with comparative performance data to inform their own development process. Simultaneously it can be used to demonstrate market value to potential clients.

Such integrated partnering will also promote more cost effective and affordable investment in world class best practice business processes, procedures and systems. It will also provide an increased need for product facing training, research and development and marketing skills.

It is on this basis that other industries such as the automotive, off-shore oil & gas and pharmaceutical industries have reduced costs and time to market by over 50% in real terms over the last decade.

There are obvious categories of construction customers for whom this approach could be aimed in the first instance, for example the health, education and leisure sectors.

Summary

To date, the construction industry has shown not just the ability, but some enthusiasm, for the radical change necessary to secure a sustainable industry.

Partnering in its varied and proposed forms offers not just a radical change in procurement method, but, by virtue of its form, will drive the required change in culture, process and service delivery. The collaborative form of procurement will progressively diminish the adversarial habits and nature of the industry which are inherent in the old style traditional procurement methods.

Open-book arrangements are a necessity of partnering, and will provide for transparency of costs and all other risk areas in the design and construction process. This will promote development of more efficient cost effective methods and help in driving out waste.

THE NEXT STEP FOR THE CONSTRUCTION INDUSTRY

Contributed by Richard Saxon, CBE

The movement *Rethinking Construction*, and the Latham reforms that preceded it, have had limited impact because of their concept of the construction industry. A broader definition, embracing the provision of the total built environment over its lifecycle, opens up more productive viewpoints for providers and the potential of greater stakeholder satisfaction. The definitional change proposed in this section of this chapter will need changes in the legal framework to support success in the built environment solution being proposed.

The construction industry is criticised for many things. It scores poorly in every results box of the European Foundation for Quality Management's Excellence Model: Business, Customers, Society and People. The excellence model has the overall objective of striving for excellence. It is a framework within which the activities and results of any organisation can be assessed internally or by an external assessor. The model has been adopted and promoted in the UK by the British Quality Foundation.

Whilst it is not within the scope of this section of the chapter to provide an in-depth description of the strategy and techniques comprised in the model, the initiative identifies five "enabling" criteria, perceived as enabling the achievement of excellence. In summary these are:

- the way in which an organisation supports a culture of excellence;
- the organisation's formulation of policy and strategies and subsequent deployment of those into plans or actions;
- the way in which an organisation realises the potential of the workforce;
- the way in which an organisation manages its resources effectively and efficiently; and
- the way in which an organisation manages and improves its processes.

In addition to the enabling criteria, there are four "results criteria", including:

- the perception of both the customers and employees of the organisation;
- the perception of the local community; and
- the achievement by the organisation of performance targets.

These results criteria are an attempt to define and track what the organisation has actually achieved.

Apart from scoring poorly in every results box of the excellence model, the construction industry's enablers of performance are currently weak and its vision and values severely underdeveloped. Sir John Fairclough, in his valuable 2002 report *Rethinking Construction Innovation and Research*, as published by the DTI/DTLR, said:

"Construction should be seen as central to a better quality of life for everyone, and concerned with a sustainable future. It needs to develop its vision, get widespread buy-in, and communicate it to all stakeholders."

For the industry to score in all the excellence model results boxes it would need to be growing and profitable, have a well satisfied customer base, be accepted in the wider community, and contain an enthusiastic workforce. It is clear there is some way to go in realising these qualities in most areas of the industry.

The profit to enable better sustainability and human resource policies can only come from stronger value added for customers which is then partially captured by construction. Sir John Egan's accusation that the industry is not sufficiently customer focused then becomes the main issue. In short, how can much more value can be created for customers and society?

This inevitably leads to the debate over value definition. Value can be defined as the relationship of "benefits" to "costs". Facilities are needed to deliver benefits, but often entail costs of many kinds. The construction industry tends to focus on costs and on improving value by lowering costs. Consultants and advisers spend much time on the subject of risk, but this is simply one of the forms of cost.

The "cost fixation" in construction holds back the industry. In contrast, the benefit side of the equation is insufficiently examined.

The starting point for benefits is how a facility delivered by the industry serves its customer in functionality, quality and impact terms. This area is capable of far more development than it has traditionally received. For example, other industries typically start from a development premise of looking at what the customer wants or needs, and then engineering it to their price point to make it viable.

Construction has tended to take the "need" for granted. It is treated as something the customer defines with its consultants help, and which is then a given.

Benefit definition in the construction industry is, in fact, in its infancy. A publication produced by the Royal Academy of Engineering in 1998 (*The Long-term Costs of Owning and Using Buildings* by Evans, Haryott, Hasle & Jones) highlighted that lifetime costs of ownership and occupation dwarf construction costs, and that business operating costs over a 20-year period dwarf both the construction costs and the lifetime costs of ownership and occupation.

It follows that a building which facilitated business performance and reduced operating costs could pay for itself, possibly several times over, as against the "same" building not optimised in this way. By concentrating primarily on cost, the construction industry actually tends to increase lifetime costs and negative social impacts.

To illustrate this point, the publication by the Royal Academy of Engineering is referred to by some as the "1:5:200 paper". The "200" represents 20 years of business operating cost, not 20 years of value creation, the "5" is the 20 years of costs of ownership and occupation, and the "1" is the cost of construction.

A number from 25% higher to 10 times higher could apply as the performance figure for the occupying activity. Within the initial construction cost of the "1" sits the planning and design work of, for example, "0.1".

The leverage between thought input at the start and performance benefit generated therefore runs to a ratio of potentially 1:2500 upwards. Thoughtless downward pressure on design time is therefore more than a false economy; it is economic nonsense and at the root of our national dissatisfaction with the construction industry and with our built environment generally.

Nevertheless, the construction industry continues to think in this traditional form, primarily focused on cost. It has tended only to enter the facility lifecycle analysis after the initial business case making and conceptual thought. The industry then exits a relationship with its work product before experiencing the effectiveness of its work in value terms. It is therefore "cut off" from the very pressures and experiences which would help it understand benefit value and through-life costs.

Neither customers nor consultants are easily able to see this lifecycle scene for themselves; the latter often due to their non-customer focused professional priorities. Customers rarely see how certain facilities can add value to their businesses. Indeed many customers buy facilities as a "distress" purchase, without aspirations other than to relieve pressure (for example in relation to office size).

It is only for commercial developers that construction could be said to be their core business. There is consequently only a very small cohort of customer enthusiasts able or willing to play a part in industry strategy. Customers, who often do not even know they are customers until they have begun, are wishing in the main that construction could be like other advanced industries: easy to buy from, full of ideas to meet their special needs, needing no customer leadership.

The Built Environment is the author's preferred term for the sector that provides physical context for life and economic activity. Whilst construction is currently rated at 7% of GDP (the same size as the NHS) it is suggested that the built environment and its associated utilities could represent a quarter of the economy, supporting and enabling the rest.

The £80 billion trade spend of construction has upstream of it over £12 billion of construction consultancy work. There is then an unquantified amount of management, legal and accounting consultancy to define business cases and support customers through projects. The property industry adds about £60 billion in land, finance and management of estates. Downstream of construction comes £60 billion of hard and soft facilities management, not counting £18 billion of domestic DIY. A study is currently underway to map the sector properly, but it could easily be the case that the total sector value is over £200 billionn, equivalent to 18% of GDP.

In addition, the utilities (electricity, gas, water), sewerage, transport and telecoms are all closely associated with the built environment sector. Half of all energy production goes to service buildings and another ten percent goes to make materials. Twenty percent of all road traffic is construction related, whilst our development decisions determine the rest of traffic generation. Water supply and drainage are dictated by development; flooding problems are largely caused by poor design and development management. Information and communication technologies are largely building based and run the buildings as well as the occupier's businesses.

In this context and given the real size and implications of the built environment sector for the lifestyle, prosperity and sustainability of our economy, the current vision for construction looks exceedingly thin. Be suggests the following mission statement for construction:

"To add value for customers and society by shaping and delivering the built environment to meet their needs."

The sector should aim to take a share of value added, rather than be positioned as a cost to be minimised as the industry is positioned today.

The proposal for the industry formerly known as construction is that it should offer integrated solutions tailored to need. The phrase "integrated solutions" comes from other industries which have moved beyond selling products. (See *Integrated Solutions; the new economy between manufacturing and services*, Andrew Davies and others, SPRU, 2002.)

Where customers' real need is to have the use of a performance-enhancing facility, the integrated solution provider would finance, design, build and operate the facility. The PFI concept introduced the integrated solutions model to construction, following its emergence in the transport and defence sectors. The provider lives on stable, long-term income streams, learns to improve the product and service because it is living with it, and learns above all how it is adding value to the user. At the top end of the integrated solution provider skill set comes consultancy ability, to enable purchasers to be advised on what will serve them best and to enable the provider to develop the most attractive offers.

The PFI process has started the ball rolling towards integrated built environment solutions provision. Unfortunately, in the author's view the legal framework for PFI has become unduly complex which results in unnecessary waste. The PFI process has also created perverse incentives for providers, diverting their attention from the idea of providing innovative, performance enhancing and risk removing facilities. Quality in the design sense has been eroded by the process and its leadership style, exposing the weakness of constructors as system integraters on this large scale.

What the industry needs is the legal profession to develop tools which facilitate the success of the overall mission, aligning customer and society goals with the incentives in the process, fostering value seeking and enabling providers to share in added value. Partnership will be the style of successful customer/provider relationships and also of those within what will undoubtedly be a network of suppliers forming the branded provider offer.

A mature built environment provider will aim to offer "fitness for purpose" to its customers, ending the long-term avoidance of this issue. If such a provider were to own, design, build and operate it would have only itself to turn to for performance and consequently the chain would be in place to ensure quality, both of technical construction but also of suitability for the intended use. The industry also needs to end the "Catch-22" situation when zeal to protect the end customer from risk serves to prevent that customer gaining the full value, which might have been created by collaboration.

One paradox of the UK construction industry is that it has tended to use lowest first cost tendering and risk-transferring contracts to protect customers, yet it has achieved one of the highest construction cost economies in the OECD with a less than satisfactory built environment. Trust-based systems outperform adversarial ones, but the "Catch 22" dilemma referred to above ensures that distrust still rules. Things are changing through framework agreements, partnering contracts and supply chain management thinking. The aim should be to lift the game to a new level, embrace broader talents and unlock social and economic value in very large amounts.

The experience of Lean Construction so far is salutary. The concept of Lean comes from Toyota and is based on clear definition of value as the customer sees it, allowing progressive elimination of producer activities which do not add customer value. The construction industry has tried to apply Lean without having any grasp of customer value other than the most simplistic. Waste cannot therefore be identified unless it is glaringly obvious, such as unused site supplies being dumped.

Michelangelo ended his career with a series of "slave sculptures", figures struggling to emerge from blocks of stone. These dramatise his method of work which he said was "to see the figure within a stone and simply cut away the unwanted material". His genius in an artistic medium is a metaphor for the industry formerly known as construction: concentrate on customer and society value and you will see the waste clearly. This applies to design and to legal process equally

CHAPTER 4

CASE STUDIES

INTRODUCTION

Although partnering may still be considered as a relatively new concept of working for the construction sector, it is a process that has been adopted by a number of those operating in the industry. This is both in terms of projects that have now been completed and as part of future procurement strategies. This chapter sets out a number of case studies demonstrating how partnering can work in practice. These range from the early example of Kent Property Services dating back to 1995, through to a recent arrangement concluded by Scottish Water that, at the time of writing, is about to get underway.

CASE STUDY 1 – KENT PROPERTY SERVICES

Information provided by Geoff Rutt, formerly Head of Property Services, Kent Property Services

Kent Police Strategic Partnering

An early example of partnering in the public sector is the construction of Tonbridge Police Station. In 1995, Kent Property Services (KPS), the consulting division of Kent County Council persuaded the Kent Police Authority to procure their construction works under a strategic partnering framework. It was proposed that this should run for three years with a two-year extension to deal with a capital programme then valued at £8m.

Framework agreement

The framework agreement was based on model specifications derived from existing examples of similar work together with a back up of a schedule of rates and prices to be used to build-up prices for specific work. It was envisaged that this would cover the majority of the types of work that might be procured under the framework agreement. It also incorporated a service agreement so that contractors could be paid for work prior to starting on site and these costs would be deducted from the works costs. Whilst the framework was in essence an agreement to do business without any guarantee of work, it detailed how the parties were expected to work together and the levels of expected performance. The underlying contract was to be the JCT 1980 Edition Standard Form, with overriding clauses to some of the core aspects such as architect's instructions, extensions of time, retention and liquidated and ascertained damages. Overriding clauses were made on the basis that all these matters potentially undermine the philosophy of partnering. The framework agreement was then advertised in accordance with EU public procurement rules and some 42 companies responded to the advertisement. The pre-qualification criteria included factors such as:

- the organisation and structure of the company;
- relevant project experience;
- experience of framework agreements and partnering;
- quality management systems;
- financial status;
- health and safety management systems.

Bidding process

This process led to a short list of 12 and then eventually, by a quality analysis to a tender list of eight. By April 1996 the framework agreement had been put in place with four contractors. These contractors were of differing sizes so that there could be an appropriate match to the size of contract that was likely to arise in the capital programme. There were also eight specialist contractors in areas such as mechanical and electrical work.

Once the contractors had been selected, it was expected that, on a project-by-project basis, they would have input into aspects such as design, cost models/budgets, the early introduction of specialists and suppliers, the supply of up-to-date market information and to generally have an impact at the formative stages of any given project. Partnering workshops were held involving all the 12 main and specialist contractors and a strategic partnering charter was agreed and signed by all. This process was repeated for each of the separate contracts awarded under the overall framework agreement. By the end of the five years, £22m had been spent as the programme rapidly expanded and the Kent Police Authority Estates were happy to spend the extra funds through the framework that had been set-up.

Award

The first contract carried out under the strategic partnering framework was the largest at £5.75m. The project involved the procurement of a new police station in Tonbridge (one of the first above ground M4i public sector projects). It involved a four storey Police Station with a two storey 100-space car park. It was built between November 1996 and January 1998.

Out of the four main contractors selected under the framework agreement, Wates Construction was selected as the main contractor. Alongside KPS, the Kent Police Authority and Wates, the remaining partners were the subcontractors Dennes Building Services (mechanical) and Gilbert & Stamper (electrical). Each of the partners, including the Kent Police Authority as the client, nominated a senior representative of their organisation to act as "champions". These representatives were charged with leading the project and generally promoting effective communication between the partners. They were very effective, meeting on a regular basis to monitor the partnering process, to talk about issues informally and raise issues in a non-confrontational forum so that these issues could be sorted out before they developed into problems that could disrupt the project. At the same time, Wates Construction, Dennes Building Services and Gilbert & Stamper undertook to promote similar partnering principles within the overall supply chain.

Management support

As Head of KPS for the duration of the Tonbridge Police station project, Geoff Rutt was particularly proactive in persuading the Kent Police Authority to adopt the partnering procurement option in place of the more traditional forms of procurement. Commenting on the experience gained from this project, it is Mr Rutt's view that had it been carried out under a traditional form of contracting, this would probably have led to major problems. Amongst those factors with the potential for dispute was that the project involved a lot of accommodation in a very confined site, with access therefore causing problems. Other issues arose such as the necessity to move two water sewers, followed by a third that even the relevant water company was not aware of.

However, during the project, partnering workshop team building meetings were arranged to canvass ideas and views from everyone on site. An example of such a workshop was one entitled "achieving exceptional success". Those taking part included representatives of all the finishing trades, the police and the mechanical and electrical specialist to discuss how each party could assist the others to save the police time and money in making the buildings operational in the shortest period possible by the overlapping of the trade programme with communications and the like. These workshops encouraged a positive atmosphere on the site attributable to the impression of there being only one team on the site as opposed to several.

The dispute resolution strategy also worked well, the principle being that responsibility was handed to the lowest management level possible with strict rules about passing disputes up the line. In the event, no dispute reached the highest level of management within the respective structures: there were no claims and the final account was settled in a matter of weeks. Levels of paperwork were slashed with all the effort going into working for the client and producing a product that all the partnering team owned and was proud of.

Achievement

In the event, Tonbridge Police Station was completed 12 weeks early with minimal defects. The team absorbed over £100,000 of client changes within the original budget and managed handover so that the police station was operational within two weeks – in the past this could have taken three months. The client was involved at all stages. This experience was repeated at other Kent Police projects, such as the Headquarters for Specialist Crime and Margate Police Station, where substantially the same team was involved.

Swan Valley Secondary School

During his time as head of KPC, Mr Rutt was involved in a number of project-specific partnering projects, such as the construction of the Swan Valley Secondary School. Kent County Council required the construction of a new secondary school in the Swanscombe area within the relatively short period of 24 months. The school was to cater for 500 students, with a budget of £6m. It was built between July 1997 and August 1998. Wates was again selected as the contractor, with a price, which although not the lowest represented as an overall package, value for money. By reason of the speed with which the project was to proceed, much of the design work was carried out in the hope of obtaining planning permission. This meant that Wates was involved in the initial design and made a contribution from that point on.

Achievement

The team managed to complete the work in just over 24 months when it would be more usual for such a scheme to take up to five years. The finished product was handed over with minimal defects and within the budget so that the school was open to the students on the required date. This was despite the discovery during construction of a significant archaeological area, which ordinarily could have had the potential to close the site for several months, with the necessary suspension of the work. Under the partnering arrangements, the team was extended to include an archaeologist and the work reprogrammed so that the archaeologist could work along side Wates. If problems arose, a meeting was held and a way forward was agreed by the site operatives. No time was lost as a result. In addition, the newly appointed school headmaster provided active client/end-user involvement. This project also mirrors the experience of Tonbridge Police Station in that there was a significant reduction in paperwork and no claims.

From these projects, Mr Rutt identifies five key elements in a successful partnering arrangement. These are that the project should command the following:

- total involvement of all;
- earliest involvement of all;

- maximum communication;
- empowerment of all so that problems are solved at the lowest possible level;
- ownership and pride.

CASE STUDY 2 – MINISTRY OF DEFENCE AND BUCKNALL PRIME SOLUTIONS
Information provided by Tony Brown, Partner, Bucknall Austin

Achievement

Set to be a model for future Ministry of Defence (MoD) schemes, Defence Estates' £40m Andover North Site Redevelopment project was the first "Prime Contract" let by MoD, and the first one to be completed. The project has been innovative in the approach taken in the management, design and construction process and sets new standards for collaboration. Bucknall Austin adopted a consultant led "virtual company" approach, supported by an innovative IT approach utilising web-based communication technologies.

Background

As a public sector organisation, a key priority for Defence Estates (an executive agency of the UK MoD) is to design, construct and manage its construction schemes as efficiently as possible, and it has therefore taken a lead in adopting partnering-type approaches – such as "prime contracting" – to its projects.

A prime contractor takes single, overall responsibility for the management and delivery of a project to meet the required specification efficiently, economically and on time and brings to play the full talent of the supply chain. Responsibilities include selection and management of the supply chain, design and works co-ordination, planning, cost control and working with the client to ensure a fit-for-purpose outcome.

The Andover North Site Redevelopment, providing new facilities for the Defence Logistics Organisation (DLO), was procured as a Prime Contract. The project brief required construction to be right first time and provide best value for money on a through life basis. The successful contractor would also be responsible for post-construction maintenance of the structures and building services for six-and-a-half years (known as the compliance period), so design durability and reduced whole life costs were key elements of the brief.

A former air base, the 34-acre Andover North Site Redevelopment provided 26,000m^2 of new accommodation, including an office building for 780 staff, a warrant officers' and sergeants' mess with 68 live-in members, technical and sports facilities, a day nursery, gatehouse, and associated infrastructure and external works.

Bucknall Austin have been working with Defence Estates for many years. Key projects include the ground-breaking Abbey Wood HQ for the Defence Procurement Agency, and also their Project Partnering Agreement (South-West Region) which has to date involved over 70 projects throughout South-West England.

After a 17-month selection and tender period (from initial OJEC), Bucknall Austin was awarded the Prime Contract in January 2001, and construction started in April 2001.

There was a single contract between Defence Estates and Bucknall Austin Prime Solutions; Bucknall Austin then agreed contracts with each member of a supply chain. Key members included the three main cluster contractors C. H. Pearce, Thomas Vale and Southern Electric Contracting (SEC), architect Percy Thomas Partnership (including landscape architect, Fira), M&E engineers Hoare Lea & Partners and Torpy & Partners (now part of Halcrow), structural engineer URS Thorburn Colquhoun and civil engineer Hyder Consulting. Integral members of the team were staff from the DLO, representing the client.

MPTC

An important principle behind Prime is the concept of MPTC (maximum price, target cost) in which:

- the Prime team declare a single "ring fenced" profit;
- the team establish a target cost;
- a pain/gain sharing mechanism is agreed between MoD and Prime Contractor to share any actual cost savings/overspends below or above target;
- a maximum cost is established above which the Prime Contractor takes 100% of pain.

The virtual company approach

From the outset, Bucknall Austin recognised that the key to delivering Prime successfully was going to be mutual trust and co-operation and developing seamless collaboration between team members. Great emphasis was placed on working closely together in an atmosphere of honesty, trust and openness.

A virtual company approach for the project was developed, reviewing areas of available best practice and developing new approaches to suit the Prime Contracting requirements. Key aspects of this approach included:
- Each of the core team took "shares" in the Prime Contractor's pain/gain costs. In this way the team became jointly accountable for the success or failure of the project.
- The whole team adopted a completely open-book approach between team members and client.
- A partnering charter was developed in a partnering workshop and signed by all team members and client.

- A single project professional indemnity insurance policy was taken out, spanning the construction and Compliance Period and covering the whole team for design and for fitness for purpose.
- Bucknall Austin developed a whole suite of contracts for the team and supply chain.
- With the help of Hammonds, an umbrella contract was developed (termed the Integrated Project Agreement) which spelt-out the working arrangements and partnering principles and identified the core team members shares in the pain/gain arrangements.
- A joint steering committee was established enabling a meeting of the senior directors of each of the core team members' companies. These meetings were held monthly throughout the project to review progress, finance and any other issues, and to agree a common way forward.
- Bucknall Austin established a project bank account, which enabled payments to the whole core team and Prime Contractor to be made simultaneously. The original Prime Contract required the Prime Contractor to demonstrate that they had paid their supply chain before applying for payment themselves (i.e., requiring the Prime Contractor to effectively "fund" construction). The project bank account created certainty of payment to the supply chain but retained a "cash neutral" position for Bucknall Austin as Prime Contractor – whilst it was agreed to forego any potential cash flow benefits, Bucknall Austin were also not penalised for negative cash flow.
- Key team members were co-located in offices on site at Andover, but others continued to work from other locations. To support the partnering culture of openness and transparency, the team agreed to use a web-based collaboration system, a project extranet, to provide a communication platform to share and exchange all documents, drawings and other information relating to the project. This agreement was written into a key document, the project execution plan.
- Bucknall Austin developed a knowledge management system for Prime Contracting (Prime Values) that was made available to the whole supply chain via the collaboration system.

The information channel

BIW Information Channel, from BIW Technologies, makes data available to every team member through a secure, project-specific website – accessible by authorised individuals from any location 24/7. Users are able to create, and have access to, information on the site including drawings, specifications, comments, notes of meetings, schedules, photographs, team member details, etc. The system provides a transparent, single repository of the most up-to-date information, and all user activity is tracked and recorded, providing an audit trail detailing who did what and when.

Training for key users was provided at the outset; each key user attended a two-day course that equipped them to then train other users within their company. To accommodate team changes and additions as the project progressed (e.g., short-term use by a cladding subcontractor), additional training days were provided at appropriate intervals throughout the project.

The site offices were equipped with a network, a 2Mb MegaStream tele-comm connection, plotters and a shared CAD facility; all other team members could use their existing company networks and/or internet connections to access the Information Channel (some even started to use the system from home). The system utilised a "HTTPS" site (a secure server certificate provides 128-bit high security level encryption). The client team accessed the Channel via a dedicated PC.

The Channel usage grew rapidly, averaging more than 2000 log-ins every month throughout the peak. One factor in this rapid adoption was that design work continued in parallel with construction for some months, so the Channel became a vital conduit between designers, constructors and suppliers. In 20 months, there were over 23,600 system log-ins; 1,733 documents and 4,072 drawings were published, over 1,300 comments on these were made, and all were accessible to over 170 users from 27 organisations.

Instead of designers distributing multiple packages of drawings to lots of individuals, drawings were published once – to the Channel – and individuals could then view, comment upon and, if necessary, print off just the drawings or details they needed. This drastically cut the volume of paperwork produced, distributed and stored (team feedback suggests this reduction was also partly due to the partnering ethos; the absence of an adversarial culture removed the need for the many contract letters found on more traditional projects). Information could be found more readily (some team members contrasted ease of access to a single repository with searching through email attachments or filing cabinet drawers), and the client was able to produce vital monthly reports based on information published to the Channel (the client team logged-in nearly 900 times).

Following completion in October 2002, the Channel created an efficiently searchable electronic archive of all information relating to the buildings, for future operation and maintenance purposes.

Did the approach succeed?

In a word – yes. The virtual company approach enabled real innovative solutions to be realised in the project design and delivery, including:

- Electrical wholesaler on site. SEC, the M&E services Cluster leader, appointed an electrical wholesaler on site. All components were ordered "live" via the wholesalers' computer terminal on-site and delivered "just in time" on an open-book basis.
- SEC erected a prefabrication workshop erected on site to fabricate ductwork, pipework, conduits etc. in a controlled, safe environment.

- Building structure design, building orientation, and structural components were specifically designed and selected to assist the thermal control of internal environment.
- Heat pumps were utilised in lieu of chillers.
- Intelligent lighting utilised throughout the offices, eliminating light switching and enabling lights to dim to provide correct illumination.
- Office interiors, IT, partitioning and structure designed to reduce churn costs.
- Low energy buildings – excellent BREEAM rating achieved on offices.
- Fabric roof to streets.
- Enclosed steelwork left unpainted.
- Site levels optimised – minimising material off-site.
- Re-use of topsoil, minimising imported material.
- Material and component selections were made utilising a "Balanced scorecard" approach – this encompassed not only capital costs and through life costs, but also programme impact, risk, health & safety, environment, aesthetic.
- Pro-active approach taken in respect of health & safety, sustainability and environmental issues both in the design, construction and management of the facilities.

The project bank account has been a real success (and is mentioned in *Accelerating Change*). Bucknall Austin will be seeking to extend the account to the whole supply chain – which will effectively bring the added advantage seen in construction management, such that the supply chain (and Prime Contractor) are effectively paid direct by the Client.

The strength of the collaborative "virtual company" approach was put to its ultimate test when a real problem occurred. Normally, the result of this would have been delays, litigation and cost escalation where no-one wins. In reality, what happened was that an emergency meeting of the joint steering committee was called, the options were examined and a conclusion was agreed by all in 20 minutes! As a result – everyone won!

The project was handed over on time, on budget and to a high standard.

The project and the team approach has been recognised by our peers.

- The project won the BIFM PFI/PPP project of the year award 2002.
- CABE have commented favourably on the designs.
- The team were finalists, coming third in the Building "Contractor of the Year Awards" 2003.

Most importantly – the end-users from DLO have been delighted with their new facilities.

Bucknall Austin and the Prime Solutions team are tendering for several other prime contracts and are formalising their working arrangements within a new joint venture company.

CASE STUDY 3: TAYLOR WOODROW STRATEGIC ALLIANCE PARTNERSHIP

Information provided by Charles Lever, Director of Building Services, Taylor Woodrow

The Strategic Alliance Partnership is an example of the benefits of long-term strategic alliancing.

Background

In 2000 Taylor Woodrow's construction arm undertook to develop and implement a strategy that would provide significant improvements to Taylor Woodrow's building services design, procurement and installation. After an extensive programme of interviews, interrogation, visits and presentations Taylor Woodrow created a Strategic Alliance Partnership with three major building services contractors (N G Bailey, The Rotary Group and Staveley Industries) in the autumn of 2001. The aim of the alliance is to work in an integrated manner, to share knowledge, labour, resources and technology in order to enhance performance and provide continuous business improvement.

This integrated approach is intended to enable the Alliance to perform value engineering during design development, thereby reducing risk, saving time and achieving cost efficiencies.

In the past, Taylor Woodrow had worked with some 200 individual building services companies so the establishment of the Strategic Alliance Partnership represented a radical approach to procurement for them.

The Partnership Charter

All four companies have signed up to a Strategic Alliance Partnership Charter, which sets out the vision of the Alliance which is "to be the premier collaborative force for a new generation of creative built environments". The Charter puts the interests of the customers first and bases its approach on trust, shared objectives, collaboration, continuous improvement and sharing of risks.

Cost services

One of the drivers behind the creation of the Strategic Alliance Partnership was the fact that 34% of the construction prime cost spend is made up of building services systems. By offering an integrated approach cost savings and continued development of best practice can be offered to clients.

Strategic Alliance Board

The Alliance is headed by a Strategic Alliance Board (which meets monthly) consisting of a director from each of the four parties with an additional Taylor Woodrow director acting as a Chairman. The Board determines the allocation of tender negotiated works during that period. Wherever possible the Alliance is put forward for the services element of a project that is being tendered. The nominated services contractor acts with Taylor Woodrow to advise and input on the services portion of the tender. If significant projects are to be let, a combination of all three building services contractors may be used.

Alliance Implementation Team

Under Board level is the Alliance Implementation Team who are responsible for the implementation of policy and strategy, monitoring project delivery activities and reporting to the Board. The Alliance Implementation Team is split into a number of groups each made up of one of the four alliance members with one of the Board members as a facilitator. The groups are Project Management, Communications and Marketing, Procurement and Design and Research and Development. Each group meets monthly to share and review best practice and monitor and update Alliance procedures. This ensures that the Alliance continues to work on strategies to share knowledge, provide continuous improvements, develop best practice, promote a non-adversarial culture and promote performance monitoring. Current Alliance strategies include working to reduce the number of second tier suppliers being used by the Alliance and to enhance benchmarking, improvement targets and key performance indicators.

Since the development of the Strategic Alliance Partnership Taylor Woodrow has let contracts more effectively and has 25 live projects with the alliance and over 40 live bids (March 2003).

Four of the Strategic Alliance Partnership projects include:

Greenwich Millennium Village

Taylor Woodrow worked with N G Bailey on this project to design and construct a unique housing development which is well-known for its sustainable construction and construction best practice (£30 million). The early appointment of N G Bailey before the M&E design was finalised has led to greater co-ordination of services drawings and the advice of key suppliers prior to manufacture and assembly has led to valuable savings for example by installing prefabricated bathroom pods in each apartment.

Tidworth Primary Healthcare Centre

The early involvement of Staveley Group company, MJN Colson, enhanced cost certainly for this MoD project and ensured that the project benefited from their expertise particularly in areas of modularisation brought across from the Bromley Hospital Project.

The Green Building, Macintosh Village

This is an 11-storey circular block with 32 apartments, over a triangular podium, which includes a nursery and doctor's surgery. The early input of Alliance member N G Bailey at design development changed the original ground sourced heat pump design to gas boilers on the roof linked to solar collectors, creating a unified heating system and reducing the need for a hot water cylinder in each apartment, thereby increasing net available area and creating cost savings.

King William Street, London

Taylor Woodrow is working with The Rotary Group on this £6 million refurbishment of an eight-storey office building. The early involvement of The Rotary Group enabled Taylor Woodrow to recommend the early ordering of critical fan coil units and rapid turn around of the building services tender.

There are many other projects on which the Alliance is working and as for the future, Charles Lever, Director of Building Services at Taylor Woodrow has said that "SAPs targets include further reductions in prime cost, ability to attract quality resources from diverse backgrounds, zero accidents on SAP sites and a significant reduction in waste".

CASE STUDY 4: THE DURHAM SCHOOLS PARTNERING PROJECTS

Information derived from Rethinking Construction Case History, January 2003 and the Durham County Council Information Service at *www.durham.gov.uk*

Background

Following an audit of schools construction in the county of Durham, the Council looked to partnering as a method of procurement to solve problems of inadequate control of capital cost, construction delays and an unacceptable number of defects. All of these deficiencies had been brought to light in the course of the audit. Using partnering as the preferred process, the Council procured two new-build projects and two refurbishment projects.

Selection of the partner

To address the problem of capital cost control, Durham's selection process included a tender assessment on quality and price, which incorporated the securing of a guaranteed maximum price and the sharing of savings from an agreed target price. The target cost was ascertained by reference to value engineering to ensure that the guaranteed maximum price did not exceed the budget. Looking at issues related to delay, provision for liquidated and ascertained damages was retained so as to maintain pressure on construction time. Finally, with reference to defects, it is understood that Durham was confident that the partnering process would foster an environment within which defects would be kept to a minimum.

The selection of a contractor involved the Council in inviting submissions from contractors approved for projects of more than £2m. From the responses received, a tender list was prepared of those of companies who could satisfy certain essential criteria including previous school building experience and involvement in other partnering projects. The top four tenderers were short-listed for interviews by the project stakeholders, which would include the schools. It was a stipulation that attendance at the interviews with the project stakeholders was restricted to personnel who proposed to work on the project. Miller Construction was selected for the new-build projects and Shepherd Construction for the refurbishment projects.

Thereafter, the contractor, Durham County and the major stakeholders developed a Stakeholder Project Charter that set out their objectives and how they intended working together. The Charter which included a "Mission Statement" was signed by everyone to underline their commitment to its success.

The new build projects

The new build projects were Middlestone Moor School and Catchgate Primary School, both of which involved Miller Construction.

Middlestone Moor

Middlestone Moor was a new school built on the site of the former Spennymoor West School. The old school premises were demolished. The project's mission statement was "By Teamwork and innovation we will create new schools which will provide an environment for excellence and opportunity".

Catchgate School

This school has been built on the site of a reclaimed colliery spoil heap, adjacent to the site of the original school. The old school building was demolished and the site transformed into playing fields. The agreed mission statement was "By Teamwork and innovation we will create new schools which will provide an environment for excellence and opportunity". The new purpose-built £2.1m school was officially opened in June 2002.

Financial initiatives

The partnering framework between the Council and Miller promoted a number of value-engineering initiatives. The Rethinking Construction Case History cites that "For example, at Middlestone Moor they needed to reduce costs by £100,000 otherwise the project would stall. They did this by adapting the original linear building concept to cluster classrooms around shared practical spaces. This had the benefit of optimising roof spans and circulation space that reduced costs. Miller and Durham also agreed the GMP, target price and incentives following extensive value engineering. Only then was a contract signed. At Catchgate they saved £30,000 off the target cost by value engineering the groundworks with the specialist to reduce gradients and fill volumes. The Council reinvested their share in improved acoustic finishes and tree planting to reduce exposure to wind at Catchgate."

Technical innovation

The innovations and improvements cited by Durham Council (*www.durham.gov.uk*) include:

- "*Sustainable Urban Drainage System*. Middlestone Moor Project in Partnership with Northumbrian Water has developed a rain water collection system. The system works by channelling the water draining from the roof and land areas into an external underground tank. The water collected is used for flushing WCs and urinals. Northern Electric and Gas supplied a solar cell to power a pump, which in turn assists in the movement of rainwater from the collection tank to the school."
- "*PVC-free wiring*. PVC is a toxic substance. To make the school even more environmentally friendly, AEI cables supplied PVC free wiring to Catchgate School."
- *Natural lighting*. Natural light is used to maximum advantage, so reducing artificial lighting running costs. Automatic lighting controls, using presence and daylight level detectors, are installed in all classrooms and switch off when rooms are unoccupied or sufficient natural lighting is available."

It is understood that by reason of the Council's positive experience of partnering by reference to this two-project partnership with Miller Construction, the Council will take forward the concept of long-term, strategic alliances for building and civil engineering design and construction.

The refurbishment projects

The refurbishment projects were carried out at Chilton Primary School and Tanfield School by Shepherd Construction.

Chilton Primary School

The refurbishment work involved the amalgamation of the old Chilton Junior and Infant Schools to create a new primary on the site of the existing junior school, a project carried out in three phases. The first phase focused on building a new infant and nursery block, and was completed in December 2001. The second phase involved the refurbishment of the existing junior block, comprising eight classrooms, adding further classrooms and two joint use rooms. Phase 3 again involved the construction of additional facilities. The works were completed in August 2002. The new primary school caters for 420 pupils.

The project workshop included representatives from the school, the design engineers, and the builders and education advisors. The project Charter included an agreed mission statement, which stated that "The Chilton Primary School Partnering Team will by team commitment and creativity, deliver a quality life-long learning environment for the community of Chilton".

Tanfield School

Internal work included the addition of new classrooms, toilet facilities, a student social area and an office for the Heads of Year. The external refurbishment comprised essential restoration repairs so that the building has a minimum life expectancy of 10 years. The mission statement set out in the project charter was "To work in partnership with a spirit of mutual trust, co-operation and respect, to provide the best possible improvement to the learning environment for the community and users of Tanfield School".

CASE STUDY 5 – SCOTTISH WATER
Information provided by Charles Brien, Senior Commercial Lawyer, Scottish Water

Background

Scottish Water was formed in 2002 and brought together the three pre-existing Water Authorities which had all been local authority based. Although Scottish Water is still publicly owned it was created with the intention of providing Scotland with a more efficient water and waste water provider and to allow Scotland to benefit from the efficiencies which had been generated in England and Wales following the privatisation of their water and waste water industry.

In the months preceding the creation of Scottish Water the three Water Authorities met and considered how they could start to deliver the efficiencies that the Scottish Water Regulator, the Water Industry Commissioner, would require. In the next regulatory period, 1 April 2002 to 31 March 2006, the Regulator was going to require Scottish Water to deliver assets that had previously been costed in the region of £2.3billion for £1.8billion. This level of efficiency, which had been achieved in England and Wales, could only be achieved in Scotland if a different model was used to deliver the Capital Programme.

In considering how the efficiencies could be delivered Scottish Water initially considered simply operating their business in a more efficient way but that in itself would not produce the almost 30% efficiencies that would be required. What would be required would be a step change in the way the Capital Programme was delivered. The new delivery model would require a more streamline decision making process, with the right answer being found first, more frequently and at a lesser cost. It was further noted that true efficiencies could only be achieved at the programme level rather than at the project level. When a budget had been determined for a particular project there was little or no scope for further savings to be identified. Those savings had already been determined in reaching the target cost. Accordingly, for the efficiencies to be achieved, the identifying of those target costs throughout the programme and the combining of diverse projects to produce a better solution were seen as being a more likely source of efficiencies.

Scottish Water is subject to the EU Procurement Rules and in December 2002 the placing of an advertisement commenced the process. Seventeen notes of interest were received and using high level differentiation five consortia were short-listed to enter into Stage 2 of the process.

At the same time it was decided by Scottish Water that they would wish to have two partners so that there would be a wider sharing of risk. Each partner would have a delivery capability and in total that would amount to 50% of the total delivery.

Alternative structures

In addition, two models were proposed. The first structure was based on the two successful consortia forming a separate legal identity through a limited liability company, the shareholders of whom would be Scottish Water and the two partner consortia. This model assumed that there would be a Services Contract between Scottish Water and the Company setting out the scope of each parties responsibilities, detailed methodologies on the day to day implementation of the Capital Investment Programme and the flow of funds throughout. There would be a separate Shareholder Agreement between Scottish Water and the two partner consortia governing the day to day management of the company, setting out the responsibilities of each of the Directors and Shareholders with particular reference to matters which would be subject of unanimous or majority approval of the Directors and identifying areas that would be reserved for Shareholder approval and determining the exit strategy both at the natural expiry of the Services Contract or earlier in circumstances where either of the partners was failing to perform.

The second structure was essentially based on a contractual arrangement among Scottish Water and the two partner consortia. The rights and responsibilities of each of the parties would be based solely on a single agreement among the parties. The contract would encapsulate all the provisions concerning implementation of the Capital Investment Programme including constitutional arrangements for decision making, approval process, day-to-day management and monitoring of the relationship and exit strategy.

At this time Scottish Water had not determined which would be the better option. However, it was noted that the first option had not to-date been tried elsewhere and might thus be too innovative. Equally, it was feared that the second option being a wholly contractual matrix would involve such a complicated structure, having to deal with such a large and complex matter, that it may itself not produce the required efficiencies.

Bidding process

During the bidding process Scottish Water determined on the first structure and advised the tenderers of the model against which their bid had to be made. The model (see Figure1) has developed over the negotiation period but it is materially the same and involves a company being formed, Scottish Water Solutions Limited, of which Scottish Water owns 51% of the shares, the remainder being owned equally by the consortia partners. At the design, programme and procurement level there is total integration. Below that, but still within Solutions there is 50% delivery by the partner consortia with the remaining 50% being delivered by third parties but through a partnering based contract.

Figure 1

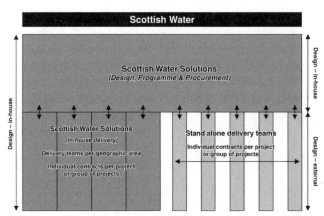

It had always been a desire of Scottish Water that the indigenous construction industry would be maintained and used and hence it was important to ensure that work would be available to the Scottish Construction Industry. This is to be protected through the third-party delivery chain.

The critical issue for Scottish Water was to identify the correct partners who would not only have to be able to work together but work with Scottish Water and within the legal identity of Scottish Water Solutions Limited.

As part of the tendering process Scottish Water carried out site visits to identify on the ground how the consortia and individual companies that made up those consortia operated. The consortia were required to produce a business plan indicating how they would deliver the Capital Programme. Representatives from the consortia were called to assessment centres to monitor how they would work together. It was not simply the one consortia working together but how would the members of that consortia gel with the other consortia. The tenderers were also required to produce cost base scenarios and cost schedules in order to create a mechanistic method to calculate cost. It should be noted that the tenderers were not to be assessed on the cheapness of their prices and costs but much more fundamentally on the robustness of their solutions to problems and their ability to deliver the programme within the recognised budget.

Evaluation

In respect of all this work the tenderers were scored on a variety of matters:

- partnering – how open, adaptable, collaborative, willing to listen and challenging they were;
- quality and robustness – to what extent did they understand key aims and objectives of Scottish Water, how practicable were their solutions;
- deliverability and sustainability – what was the quality of the people that they would bring to the new company; what was the quantity of the people; what was the quality of the processes that they would bring and what was the extent of the process coverage; what was the quality and quantity of the supply chain that they already had in place; how realistic were they when considering issues of risk;
- Innovation – how innovative would our partners be, would that innovation tend to drive up cost because the company would be seen as a test bed;
- Risk – could our private sector partners meet the challenge of risk.

Finally, surrounding all this the partners were measured in relation to trust because partnering comes down to trust. If you trust somebody you can partner with them, if there is no trust, then partnering cannot properly take place.

It should also be remembered that in moving from five to the final two, Scottish Water was not simply looking for a winner. This is not a case where lowest price would or could be the deciding factor. Scottish Water was looking for the best fit between the two partners and between the partners and Scottish Water.

Having identified the two preferred partners Scottish Water had then to align those partners so that the company, Scottish Water Solutions Limited, would act as a single entity. It was being created as single legal entity and it would have to manifest all the characteristics of such an entity. In addition, there was to be partnering at all levels, within Scottish Water Solutions, between Scottish Water and Scottish Water Solutions and within the third party supply chain. The consequence for Scottish Water Solutions and hence for the partner consortia is that there is a pain/gain mechanism. If the programme is delivered for less than the costs in the Capital Programme then all partners in Scottish Water Solutions, including Scottish Water, will benefit and likewise if the delivery is more expensive then all partners will suffer.

Achievement?

Solutions is about to commence business and hence it has yet to be seen whether the challenges in the programme have been successfully met but it is the belief of all the partners of Solutions that a model has been created which should be able to meet those challenges.

CONCLUSION

The five studies set out above present a positive endorsement for the partnering process as an effective method of construction procurement. The indications are that, subject to the partners' commitment to a collaborative form of working, it can deliver a project to time and to budget, it promotes innovation and it can encompass circumstances that might otherwise result in the deterioration of relationships between the parties. Perhaps of particular significance are the benefits to be gained from a long-term partnering arrangement. Whilst the process undoubtedly presents challenges, most notably in terms of the legal issues discussed in the second part of this book, the affirmation of partnering by both the public sector and major industry private sector players should send a message to those who question the place of this procurement method within a legal framework.

CHAPTER 5

THE ROLE OF LAWYERS

David Jones[1] and Alan Crane, CBE[2]

As illustrated already in this book, "partnering" has emerged as an important and rapidly developing way of working in the UK construction industry. It most often starts in the form of facilitated workshops beginning in the construction phase, usually enhanced by follow-up sessions during the course of construction. In these meetings, representatives of the clients, contractors, key subcontractors and design professionals are led through a series of team building exercises designed to sharpen their communication and conflict resolution skills, and to enhance their commitment to the project and to each other. In its broader manifestation, the partnering concept involves a realignment of interests and relationships on a project-by-project basis or, more beneficially, as a strategic multiproject framework which then forms an integral part of the participant's long-range business strategy. There is a growing awareness that the greatest benefits accrue when partnering arrangements begin much earlier – preferably at the commencement of the project planning and design process.

It perhaps seems obvious to say that projects that are better planned at the outset have a better chance of remaining on time and within budget. But back in the 1980s, there was a property boom in London and the industry embarked on what was described as "fast-track construction". Many large projects were begun on a limited number of drawings and the detailed design, particularly by specialised subcontractors, was worked up as the project progressed. It was not uncommon to see a multimillion pound project let on barely a dozen drawings. However, fast-track construction caused all sorts of difficulties and ultimately many such projects lacked a co-ordinated approach. Although well intentioned, they often ended up very late, substantially over budget and heading towards litigation or arbitration.

Major employers such as the Ministry of Defence, through their prime contracting initiative, are now encouraging the partnering process to begin at the outset – that is to say, as part of the process of pre-qualifying contractors. A tenderer will work with an employer's team in building up the tender and going through what are described as a number of stages (or gateways). At the preferred bidder stage the employer and the contractor will be developing

1. Partner and Global Head of Construction, Engineering & Projects, Hammonds.
2. Special Industry Adviser, Hammonds.

what should be a long-term relationship of benefit to both parties. All this will occur before any contract is concluded. When it is eventually signed, the agreement ought to reflect the spirit of co-operation and partnering. However, as this book goes on to explore, the drafting of a partnering contract is far from easy. It is not straightforward to draft a contract which, in effect, seeks to define how parties should behave rather than spell out what they must (or must not) do.

The purpose of this chapter is to look at the phenomenon of "partnering" from a construction lawyer's perspective; to place it in the context of the major trends currently shaping the UK construction industry; and to explore a strategy by which construction lawyers can participate in partnering projects to the benefit of those in the construction industry and the legal profession.

THE CONFLICT OF VALUES IN PARTNERING PROJECTS

The central elements of partnering are often described as "goal statements", a "conflict free resolution process" and "communication procedures" – all of which are developed at an initial partnering workshop and usually summarised as "the Project Partnering Charter". A trained facilitator usually leads these workshops and lawyers are typically not invited. It is not unusual for workshop participants to dedicate themselves to the principles of partnering by symbolically signing a flipchart page or some charter document. Perhaps one of the more famous (or perhaps infamous) charters to be signed related to a civil contract on the Jubilee Line Extension, where there was a gathering of over 400 people involved on the project at Westminster Conference Centre. The outcome of the meeting was that the client, the main contractor and a number of specialised subcontractors signed a charter agreement.

Unfortunately, those who sign a project partnering charter also sign or commit themselves to another very relevant (and not entirely dissimilar) document, namely a contract. This tends to cause difficulty when comparing the contractual obligations with the principles of the partnering charter. More often than not, the charter is neither binding nor conjunctive with the contract.

This has caused judges some difficulty over how to interpret a partnering charter as it clearly has a meaning that cannot be ignored. In *Birse Construction Ltd* v. *St David Ltd*, Judge Humphrey LLoyd dealt with the effect of a "team building seminar" in the interpretation of a contract. In this case, Birse was building St David's Hotel in Cardiff Bay. The parties had attended a team building seminar, at which a partnering charter (not a contract) was signed. The terms of that charter, while obviously not legally binding, were important because the charter clearly provided the standards by which the parties had to conduct themselves and against which their conduct and attitudes were to be measured. The charter contained an expression of "mutual co-operation and trust" and relationship, which was intended "to promote an environment of trust, integrity, openness and honesty…and to promote clear and effective communication".

The case centred on the question whether there was – or was not – a valid arbitration clause, which in turn depended on whether there was a contractually binding contract between the parties containing a valid arbitration clause. Judge Humphrey LLoyd held there was a valid contract – and consequently a written arbitration clause – and ordered a stay of legal proceedings to arbitration under s.9 of the Arbitration Act 1996. In doing so, he made some interesting observations about the interpretation of the contract against the background of a partnering charter. These included the following:

- Having put forward a contract programme within the partnering ethos, the contractor naturally expected that it would be treated sympathetically when it came to extensions of time, and deduction of damages for delay, in circumstances where the contractor had been unable to maintain the programme because of the occurrence of a relevant event (as defined in the JCT Conditions) or for other reasons beyond its immediate control (such as being let down by a supplier or subcontractor, for example).
- Where the parties to a contract have made mutual commitments such as those in a partnering charter, then, while the terms of the charter will not alter or affect the terms of the contract – at least, not in cases where the charter terms are not incorporated or referred to in the contract, or are not binding in law in their own right – an arbitrator or judge will undoubtedly take such adherence to charter commitments into account when exercising the wide judicial discretion to open up, review or revise certificates afforded under the JCT Conditions.

In our view, *Birse Construction Ltd* v. *St David Ltd* was rightly decided, Judge Humphrey LLoyd reaching the conclusion that a partnering charter will influence how a contract is interpreted, while not of course changing its overall meaning. The drive by the construction and engineering industry towards partnering does not mean more flowery words and good intentions. It is setting a cultural change that a court will recognise when it comes to interpreting the financial bargains made between the parties.

Since partnering charters came into existence, the industry has now moved forward in trying to develop "partnering contracts" such as PPC 2000 and ECC Partnering Option X12. Both these forms of contract are considered later in the book but they represent the legal profession's attempt to create a contractually binding partnering arrangement, and contain the facility to set out the commercial and financial bargains reached between the parties in a partnering ethos.

Lawyers have, of course, become accustomed to hearing their clients exclaim with relief, "Well, now that the contract is signed we can put it in a drawer and forget all about it!" Until the advent of partnering, we may not have realised how many clients, designers and contractors seem to have taken this comment literally. Indeed many of the participants in partnering workshops have no apparent memory of the goals, procedures and processes they have just finished negotiating or bidding on. When it comes to partnering, their objective seems to be to reinvent at a personal level the very relationships that have been contractually established at the corporate or institutional level. By way of example, some of those involved in the construction of the Channel Tunnel felt that one of the difficulties was that people became obsessed with building a magnificent engineering structure (which it became) instead of reading the specification as to what was required at the price which the parties had agreed.

While the intentions behind such an approach are understandable, particularly in the context of an industry that is desperate for a change of culture, certain manifestations of this attitude are potentially worrying. There frequently appears to be enormous discontinuity between the world described in the construction contract documents and the world of the partnering sessions. The contractual world is replete with written notices, preconditions, deadlines, prescriptions, incentives and consequences, all of which are intended to be enforceable. The concept of compliance and breach are central to the culture of this world. The partnering world is, in a sense, countercultural. It rejects, or at least ignores, the values system recommended by the contract documents, and seeks to replace it with an alternative value system. The problem is that the contract documents cannot be made to disappear with the wave of a facilitator's wand. In the drawer or on the table, they are available to any party that wishes to enforce them in accordance with their terms.

The other related discontinuity is the chasm between the consensual conflict avoidance procedures that emerge from the partnering process and the coercive procedures imposed by the contract or by the governing legal system when the partnering procedures fail to prevent conflict. This discontinuity can prove quite a shock to a business partner who has put the contract in the drawer and forgotten about its terms and conditions, and then sees them recited in the adjudication notice, notice of arbitration or court claim form.

Drafting a contract while drafting a partnering arrangement can open the parties up to all sorts of potential difficulties as to the words used and their meaning. Contracts tend to be precise, while partnering arrangements tend to be loosely worded, describing a mode of behaviour rather than specific obligations.

Over the years there have been many fascinating cases revolving around the meaning of words and phrases. Two such cases which are relevant to the construction industry have looked at what is meant by the words "the height of a building" and, in the second case, the phrase "and other similar devices". The first set of words were drafted by a lawyer. The second had minimal legal input but were regarded as an "industry norm".

The first case centred on the Queen Elizabeth's School in Blackburn (*Queen Elizabeth's Grammar School Blackburn Ltd* v. *Banks Wilson* [2001] Lloyd's Rep PN 840, CA). In 1995, the school bought some land adjoining the school and on which stood an old nursing home, complete with chimney pots. New school buildings were to built in place of the nursing home. A restricted covenant was negotiated relating to the height of the new building. Initially, the suggestion was that the new building should not be higher than the roofline of the old nursing home. That was not agreed and instead the contract read that the school would "not construct any building on the property that shall be greater in height than the buildings now existing on the property". Did the buildings then existing include the chimney pots?

However, the case was primarily concerned with advice given by the solicitor, warning his client about the covenant. Having decided that the solicitor was negligent, the court then chose not to rule on the meaning of the phrase, "the height of the building". It conceded, though, that there was "real scope for dispute" over whether the phrase "the height of the building" was restricted to the roof height. As the words of the covenant were "not [to] construct any building … that shall be greater in height than the buildings now existing…", then the chimney and its pots were arguably part of the building and therefore formed part of its height.

In the second case (*Greenfield* v. *Philles Records Inc* (2002) 780 NE 2d 166) – dealing with the phrase "and other similar devices" – the New York Court of Appeal, the highest court in the state of New Jersey, considered a two-page contract made in 1963 by a group known as the "Ronettes" with a music production company called Philles Records. Philles was Phil Spector, who subsequently married and divorced one of the singers – Veronica – known as "Ronnie".

The Ronettes recorded dozens of songs under the contract, including "Be My Baby" which sold over one million copies and topped the charts. Twenty years after the group disbanded, Phil used a new recording technology called "synchronisation" which enabled the old recording of "Be My Baby" to be used in the film "Dirty Dancing" and to be distributed widely – again – throughout the US. However, he did not pay a cent to his divorced wife or any of the other Ronettes.

Everything turned on the wording in the contract which the Ronettes had signed, without the benefit of any lawyers, using a form that was extensively used by music producers in the 1960s. The contract said that:

- Phil Spector's company owned the recordings, and
- the objective was to record and market the Ronettes' vocal performances and "make therefrom phonograph records and/or tape recordings and other similar devices".

The New York Court of Appeal held that the words "other similar devices" included the yet uninvented technology of synchronisation. Ironically, in *Queen Elizabeth School*, a non-lawyer might well have drafted the covenant to read "not [to] construct any building… greater in height than the buildings now existing on the property" but then have added the crucial words, "including their chimney pots".

The two cases above highlight how difficulties can arise out of the use of a simple phrase, with great sums of money at stake on its interpretation. In our view, this kind of problem can more easily arise as a result of the looser wording of partnering agreements than of the disciplined drafting of formal legal documents.

Many lawyers see a clash between the New Age culture of partnering and the legal world of ruthlessly defined contracts. The truth is probably rather more complicated, so what we are observing are the fundamental and fragmentary pieces of an industry that is struggling to reconcile itself at the onset of a new century. In summary, it is the shift away from the adversarial approach of contracts to the more conciliatory approach of partnering, coupled with a move by the industry towards the provision of services and products beyond just the building itself. The typical costs of a building are generally considered to be in the ratio of 1 (construction), 5 (maintenance and repairs) and 200 (operations – many of which relate to the business functions and the technological equipment within the building and not to the building itself).

We now look at partnering, how it affects the UK construction industry and its impact on construction lawyers.

INDUSTRY TRENDS – THE BIG PICTURE

By way of background, for many years the UK construction industry operated primarily through a triangle consisting of the client, the design professional and the contractor. Initially, only the client usually had a long-term interest in the building. In the 1980s and early 1990s, this traditional approach was diluted by the trends for facilities management and/or outsourcing, third party financing and the power of developers whose interest in the project ended with a post-construction sale or lease.

Concurrently, the unitary responsibility of the contractor for constructing the building was often replaced by the more fragmented duties of the construction manager whose primary role was to programme the works for the benefit of the client but not to produce the construction, which was then divested among many trade contractors servicing and in contract with the client direct. A good example would be trade contractors for mechanical, electrical and cladding work. The design function was also often split away, with the client procuring services directly (and often separately) from a number of different design disciplines.

These trends accelerated through the 1990s, accompanied by tighter margins and shorter schedules wreaking even more havoc on relationships among project participants. New teams formed for each project and even the role of the client was probably being outsourced by the appointment of project or, more recently, programme managers who arrived and departed with everyone else. Construction sites resembled nightclubs or singles bars where strangers made it up as they went along.

It is against this background that, over the last few years, there has been a kind of cultural revolution. Increasingly, design and construction have combined in a realignment of the traditional industry participants. One has seen the changes in dispute resolution typified by adjudication, with alternative dispute resolution methods – such as mediation, conciliation and expert determination – becoming increasingly popular. The world of multiparty High Court actions, involving up to 30 parties, has been replaced by roundtable dispute resolutions of a more informal nature.

The effect has been startling. The number of disputes issued in the Technology and Construction Court has come down from 1,609 in 1996 to 386 in 2002. In many respects, partnering has prospered alongside this disputes counter-revolution, as we move forward into the 21st century. It marks the entry into the construction industry of organisational development and human resources professions, and behavioural processes from other industry sectors. It also perhaps reflects the increasingly widespread influence of the theory and practice of UK and global business generally. It can even be said that the construction industry will have to disclaim its previous difference from other industries.

INDUSTRY TRENDS – THE ROLE OF
CONSTRUCTION LAWYERS

The construction sector has traditionally been a large and profitable market for legal services. As a form of insurance, resolving disputes in the industry by way of High Court litigation or arbitration has proved to be very costly and time consuming. In the past, cases lasting many months were not uncommon. The volume of paperwork generated by such cases could also run into millions of pages. There were many legal cynics who came to the view that some cases lasted for so long that it was not possible, even with the benefit of a transcript, for the judge to remember on, say, day 200 what had happened on day 1. Some counsel would try and make a claim untriable by creating a picture of a building site with a bricklayer holding a trowel in one hand and a copy of *Keating on Building Contracts* in the other.

For many years during the 1970s and 1980s, the leading cases on the law of negligence were entirely dominated by the construction industry, being bound up with the scope of extensive duties owed by architects, surveyors and construction managers.

In no small part, the growth of alternative dispute resolution and the development of statutory adjudication (referred to later in this Chapter) has happened as a direct result of the industry's strong desire to reduce its legal costs. Anecdotal evidence indicates that it has been successful, especially given the reduced number of cases that are now heard by the Technology and Construction Court. At the same time, the proliferation of delivery systems on a project-by-project basis has made it harder and more expensive to provide comprehensive and well-documented agreements between (among others) clients, designers, contractors, construction managers, trade contractors, specialists and subcontractors. Given this background, lawyers could have proved useful when trying to sort out these kinds of issues. However, what has happened instead has been the arrival of a number of firms of consultants who are not lawyers but who nevertheless offer some form of legal advice. Many of these consultancy firms are programme managers, quantity surveyors, civil engineers, claims consultants and insurers' agents.

The turning point for construction lawyers came in 1996 with the passing of a new Arbitration Act. This superseded the Arbitration Act 1979. More than any other legislation, the 1996 Act heralded the privatisation of disputes and loosened yet further the grip lawyers had over dispute resolution.

Up until this point, the construction industry had been torn between arbitration and litigation as the best way of dealing with disputes. Arbitration tended to be favoured because cases were of a technical nature. Prior to 1979, the court could and did interfere with the arbitration process by way of case stated. This occurred when a party to arbitration asked the arbitrator for a preliminary decision on a point of law by way of case stated. This was the procedure under which an arbitrator could voluntarily seek, or be compelled by the parties to seek, the assistance of the courts in resolving a point of law which had arisen in the course of the arbitral proceedings and before any award had been made (see s. 21 of the Arbitration Act 1950).

This was abolished by s. 1 of the Arbitration Act 1979 and replaced by s. 2 (1) of the 1979 Act, which has itself now been re-enacted by s. 45 of the 1996 Arbitration Act. The position now is that any application to the court on a preliminary point of law during the course of the proceedings must be made by one of the parties rather than by the arbitrator, and the court must be satisfied that the particular question of law will substantially affect the rights of one or more of the parties. The applicant must either have the agreement of the other parties or the permission of the arbitral tribunal. In the latter case, the court must be satisfied that the determination of the question will result in a substantial cost saving and that the application has been made without delay.

In a domestic arbitration, however, the parties can agree to exclude the court's jurisdiction, provided that this agreement is reached after the commencement of the proceedings in which the question arises (see s. 87 of the Arbitration Act 1996). As regards the potential for delay, s. 45 of the 1996 Arbitration Act also provides that, unless the parties agree otherwise, the arbitration proceedings can continue, pending the outcome of the application to the court.

The 1996 Arbitration Act has severely limited the rights of the court to interfere in the arbitration process. Since the legislation was passed, case law has shown appeals from arbitration to be very much the exception rather than the rule, reinforcing the trend towards the privatisation of disputes.

The 1996 Arbitration Act undoubtedly encouraged the private sector to refer technical disputes away from the High Court and into arbitration. It was, rightly in our view, heralded as a major breakthrough for privatised disputes when (within reasonable parameters) it became possible for the parties, when entering into a commercial contract, to write their own dispute resolution procedure. This could go so far as to exclude lawyers from hearings, or to limit the time and length of hearings and the ability of parties to present their case orally in deference to the greater commitment demanded by the American form of written submissions.

Equally, the Act reinforced the right of parties in arbitral proceedings not to be legally represented. The rise of non-lawyers participating in dispute resolution continued apace. As such, rights of audience became increasingly open to non-lawyers (whereas, in the High Court, one still normally has be represented by a solicitor or barrister). In addition, legal cynics were quick to point out that, for Her Majesty's government, there would be a long-term saving of costs associated with the operation and maintenance of court facilities and judges' time.

If non-lawyers could now present cases in arbitration and non-lawyers could hear contractual disputes, some people wondered if there was still a role for the legal profession? The answer was (and remains) yes, given lawyers' specialised skills and expertise, and their much larger professional indemnity levels of cover to meet any claims. However, with the advent of ADR, the market became even more open to non-legal professionals acting for clients. The passing of Part II of the Housing Grants, Construction and Regeneration Act 1996 furthered this trend, introducing statutory adjudication as a means of resolving disputes arising under construction contracts entered into after 1 May 1998. In statutory adjudication, many disputes (especially those between a contractor and a subcontractor) now involve no lawyers at all. One of the benefits to the industry has been, of course, that the cost of managing disputes has come tumbling down, with the market open to greater and cheaper competition. However, there are major concerns that, in turn, the quality of decision-making has also declined. This is of significance, particularly bearing in mind the size of many projects, which run into tens of millions of pounds; and the amounts in dispute can also run into similar sums of money.

The rise and rise of non-legal advisers has meant that such consultants are also offering to draft documents for the construction industry more cheaply than lawyers, whose only unique credential, after all, is their exclusive right to appear in High Court proceedings – something which everyone else in the construction industry is now obsessively trying to avoid. It could also be argued that partnering represents a further excellent opportunity for the non-legal adviser to draft, participate and advise.

Further evidence of this comes in the form of the partnering adviser in PPC 2000. The *CIC Guide to Project Team Partnering* (second edition) recommends the appointment of a partnering adviser "to facilitate the smooth creation and development of the project purchasing team".

In line with the *CIC Guide*, the *Guide to PPC 2000* (published by the ACA) proposes the appointment of a partnering adviser, and clause 5.6 sets out the range of the partnering adviser's advice and support role which includes, by way of example:

- selection of partnering team members;
- review of specialist contracts for consistency with the partnering documents;
- preparation of the project partnering agreement and any partnering charter;
- provision of fair and constructive advice as to the partnering process;
- assistance in the solving of problems and avoidance or resolution of disputes.

The *Guide to PPC 2000* cites the following extracts from the *CIC Guide*: "the partnering adviser would not be a party to the partnering contract" and "it is imperative that the partnering adviser is not the client's representative, as trust within the project partnering team will be threatened if the adviser is not regarded as an independent authority with an interest in the success of the project as a whole".

At first blush many of the obligations of a partnering adviser under PPC 2000 would be viewed as coming within the professional expertise of a lawyer. In particular, the obligations to give fair and constructive advice and assistance in resolving disputes. However, it is clear that this is not necessarily so. The *Guide to PPC 2000* states in express terms that this role could be undertaken by someone with experience of the needs of the partnering team and the project. The *CIC Guide* says that this person "can come from any suitable discipline, but his or her skills set must be right for the role and the proposed project". This clearly paves the way for the non-lawyer (be it quantity surveyor, claims consultant or whoever) to actively participate as a partnering adviser. Any doubt is removed by two factors.

First, the *PPC 2000 Guide* goes out of its way to stop the partnering adviser from being retained by the client. Unfortunately, it fails to give definitive guidance as to whom the partnering adviser acts for and whom pays his fee. Clause 5.6 of the *Guide to PPC 2000* anticipates that the partnering team members "may together or individually utilise the advice and support of the Partnering Adviser". By implication, this may permit an approach by one partnering team member for a unilateral piece of advice on another partner's approach to the partnering process. If so, would an individual approach have to be made known to the other team members? The use of the partnering adviser is made subject to the prior agreement of costs and his "duty of care". Presumably, it will be for the partnering team as a whole to agree whether his fee will be split equally or allocated between them by some alternative formula. What may be more problematic is the exercise of defining the duty of care owed by the partnering adviser, given that that advice may be provided to the team as a whole or to individual members. (As the partnering adviser is not a party to the contract, he or she will not be covered by clause 22 of the *Guide to PPC 2000*, which deals with duty of care and warranties.) This would cause a construction lawyer difficulty in terms of confidentiality and conflicts (see the subsequent section on the Single Project Lawyer) provided he or she was acting in their capacity as a lawyer. Equally, this loose arrangement is likely to cause a ripple or two within the professional indemnity insurance market if a professionally qualified (legal or otherwise) partnering adviser was held to have given negligent advice to the partnering team.

Secondly, having created a new industry role, namely a partnering adviser, it comes as no surprise that there has now been created an Association of Partnering Advisers ("The APA") which inevitably includes for each member a code of conduct.

It is in our view worrying that in an industry where substantial multi-million contracts are let that the professional disciplines and expertise able to advise and/or assist are becoming increasingly blurred and/or diluted. One senses that ultimately the quality of such professional advice and assistance will be sacrificed on the altar of reducing costs as against improving value.

Integrated information and technology are also affecting the role of the construction lawyer. Object orientated or intended CAD systems give designers, contractors, subcontractors and suppliers the ability to communicate and make project decisions in real time (for instance, opening doors can be checked for code conformance, co-ordinated with adjacent structural elements, priced and even procured from the designers' CAD station as soon as the door schedule has been finalised). This integration and the integrated teams at the heart of partnering and the government's "Rethinking Construction" culture threaten not only to have a profound effect on the process by which liability is determined and allocated, but could potentially marginalise lawyers as the only off-line construction professionals.

Lawyers are often seen as part of the problem within the construction industry and not part of the solution. They have been called upon to demonstrate that their contribution to the construction process is commensurate with their cost and perceived value. Construction lawyers are finding themselves in a similar position to that occupied by other professionals in the industry who are faced with increased competition and widespread challenge to their professional value systems.

Of course, it would be premature to declare that, thanks to partnering and the industry's perceived new culture, the old adversarial system and culture has been banished altogether. The industry remains a revenue – rather than a capital – generating industry. It is possible for a construction company to sign a contract for, say, £500 million and then employ directly only 10 members of staff to manage the work, with the rest being subcontracted out. The company's margins remain tight and it will monitor very closely each month what it pays out as against what it receives. Given a serious financial shortfall, the company will remain ready to press the dispute trigger (now dominated by statutory adjudication) when it comes to fighting the smaller companies at the end of the food chain – that is to say, the subcontractors that will feel the financial pressure most.

For the industry, cash is a drug to which it remains addicted. With low margins, it often seeks to make more money by holding onto cash rather than paying it out. It is this environment which has, for so long, generated substantial work for construction lawyers. While the basic structure of the industry has not altered, it is clear that its culture is changing, and many within it are conscious that, in seeking redress, the industry has in the past often thrown good money after bad.

In this new environment, what is the role for construction lawyers? They should be perceptive and nimble in identifying and seizing opportunities to offer a changing market the services that it actually wants to buy. Partnering can provide these opportunities. One such service the construction lawyer could move into, under the umbrella of partnering, is the role of the single project lawyer. This concept is discussed below.

THE SINGLE PROJECT LAWYER

The single project lawyer (SPL) would be engaged to improve the process of project deliveries, rather than advance the immediate interests of any particular project participant. SPL services for a particular project, might include some or all of the following elements:

(1) At the earliest possible time, the SPL would work with the client and any of the other project participants who may be involved to identify (among other things) their goals, directives, financial resources, management and technical capabilities. On the basis of this analysis, the SPL could then help to select a delivery system for the design and construction of the project.

(2) The SPL would advise the client on procedures for selecting other project participants who would be appropriate for – and could co-ordinate with – the recommended project delivery system. SPL services would include developing selection criteria, drafting and requesting qualifications and/or proposals and administering the selection process.

(3) On the basis of information developed during the initial phases of the project, the SPL would produce an integrated project-specific draft contract for all the key project relationships. These draft contracts would embody the principles of consistency, fairness and equity. They would incorporate (among other things) proposed financial incentives and risk allocation provisions, with the goal of maximising the success of the project as a whole. Ultimately, they could be produced with the assistance of document assembly software so as to enhance the efficiency

and effectiveness of the role of the SPL.

(4) The SPL would participate in an interactive team-building process that combined the current elements of contract negotiation and partnering. Using the lawyer's mediation abilities, together with the skills of experienced partnering facilitators, the SPL would help to guide the parties through procedures that affirmed and developed their relationship. This would take the place of the current, near-adversarial process in which the lawyer-assisted parties first go through an intensive and, at times, acrimonious negotiation, followed by a lawyerless partnering retreat at which the parties try to build productive "off-contract" working relationships.

(5) The SPL would work with the parties to develop a project-wide conflict avoidance / resolution system that could be administered, if appropriate, by the SPL. The system would involve the establishment of channels of communication, standardised documentation, step and/or facilitated negotiation, mediation, standing neutrals, binding arbitration and/or other binding or non-binding elements. This is one of the most important ways in which the legal and facilitation skills of an SPL could be placed at the services of the project participants, since it would integrate their informal conflict resolution efforts with more formal ADR and legal procedures.

(6) The SPL would seek to harmonise the contractual and administrative structure of the project with insurance, bonding and other risk management devices. Ultimately, any software that was developed for contract drafting could be co-ordinated and integrated within the various risk management documents in a way that would mirror the interactive CAB advances described above.

(7) The SPL could also play a particularly important role in the project close-out process, facilitating and documenting the efficient resolution of any open issues that have not been settled during design and construction. The goal would be to close out the project on a positive note and to avoid an end-of-project dispute. The SPL would be available to address post-construction disputes arising out of building failures (whether of workmanship or design), dealing on behalf of the partnering team members with (among others) funders, future tenants and purchasers.

(8) The SPL could play an important role too in the resolution of third-party claims relating to, for instance, personal injury or employer's liability. The SPL, being scrupulously neutral and familiar with the design and construction of the project, could be an important resource when it comes to resolving such project-related claims.

The above represents possible roles for the SPL, but do they also present possible problems for the future? In answering this question, there are in particular two matters to consider: the issues of conflict (which implies questions regarding duties of care) and the duty to warn.

On any view, some of the roles that the SPL could be asked to play are more commercial than legal in nature. This is particularly true when it comes to identifying goals, objectives, financial resources and management capabilities, and advising on procedures for selecting other project participants. In addition, under the partnering arrangement, there would be not only a number of immediate participants but also other parties joining in as the project developed. A good example might be an M&E contractor coming into the partnering arrangement some months after the project has started. Under the Law Society's rules governing the conduct of solicitors, it is fundamental to the relationship between the solicitor and the client that the lawyer should be able to give impartial and frank advice to the client free from any external or adverse pressures or interests which would destroy and weaken the solicitor's professional independence, the fiduciary relationship with the client or the client's freedom of choice.

So the two key issues for the SPL are these: Who is the client? And can the SPL give impartial advice? Turning to the first issue, is it possible for each member of the partnering team to be a client? Under the Law Society rules, it is clear that a solicitor (or firm of solicitors) should not accept instructions to act for two or more clients where there is a conflict or a significant risk of conflict between the interests of both clients.

Accordingly, if there was a potential conflict between two members of the partnering team (for example, between a designer of a cladding system and the cladding contractor in circumstances where the cladding has failed), does the SPL have any role to play, given the rules of the SPL's professional body?

It is, of course, widely recognised that members of an association, parties in multiparty actions or a common interest group between one or more individuals (even where there is no formal association) can be represented by a solicitor that acts for those individuals whose rights are affected. (Among other things, this is likely to lead to a saving of time and costs). Examples include common claims arising out of an air crash or neighbourhood disputes. A solicitor may also be instructed to act in a matter both for an association, club or trade union and for members (or a number of the members) of that association, club or trade union. However, the solicitor should be alert to the possibility of conflicting interests arising out of these arrangements. Given this background, though, is it possible for the SPL to exist in circumstances where there may be difficulties of identifying who is the client and the possible conflicts that could arise?

As to the client's position and the ability of the SPL to give the client impartial advice, one solution might be for the SPL to act for the employer/owner of the project. In those circumstances, the solicitor would have to give frank and impartial advice to the owner/employer, which would make it much harder for the solicitor to help the partnering team as well. The lawyer would not, for example, be obliged to give frank and impartial advice to the project team because they would not be the lawyer's client and not paying the lawyer's fees.

Equally, if all the project partners paid the legal fees on a pro rata basis, could the solicitor nevertheless continue in the role of SPL in circumstances where he or she had a number of clients where conflicts could easily arise?

Furthermore, in any partnering arrangement, a project lawyer could become much more vulnerable to a claim for a duty to warn. There are many cases dealing with this concept including the following:

- An architect has a duty to warn a client that the design specification would not be met (see *HOK Sport Ltd* v. *Aintree Racecourse Co Ltd* (2003) BLR 155).
- If in the course of doing the work for which a solicitor is retained, the solicitor becomes aware of a risk (or a potential risk) to the client, it is their duty to inform the client about it (see *Crédit Lyonnaise SA* v. *Russell Jones & Walker* [2003] Lloyd's Rep PN 2).
- A contractor was held to be under a duty to warn about the suitability or safety of work which it was asked to undertake. However, this duty could not be extended so as to require the contractor to warn about the feasibility of work which might be done by others in the future and could affect the state of the work that the contractor had carried out (see *Aurum Investments Ltd* v. *Avon Force Ltd* (*in liquidation*) [2001] Lloyd's Rep PN 285 and (1) *Knapp Hicks & Partners* (2) *Advanced Undertaking Ltd* (*Part 20 defendants*) [2001] 2 All ER 385).
- Even where it is not liable for design faults, a subcontractor who is acting on the employer's direct instructions still owes a duty of care to point out such faults to the contractor by protesting as vigorously as possible (see *Plant Construction Ltd plc* v. *Clive Adams Associates and JMH Construction Services Ltd* (1997) 86 BLR 119).

Perhaps one of the solutions to the regulatory difficulties affecting a SPL could be membership of a virtual company. As discussed later in the book, one of the more advanced partnering arrangements is the development of a virtual company, with a number of participants in the project (such as contractors, specialised contractors and developers, for example) taking a share in the virtual company, with profits and losses being capped at a certain level. Is there any reason why a firm of solicitors should not be a member of such a virtual company, recovering a fee by way of equity participation rather than an hourly rate?

If a law firm were to act in that way, the problems discussed above about giving impartial advice and the duty to warn could still arise. However, the issue of who is the client would probably not be a difficulty since the firm would, in effect, be its own client, having taken an equity participation in the virtual company. However, the point is not free from doubt and would probably create an interesting dilemma for the law firm involved!

The concept of partnering has yet to be fully developed, as has the role of the SPL. There are clearly a number of obstacles and difficulties as to whether a project could take an SPL on board. Equally, there is much that a SPL could do to help – particularly when it comes to comparing the strict legal obligations of a contract and the more wide-ranging behavioural patterns set out in the partnering arrangement.

The main area where difficulty is likely to arise is an unresolved dispute between two or more parties who are engaged in a single partnering project. What are the applicable principles governing such matters as confidentiality, duties of disclosure and reliance? To what extent could such problems be solved by engagement agreements, all-party consent and / or representation of each party? Clearly there may be circumstances where the SPL would have to withdraw – for instance, where a dispute escalates to the point where both sides are separately represented by other lawyers.

As to the role of the SPL, is it something that could be covered by professional indemnity insurance or might there be aspects of the service (particularly in relation to the giving of quasi-commercial advice) that insurers would not underwrite?

If it is found that because, of the obligations imposed by Law Society rules, an SPL cannot deliver the service required, will members of a partnering arrangement seek to fill that gap with management consultants, design professionals and/or construction managers? Such professionals may well have certain capabilities but, more significantly, they may not be subject to the same (or even similar) codes of ethics and rules of professional conduct.

It would appear that the virtual company probably offers the best solution. If it is set up with capped liability, it may be easier to reach a resolution between members of the partnering arrangement, particularly in circumstances where no-one is faced with unlimited liability, thereby avoiding any conflict. However, this presupposes that even capped levels of risk are financially manageable. This may not be the case with large projects.

CONCLUSION

This chapter has sought to highlight the trends within the industry as regards partnering and the possible role of a single project lawyer. On any view, there are challenging issues which need to be determined in order to ascertain whether the concept of an SPL is feasible, marketable and an effective contribution to the benefit of both the construction industry and the legal profession. There is obviously an element of crystal-ball gazing. Although everyone will try to achieve a satisfactory solution, it is unhappily not always possible – if people insist on it – to end up arguing about whether the height of a building should include its chimney pots or whether yet-to-be-invented technology is within the meaning of other similar devices.

CHAPTER 6

PROCUREMENT AND COMPETITION ISSUES

Richard Cooke,[1] *Brona Heenan*[2] *and Corin Ramsden*[3]

INTRODUCTION

This chapter addresses partnering from the procurement viewpoint. Firstly, it looks briefly at partnering compared to more traditional forms of construction procurement, identifying the perceived advantages of partnering and seeking to provide some practical advice as to how partnering arrangements should be procured.

The differences between strategic partnering and project-specific partnering are then examined so as to provide an understanding of how the two types of partnering should be treated. Finally, the chapter provides a detailed review of the regulatory aspects relating to partnering, including the EU procurement rules, together with EU and UK competition law, so that those thinking of using partnering arrangements can structure contracts and partnering relationships in such a way as to minimise the adverse impact of these regulatory controls. The chapter also addresses topics – such as, for example, merger control – that do not regularly need to be considered when thinking about partnering but which in certain circumstances can have considerable implications.

PARTNERING DEFINED

Before comparing and contrasting the concepts of strategic partnering and project partnering, it is worthwhile reflecting on what we understand by the term "partnering". It is widely accepted that partnering means different things to different people and that the term is far from being a term of art. (According to R. K. Lorraine in *Partnering in the Public Sector* (1993), "partnering is an imprecise term covering a range of different arrangements of varying degrees of intensity".) Two generally accepted definitions of partnering in the construction sector come, firstly, from the National Economic Development Council (NEDC) Report of June 1991 and, secondly, from the Reading Construction Forum. The NEDC Report defined partnering as:

1. Partner, Construction, Engineering & Projects, Hammonds.
2. Solicitor, Hammonds, Brussels.
3. Solicitor, Construction, Engineering & Projects, Hammonds.

"... a long term commitment between two or more organisations for the purpose of achieving specific business objectives by maximising the effectiveness of each partici-pant's resources... The relationship is based on trust, dedication to common goals and an understanding of each other's individual expectations and values. Expected benefits include improved efficiency and cost-effectiveness, increased opportunity for innova-tion, and the continuous improvement of quality products and services." (See the NEDC Report *Partnering Without Conflict*, June 1991.)

The NEDC definition is a useful starting point but the definition has been built upon. Another useful definition of partnering, adopted by the Partnering Task Force, is that provided by the Reading Construction Forum in 1995:

"A management approach used by two or more organisations to achieve specific busi-ness objectives by maximising the effectiveness of each participant's resources. The approach is based on mutual objectives, an agreed method of decision making and an active search for continuous measurable improvements".

(See *Trusting the Team* by the Reading Construction Forum – The University of Reading with the Partnering Task Force. See also *The Seven Pillars of Partnering – A Guide to Second Generation Partnering* published as a compan-ion to *Trusting the Team*.)

From these definitions we can see that common themes exist:

- The aim to achieve specific business objectives.
- The aim to maximise the effectiveness of each participant's resources.
- The aim of mutual objectives, or common goals.
- The aim to secure continuous improvements.

We can see that the Reading Construction Forum also places value on the management approach and on the provision of an agreed method of decision-making. While these features are perhaps implicit and therefore not contentious, the NEDC definition also includes reference to a long-term commitment between organisations and there is, in some quarters, debate about the impor-tance of having a long-term relationship in a successful partnering process.

Strategic long-term partnering and project partnering

To meet the demands of the construction sector, partnering has developed into two forms; traditional, long-term (or strategic) partnering must now be compared with one-off (or project-specific) partnering. While some commen-tators argue that project-specific partnering is not partnering in the strict sense of the word, it nevertheless contains many elements of good industry practice and has been embraced by the industry. Standard forms, such as PPC2000 (see PPC2000, ACA Standard Form of Contract for Project Partnering 2000), NEC Partnering Option X12 (see The NEC Partnering Option, Option X12, First Edition, June 2001) and JCT Practice Note 4 (see the JCT Standard Forms of Building Contract 1998 Editions, Series 2 Practice Note 4, Partnering 2001) all address partnering in very different ways. This ranges from PPC2000's legally binding multiparty agreement, to the NEC's additional secondary option included within the NEC's discrete Own Contracts where parties have obligations solely to the other party to the Own Contract, to the JCT's two page non-binding partnering charter. If none of these standard forms provide the desired framework, the parties should create their own agreement tailored to reflect what they think is the most effective approach towards partnering.

Partnering arrangements can be intentionally legally binding or alternatively non-binding. This chapter does not address these differences in detail. However, parties should be aware that in certain circumstances a non-binding agreement could even fall within the EU procurement and competition regimes.

The traditional approach of the construction sector is based on the choice (or balancing exercise) of three key elements – quality, time and cost – and traditional standard form contracts are designed to manage the perceived conflict between these competing elements. The main idea behind partnering is that the industry can provide a service where the quality, time and cost elements all demonstrably improve to the benefit of everyone involved in a project. Partnering not only addresses the on-site construction process itself but also contemplates early co-operation in a project. This includes aspects of developing the business case, planning, design and contract drafting – aspects previously dealt with separately under the traditional procurement approach. If the creation of a partnering arrangement is considered beneficial to the project, then the parties should implement a procurement regime that embraces the partnering approach, thereby achieving the best results in terms of quality, time and cost.

The procurement process must therefore begin with the employer having a clear idea of how it wishes to use partnering. Ordinarily, there is nothing particularly unusual about an employer seeking to procure a project under partnering arrangements. It is simply a question of making the requirements clearly known at the time of tender.

In many respects, procuring a partnering arrangement is no different to procuring any other construction contract. Ignoring, for the moment, EU procurement rules, an employer can follow one of the three following procurement routes:

- open competitive tender (using the word "open" here in its normal sense rather than its specialised meaning under the EU procurement rules);
- competitive tender from a pre-selected short list; or
- direct negotiation with a preferred contractor.

Here, the important point to note in respect of partnering is that the employer must make his requirements clearly known to the tendering contractors at the beginning of the process. In theory, it is possible to agree a non-binding partnering arrangement separate from the tendering process, but it is recommended that, even in non-binding partnering situations, the employer's desires are made plain at the outset and within the tendering process so as to ensure that the pricing properly reflects the overall relationship.

As in any tendering situation, the employer is well advised at the pre-bid stage to issue a questionnaire to the potential contractors. The questionnaire should set out, among other things, questions relating to partnering – questions, for example, regarding the contractor's previous experience, and how its business is geared towards incorporating partnering into the corporate structure. This would include addressing matters such as the contractor's previous experience of partnering, the flexibility of personnel and internal attitudes towards partnering. Furthermore, depending upon the particular requirements of the partnering relationship, it might be relevant to raise questions relating to supply management techniques.

As the success of any partnering relationship will largely depend on good personal relationships, there are real advantages in setting up meetings or interviews so that key personnel from the various parties can meet. Depending upon the nature of the partnering relationship, it may make sense for these meetings to be widened so that they include not only the employer and contractor but also consultants, key subcontractors and suppliers. As with other tender situations, it is recommended that a detailed record is made of these discussions, particularly if the contract is being awarded on the basis that the contractor is able to work within a partnering arrangement. The employer must be clear as to how the potential partner would go about achieving its objectives. Notes of such discussions may also provide a helpful checklist to all parties on whether initial expectations regarding the project have been fulfilled.

While employers may prefer entering into partnering relationships with existing long-term suppliers or contractors, this may not always be possible because of regulatory restrictions. Furthermore, it may well be in the interests of the employer to test the market in order to achieve best value.

As pricing is likely to remain important, parties should be firmly agreed on a schedule of rates, a guaranteed maximum price or some other agreed pricing mechanism at the beginning of the project. Parties must also be aware that open book arrangements are likely to be adopted to help monitor actual costs. Such arrangements help the parties understand the true position and to determine whether best value is achieved. All parties will expect to benefit over time from any continuing improvement on price due to economies of scale or other efficiencies made during the contract term. The partnering arrangement should reflect that all parties share in improvements instead of creating a mechanism that simply pushes down prices to the benefit of the employer.

Which type of partnering arrangement is best?

Strategic and project partnering share a number of common attributes but, equally, there are several differences. This chapter is not intended to provide a detailed analysis of the two types of partnering but the table below summarises some of the key similarities and differences. It should also be noted that the standard form project-specific partnering forms vary widely in their provisions. Similarly, many partnering arrangements are structured according to bespoke agreements, or charters, and all partnering arrangements therefore need to be examined in detail to fully appreciate their individual character. Nevertheless, the key similarities and differences between strategic partnering and project-specific partnering can generally be summarised as follows:

Attribute	Strategic partnering	Project-specific partnering
Long-term commitment between the parties.	The main purpose of a strategic partnering arrangement is to induce benefits that only come from such a long-term commitment.	Whilst project-specific partnering arrangements can be used on a number of linked projects, in general projects will be stand alone, or one-off, and there is unlikely to be any long-term relationship made.
Aim is to achieve specific business objectives.	Yes.	Yes.
Aim is reached by max-imising the effectiveness of each participant's resources.	Yes.	Yes.
Aim is based on mutual objectives, or common goals.	Yes.	Yes.
Based upon a management approach.	Yes.	Yes.
Adopts an active search for continuous measurable improvements.	Yes.	Possibly. The more limited duration of project-specific partnering necessarily lim-its this potential benefit but it may exist in some project- specific arrange-ments, particularly on larg-er projects.
Adopts an agreed method of decision- making.	Yes.	Yes.
Adopts key performance indicators (KPIs).	Yes, however it is possible that the nature of a strate-gic partnering arrangement may be applied to a less traditional construction project and hence relevant KPIs may not be readily available for comparison. Parties can nevertheless develop their own KPIs to be reviewed over time.	Yes. Movement for Inno-vation and Construction Best Practice have been instrumental in developing a range of construction related KPIs. (See "Rethinking Construction: 2002" and also websites for Movement for Innovation at *www.m4i.org.uk* and Construction Best Practice at *www.cbpp.org.uk*).

Attribute	Strategic partnering	Project-specific partnering
Mix of works supplies and services.	A strategic partnering arrangement could cover the provision of works, the provision of supplies or of services, or a mixture of all three.	It is possible that a project-specific partnering arrangement could apply to a contract where services are the main object of the contract. Generally, however, the main object will be the provision of works.
Duration.	Generally either open-ended or for a given number of years rather than the duration of a specific project. Procurement and/or competition rules can apply as duration can often be lengthy.	Usually for the duration of the project. May include pre-construction activities such as feasibility and design (e.g., PPC2000), or may be limited to the on-site construction phase only.
Value.	Value will vary from project to project. Individual projects can of course be of sufficient value to exceed EU procurement thresholds, but projects might fall below these thresholds.	Value will vary from project to project. Individual projects can of course be of sufficient value to exceed EU procurement thresholds, but projects might fall below these thresholds.

From the above, it can be seen that strategic partnering and project-specific partnering have different aims, are intended for different uses and have different benefits. If an employer is to adopt partnering, the first important decision is whether to adopt strategic – or project-specific – partnering. While project-specific partnering has a number of standard forms available, there are no standard forms for strategic partnering. If the project-specific standard forms are not appropriate, or an employer wishes to adopt strategic partnering, a useful starting point is the Construction Industry Council's *Guide to Project Team Partnering* published in June 2000.

In many instances, it may be possible to adopt partnering techniques without having to consider EU procurement and competition law points, but the size and nature of many proposed partnering relationships will mean that these regulatory areas need to be considered in detail.

REGULATORY ASPECTS OF PARTNERING

A partnering arrangement, depending on its structure and legal standing, requires analysis from a wide array of legal as well as practical viewpoints. There are two areas of law – public procurement and competition – that can impact on the actual partnering route itself. These are examined in detail below.

The aim of both procurement and competition rules is to maintain competition in the market place to the benefit of consumers. However, the routes taken to achieve this aim are different. The origin of these sets of rules helps to explain this.

Origin of the procurement rules

The purpose of the procurement rules is to open up the Community markets to the procurement by public sector bodies of the goods and services they require. In order to ensure that national markets were opened to companies from all member states, directives were adopted at Community level. The directives were designed to harmonise the rules applying to all public tendering throughout the Community, with the aim of achieving transparent and competitive purchasing behaviour throughout all the member states.

Origin of competition rules

By way of comparison, the EC competition rules can be found in the EC Treaty itself. EC competition law applies where there is, or may be, an effect on trade between member states. National competition law can be applied in cases where the effects on trade relate solely to the domestic market. Another role of EC competition law is to promote market integration by eliminating barriers to trade. In this respect, its role is akin to the objectives of the procurement rules.

Why is competition law and public procurement relevant to partnering?

The partnering relationship creates and restructures relationships between different purchasers and suppliers. Often the idea behind this relationship is to create long-term profitable alliances between different sectors in the industry. In creating these new relationships, partners need to be aware that the competition and procurement rules may apply in certain situations. The aim of this section is to highlight where these situations may arise.

There are severe penalties for infringements of competition law rules, which can result in companies being fined up to 10% of their worldwide turnover, depending on the gravity and duration of the particular infringement. For simplicity, throughout the text we have referred to those involved in partnering arrangements as "companies". However, in Community law, the term "undertaking" is used. That term is very widely defined and includes almost any legal or natural person engaged in an economic activity regardless of its legal status or the way in which it is financed. Thus the term includes sole traders, companies, partnerships, trade associations and state corporations. It is immaterial whether the undertaking is profit-making, provided that it carries out economic or commercial activities.

Competition issues can arise when companies are merged, taken over or where they are setting up joint ventures to operate in the marketplace. Merger control rules are not found in the EC Treaty itself but rather have come about through secondary Community and national legislation. If the parties to the partnering arrangement consider that the most effective way to create a successful partnering arrangement is by way of a joint venture, then the parties must be aware of these rules and their implications.

The EC Treaty also contains rules on state aid. These rules are applicable where government provides financial assistance of any kind that distorts, or threatens to distort, competition by favouring certain companies or the production of certain goods or services. Again, for the state aid rules to apply, there must be an effect on trade between member states, but this condition is easily satisfied. If the state aid rules are found to have been contravened, the sums granted by the state must be repaid. Obviously, this will have a significant effect on the profitability of any project. All the parties involved in a partnering arrangement must therefore be alive to the possibility of state aid issues where some or all of the funding comes from the state or through state resources.

Clearly, there will be some partnering arrangements to which both the procurement rules and the competition rules apply. While the procurement rules apply to the procedures that lead up to the actual award of a contract, the competition rules apply throughout the entire process. For example, competition law would be infringed if bidders were to collude in the bidding process, something which would undermine the procurement procedure as well. In addition, just because a contract has been awarded through the correct procurement procedure, it does not automatically mean that it will not infringe EC or national competition rules. For example, procuring entities can find themselves in a position of dominance in a purchasing market and attempt to abuse this through the inclusion of onerous conditions in the contract put out to tender. Merger control rules may also be triggered by setting up a joint venture or by awarding a contract to a joint venture following an open competition.

We will illustrate the potential application of the procurement and competition rules to typical partnering arrangements by using the following set of hypothetical examples and indicating, throughout the text, where these rules have an impact on the scenario.

EXAMPLE 1

A large international construction company (High Rise Co.), which mainly builds high-rise office blocks, does not have any expertise in the installation of lifts in its buildings. Consequently, it is obliged to enter into negotiations with lift providers on each individual project. In order to save costs, maximise resources and benefit from continuous improvements in lift installations in its buildings, High Rise Co. decides to enter into a strategic partnering arrangement with Lift Co., one of the three existing lift suppliers in the market. This will be an open-ended exclusive arrangement whereby neither High Rise Co. nor its subsidiaries worldwide will use competing lift suppliers on any future projects.

EXAMPLE 2

A local authority is considering possible options relating to the construction of a number of different projects. It may not wish to carry out all of these proposed enterprises as the funding position is unclear and there is no certainty that every one of the projects will be carried out.

Option 1 is to let discrete design and build contracts for each project, possibly based on project partnering arrangements under PPC2000 or NEC incorporating Option X12.

Option 2 is to set up a framework agreement for both design and construction elements on a strategic partnering basis over, say, seven years. Historically, because of spending constraints, the local authority has spent more on its design team than it has on the construction of projects and it cannot be clear what the construction spend might be throughout the duration of the agreement.

EXAMPLE 3

The government decides that it wants to install a toll system on its motorways as a way of ensuring that road users pay for the maintenance and upkeep of the motorways. However, the government has no expertise in this area. It also has limited finances to invest in such a system. It wants the private sector to provide the entire system (infrastructure, tolling stations, employees, hardware and software) in return for a 20-year concession under which the private sector is able to exploit the revenue paid by road users. The winning bid will be required to set up a joint venture company and post various bonds and guarantees as to its performance throughout the 20-year concession period. The concession is to be based on partnering principles.

Please note that the above examples are not based upon real companies and any similarities are entirely coincidental.

APPLICATION OF THE PROCUREMENT RULES TO PARTNERING ARRANGEMENTS

What are the procurement rules?

There are two sets of public procurement rules:
- Those that apply to works, services and supplies contracts entered into by contracting authorities in the public sector. See the Works Directive 93/37/EEC, Supplies Directive 93/36/EEC and Services Directive 92/50/EEC (all as amended by Directive 97/52/EEC) and the Public Remedies Directive 89/665/EEC. These Directives have been implemented in the UK by the Public Works Contracts Regulations 1991, the Public Supply Contracts Regulations 1995 and the Public Services Contract Regulations 1993 (all as amended).

- A second, more flexible set of rules that apply to contracting entities operating in the water, electricity, transport and telecommunications sectors (the utilities sector). See the Utilities Directive 93/38/EEC as amended by Directive 98/4/EC and Remedies Directive 92/3/EEC. These Directives have been implemented by the UK Utilities Contracts Regulations 1996 (as amended).

How are the public and utilities sectors defined?

Public sector

The public sector rules apply to the state, regional and local authorities and bodies governed by public law, as well as to associations formed by one or several of such authorities or by one or several of such bodies governed by public law.

The category of bodies governed by public law is often difficult to identify. However, for a body to qualify, three conditions must be met:

- It must be set up with the specific purpose of meeting needs in the general interest, not having a commercial or industrial character.
- It must have legal personality.
- It must be financed, supervised or appointed for the most part by the state, regional or local authorities or bodies governed by public law.

Utilities sector

The utilities rules apply to contracting entities when they carry out certain specified activities (known as "listed activities"). A contracting entity includes contracting authorities normally subject to the public sector rules, public undertakings (bodies over which a public authority exercises a dominant influence) and bodies which enjoy "special or exclusive rights" from government relating to one of the listed activities. This means that wholly private companies can be subject to the utilities procurement rules.

However, the utilities rules only apply when the contracting entity is carrying out a listed activity. Thus, for example, a wholly private company that holds exclusive rights to provide (or operate) a fixed network for the supply of drinking water is subject to the utilities rules when it purchases water pipes. However, it is not subject to the utilities rules when it buys stationery supplies. While a public sector contracting authority that purchases water pipes to provide a water supply network can use the utilities regime (as this is a listed activity), it would still be subject to the public sector rules when it buys stationery supplies. Thus, in the context of a partnering relationship with a contracting entity subject to the utilities rules, it is necessary to consider whether the contract in question falls with the scope of a relevant activity. A list of the relevant activities in the water, transport, energy and telecommunications sectors can be found in Schedule I to the Utilities Regulations 1996 (as amended).

The procurement process

The procurement rules require that both the public sector and utilities contracts must be advertised and put out to tender throughout the European Community. The various directives set out the requirements relating to the objective and non-discriminatory selection and award criteria to be used by such entities. Calls for tenders must be published in the Official Journal of the European Communities (OJEC Notice). In addition, the procurement rules set out the appropriate procedures to be used at all stages in the bidding process along with specific time limits, which must be respected.

The selection criteria which may be used differ under the public sector and utilities rules. Utilities are free to chose the selection criteria that suit them best, provided of course that the criteria are objective, non-discriminatory and relate to the subject matter of the contract in question. However, public sector bodies have far less room to manoeuvre because, for the most part, the selection criteria are exhaustively set out in the rules. This was done to ensure that contractors bidding across borders would not be discriminated against in the selection process and thereby eliminated from participating in the tendering process.

In both public sector and utilities cases, authorities have a choice between awarding a contract on the basis of the lowest price or the most economically advantageous tender. However, bidders must be advised in advance which of these standards will be applied. In the event that the most economically advantageous tender principles are to be used, the contracting entity must choose the criteria that will be relied on in evaluating the tenders and, where possible, list these criteria in descending order of priority either in the contract notice or in the contract documents.

In the public sector, the rules require the contracting authority to use the open or restricted procedure, while the use of the negotiated procedure with advertisement is limited to certain exhaustively defined exceptions. The rules are more flexible in the utilities sector where there is complete freedom about which procedure is used.

In broad terms, the differences between these three different procedures are as follows. Under the open procedure, all interested providers may tender. Under the restricted procedure, only those providers who are invited to participate by the contracting authority may submit a tender. There are two distinct stages here. Following the call for competition, the contracting authority considers the expressions of interests, excludes those who fail to meet the eligibility criteria and finally selects a minimum of at least five providers who are then invited to tender.

In the case of the negotiated procedure, direct negotiations take place between the contracting authority and one or more suppliers of its choice. Depending on the circumstances, the negotiated procedure can then be used with or without advertisement. Where advertising is used, strict time limits apply. However, there are no applicable time limits if advertising is not in fact used.

Consequently, when considering entering into a partnering arrangement with a public authority or utility, it is important to establish whether the party procuring the works, supplies or services is subject to the public sector or the utilities procurement rules. If the procuring party is subject to either set of rules, then consideration should be given to the application of the procurement rules as part of the initial selection process. If the contract is not concerned with public authorities or utilities, then the public procurement rules will not affect the partnering process at all.

Defining contracts

When analysing the procurement rules, the general approach is first to consider whether a contract is one for works, supplies or services. (Two different regimes apply in relation to services contracts depending on whether the services are listed in Annex IA or Annex IB of the Public Services Contract Regulations. Annex IA services are subject to the full procurement regime whereas Annex IB services are subject to the rules on technical specifications, and the requirement to publish notice of having awarded a public contract within a set period of time.)

When first enacted, the procurement rules were designed to apply to single contracts. A series of contracts covering individual supplies or services was to be dealt with either as separate contracts, each subject to the rules where the thresholds were exceeded, or a single contract divided into lots. This type of simple procurement is no longer a market reality, as now providers are expected to take over and run the provision of works, supplies and services contracts.

More efficient methods of procurement require companies to design, build and operate plants, often over lengthy periods and in a way that frequently requires the provision of a mixture of works, supplies and services. In general, the main object of a project-specific partnering arrangement will be the provision of works, but it could just as easily be the provision of services. On the other hand, strategic partnering may well cover a mixture of works and services. There is a degree of uncertainty about how to define mixed works/ services contracts for the purposes of the procurement rules. When considering the boundary between mixed works and services contracts, the approach of the European Court of Justice has been to consider whether any works involved were incidental to the services to be carried out. If the answer to this question is yes, then the contract should be classified as a services contract. Otherwise, it will be a works contract. The position is clearer when it comes to the boundary between services and supplies contracts because the directives have provided that the contract should be classified according to the higher value of either supplies or services. However, classification issues are relatively rare in practice due to the low thresholds which apply to supplies and services contracts.

EXAMPLE 2 – OPTION 1 (see **Why is competition law and public procurement relevant to partnering**, above)

Design and build contracts will generally fall within the definition of works rather than supplies or services. To the extent that they exceed the works thresholds (currently £3,861,932), the EU procurement rules will apply. Attention should, however, be paid to any national rules on procurement below these thresholds. If the local authority wishes to extend a contract awarded to a particular supplier without readvertising, the new works or services must consist of the repetition of similar works or services and conform to a basic project originally put out to tender using the open or restricted procedure. In addition, the original OJEC notice must have included the total estimated cost of subsequent works and negotiation of the new works/services contract must take place during the first three years following the conclusion of the original contract. There are other exceptions to the rules, which allow the use of the negotiated procedure without advertisement (such as extreme urgency and additional works that have come about through unforeseen circumstances), but the conditions are difficult to meet.

Exclusions from the procurement rules

There are numerous exclusions from the procurement rules. (It should be remembered that, being derogations from the general advertising and tendering requirements, these exceptions are interpreted strictly and the onus is always on the awarding entity to demonstrate that it was entitled to rely on a particular exception.) For example, one exception, which applies in all cases, allows the use of the negotiated procedure without advertisement where – for technical or artistic reasons or reasons connected with the protection of exclusive rights – there is only one provider which can provide the required services, works or supplies. Consequently, reliance on intellectual property rights such as patents, design rights or copyright are sometimes used by a prospective partner as a means of persuading a contracting authority that it is the only provider which can meet its requirements, thereby avoiding the procurement rules. In these situations, great care should be taken to ensure that there really is only one provider and that the technical specifications or requirements chosen by the authority have not been chosen just to arrive at this conclusion.

Another way of avoiding the application of the procurement rules is to classify a contract as a concession contract. However, while concession agreements fall outside the scope of the utilities rules, the public sector rules do apply to works concession contracts. A works concession contract is defined as a public works contract under which the consideration given by the contracting authority consists of – or includes – the grant of a right to exploit the work or works to be carried out under the contract. (Of course, concessions can mean different things in different member states and, in an effort to provide some guidance on this subject, the European Commission has published an interpretative note on concessions under Community law. See the Commission Interpretative Communication on Concessions under Community Law (OJ 2000 C121/2).)

In general, the works concessionaire is given the right to demand payment from those who use the structure for a certain period of time (for example, the right to charge tolls on a newly constructed bridge). This right of exploitation also implies that the responsibilities and risks inherent in its exploitation should be transferred to the concessionaire. On the other hand, while services concession contracts are not defined in the EC directives (and specifically excluded under the UK implementing legislation), the European Court has nevertheless decided that, even where such service concession agreements fall outside the scope of the existing procurement rules, the EC Treaty rules on non-discrimination and transparency require some advertisement before the award of such contracts. In the partnering context, it may not be feasible to try and classify the partnering arrangement as a services concession. In addition, the advertising requirement militates against negotiation with just one potential provider.

EXAMPLE 3 (see **Why is competition law and public procurement relevant to partnering**, above)

This example appears to fall within the definition of a services concession for the purposes of the procurement rules. Although services concessions fall outside the scope of the public procurement regulations, the EC Treaty rules on non-discrimination, transparency, equal treatment, mutual recognition and proportionality still apply. Transparency requires that some form of advertising should take place, although the extent of this obligation has not been defined. Following advertisement, the government would be free to choose whichever method of procurement it wished, provided of course it complied with general EC Treaty principles. Care would also need to be taken to ensure that bidders were treated equally and that national preferences were not allowed via the procurement process chosen.

What are the thresholds?

Contracts are subject to the procurement rules only when they exceed certain thresholds. The thresholds for works are considerably higher than those for supplies or services. The thresholds also vary between the public sector and utilities rules and are revised every two years (They were last revised in January 2002.) A summary of the thresholds can be found in Annex 1.

As the threshold for works contracts is considerably higher than that for supplies and services, one needs to determine whether the contract is for works, supplies or services. The procurement rules are designed in such a way that only one set of rules (public sector/utilities – works, supplies or services) will apply to any given contract.

How are the values determined?

The rules also set out how the value of these contracts is to be determined. For example, in the case of a works contract, the value is the amount the contracting authority expects to give (exclusive of VAT), whereas in the case of an indefinite services agreement, or one in excess of four years, the value is deemed to be the monthly sum multiplied by 48.

Parties should be aware that if a contract that did not originally fall within the procurement rules is extended, the overall value of the contract might exceed the relevant thresholds. In this situation, the procurement rules would apply and the contract would have to be re-tendered. Public authorities and utilities should keep a careful watch on this as, if a partnering arrangement is going particularly well, it may seem easier to continue the relationship or extend the original contract rather than procure a new contract as required by the procurement rules.

Partnering and procedural compatibility with the procurement rules

The main difficulty in pursuing a partnering relationship with an authority or entity which is subject to the procurement rules is the underlying principle that all contracts exceeding the thresholds must be put out to competitive tender. This rules out private negotiation of the terms of a partnering relationship. However, to the extent that a partnering relationship can be established within a competitive tendering process, the procurement rules can be complied with. Obviously, a partnering relationship would be more easily reached where the parties can avail themselves of the negotiated procedure. However, while this is always an option open to utilities, it can only be used in exceptional cases by those subject to the public sector rules. However, even with the free and unencumbered use of the negotiated procedure, there is still the requirement to use a competitive bidding process, which would not, except in very specific circumstances (as to which, see Article 20(2) of the Utilities Directive), be met by entering into negotiations with just one party. In this way, the procurement rules can run counter to the very intentions of the parties who would like to enter into a partnering agreement.

To the extent, then, that partnering agreements can be put out to competitive tender, there should in principle be no objection, provided the rules on advertising, selection and award are complied with. In this respect, project-specific partnering fits more easily with the existing procurement regime than strategic partnering, which by its nature is either open ended or long-term in duration.

Needless to say, should a particular partner be chosen in advance of any procurement process by a contracting authority, launching an OJEC procedure would be a mere sham, and leave the contracting authority open to legal action. Care should also be taken to ensure that technical specifications, or other requirements, are not drawn up with the intention of excluding certain parties, or designed for the purpose of awarding a contract to a preselected operator.

Future developments in public procurement

A new legislative package on public procurement is currently underway, which will result in changes to the existing directives in both the public sector and the utilities sector. One issue, which is likely to have an impact on partnering agreements, is an explicit reference to the use of framework agreements under the public sector rules.

The utilities rules provide that a framework agreement is an agreement between a contracting entity and one or more suppliers, contractors or service providers, the purpose of which is to establish the terms (in particular, with regard to the prices and, where appropriate, the quantities envisaged) governing the contracts to be awarded during a given period.

However, the public sector rules (unlike the utilities rules) do not refer to the use of framework agreements. However, it has been argued (see Arrowsmith, Issues 3 and 4 1999 PPLR) that this does not rule out the application or use of certain types of framework agreements. In addition, there is an unhelpful Commission press release dated 20 July 2002 in which it attacks a particular use of framework agreements in the UK public sector. However, there has been no evidence, thus far, of these cases being brought before the European Court of Justice. While the proposed definition of a framework agreement is the same for both the utility and public sector rules, the latter will be awarded somewhat differently under the new proposals.

Under the proposed new rules, provided the initial contract is advertised Community-wide and awarded in accordance with the usual selection and award criteria, it will be possible to conclude both single supplier and multiple supplier framework agreements for works, supplies and services. Where the framework agreement is concluded with a single provider, contracts based on the agreement will be awarded within its terms and the contracting authority can consult the provider and ask it to supplement the offer where necessary. One limiting factor is that, in general, framework agreements are not to be entered into for more than four years (save in exceptional cases justified by the contracting authority). It seems clear that by its nature a strategic partnering arrangement would be unlikely to fulfil the duration requirements of a framework agreement, while a project-specific partnering arrangement may fit more easily.

EXAMPLE 2 – OPTION 2 (see **Why is competition law and public procurement relevant to partnering**, above)

As mentioned, there is some uncertainty as to the use of framework agreements in the public sector. However, based on the fact that this is likely to be clarified under the new legislative package, a commercial decision could be taken to advertise a framework agreement. In cases where the framework agreement actually sets out the prices which are to be applied, there would be little risk in entering into a single supplier framework agreement (though the term of seven years would have to be justified by the local authority on the basis that it is three years longer than the current legislative proposal). The multiple supplier route would have the advantage of allowing competition between the providers as projects arise but would not sit well with the concept and benefits to be derived from partnering.

APPLICATION OF COMPETITION LAW TO PARTNERING ARRANGEMENTS

There are numerous ways in which the application of EC or national competition law may have an impact on a partnering arrangement. Competition law is not applied in isolation. In each case, one must consider the prevailing market conditions as well as the actions of the parties in their legal and economic context. For example, entering into a long-term exclusive agreement has a different effect on the market place depending on whether the parties have market power or not. If one of the parties has a dominant position in the relevant market, a long-term exclusive agreement may prevent other competitors entering or maintaining a presence in the market, thereby weakening competition over time.

Generally speaking, it is unlikely that an undertaking will have a dominant position where it has a market share of less than 40%. And the term "relevant market" has two dimensions: product market and geographic market. The key issue in defining the relevant product market is identifying the existence of substitutes for a given product. One test used to determine this is to consider what consumers would do in the event that the price of a product was raised by 5%–10% for a particular period. If consumers would switch to other products, these should be considered to be part of the same relevant product market. As to the determination of the relevant geographic market, a typical question would be this: if the price of a domestically produced product goes up, will customers import a substitute from another country? If yes, then that geographic area should be included in defining the geographic market.

In a publication such as this, it is unrealistic to attempt to identify every possible instance in which EC or national competition law may need to be taken into account. However, consideration needs to be given to some of the potential applications of national – as well as EC – competition rules in the context of a partnering arrangement.

The relevant competition provisions in the EC Treaty are Articles 81 and 82. These two provisions lay down the rules applicable to restrictive practices between businesses and abuses of a dominant position respectively.

Article 81(1) provides:

"The following shall be prohibited as incompatible with the common market: all agreements between undertakings, decisions by associations of undertakings and concerted

practices which may affect trade between member states and which have as their object or effect the prevention, restriction or distortion of competition within the common market, and in particular those which:
  (a) directly or indirectly fix purchase or selling prices or any other trading conditions;
  (b) limit or control production, markets, technical development, or investment;
  (c) share markets or sources of supply;
  (d) apply dissimilar conditions to equivalent transactions with other trading parties, thereby placing them at a competitive disadvantage;
  (e) make the conclusion of contracts subject to acceptance by the other parties of supplementary obligations which, by their nature or according to commercial usage, have no connection with the subject of such contracts."

Article 81(2) provides:

"Any agreements or decisions prohibited pursuant to this article shall be automatically void."

Article 82 provides:

"Any abuse by one or more undertakings of a dominant position within the common market or in a substantial part of it shall be prohibited as incompatible with the common market in so far as it may affect trade between Member States. Such abuse may, in particular, consist in:
  (a) directly or indirectly imposing unfair purchase or selling prices or other unfair trading conditions;
  (b) limiting production, markets or technical development to the prejudice of consumers;
  (c) applying dissimilar conditions to equivalent transactions with other trading parties, thereby placing them at a competitive disadvantage;
  (d) making the conclusion of contracts subject to acceptance by the other parties of supplementary obligations which, by their nature or according to commercial usage, have no connection with the subject of such contracts."

De minimis rules

Where companies have limited market power, agreements entered into by them are unlikely to have an appreciable restriction on competition. The special rules that apply to companies with a low market share are known as the "de minimis rules". In cases where the de minimis rules apply, the European Commission will not impose fines on the parties for anti-competitive behaviour. These carve-out provisions to the EC Treaty are set out in the Commission's Notice on agreements of minor importance: see the Commission Notice on Agreements of Minor Importance OJ 2001 C368/13.

The de minimis rules are based on the market shares held by the parties and different thresholds apply depending on whether the agreement has been entered into by competitors (a horizontal agreement) or by non-competitors (a vertical agreement). Reliance on the de minimis rules can be ruled out, however, if certain restrictions such as price fixing, output limitation, or market partitioning are included.

It is worth noting that in calculating the market share, one has to take account of undertakings that are connected to the parties. These include in general undertakings which are directly or indirectly controlled by that party (via voting rights/appointment to board/right to manage) as well as undertakings which directly or indirectly control it.

When talking about agreements entered into by competitors, the aggregate market share of the parties should be less than 10% on any relevant market. A company is treated as an actual competitor if it is either active on the same relevant market or if, in the absence of the agreement, it is able to switch production to the relevant products and market them in the short term without incurring significant additional costs. A potential competitor is one which, without the agreement, the company could and would be likely to undertake the necessary investments or switch costs to enter the market in response to a small but permanent increase in prices. In the case of agreements entered into by non-competitors, the market share of each of the parties should not exceed 15% on any of the relevant markets.

It seems likely that many partnering arrangements will fall within the scope of the de minimis rules, particularly as national markets become more integrated as a consequence of the Community's internal market. Smaller companies involved in partnering should be aware that if companies with a substantial market share are involved in the partnering arrangement, the competition rules will apply and the de minimis rules will not provide protection for the smaller companies involved.

EXAMPLE 1 (see **Why is competition law and public procurement relevant to partnering**, above)

In this case the relevant de minimis threshold is 15% as High Rise Co and Lift Co are in a vertical situation. Thus if each of the parties holds less than 15% in their respective markets, the EC competition rules would not apply.

Application of Article 81 to partnering arrangements

When considering the potential application of Article 81 to a partnering agreement, a first step is to decide whether the agreement is vertical or horizontal in nature. A vertical agreement is one entered into by companies, each of which operates at a different level in the market, so for example an agreement between a contractor and a cement manufacturer would be a vertical agreement. A horizontal agreement is one that is entered into between companies operating at the same level in the market place, so, for example, this would be an agreement between two or more cement manufacturers.

Partnering agreements are likely to be made up largely of a series of vertical agreements, on the basis that one party will provide goods or services, which the other party must acquire from the market place and is not in a position to supply itself.

Horizontal co-operation between companies generally leads to more serious competition problems. Such close co-operation and agreements between would-be competitors could allow the parties to fix prices, output or share markets. However, there are other instances in which horizontal co-operation can lead to substantial economic benefits, by sharing risks, pooling know how and increasing the pace of innovation. These will be dealt with separately below.

EXAMPLES

In all three examples, the partnering arrangement would appear to be vertical rather than horizontal in nature. In example 3 above, the consortia might involve companies who are normally competitors. However, in a situation where without such co-operation, the companies could not independently carry out the project, Article 81 would not apply.

Vertical agreements

Vertical agreements are considered less anti-competitive than horizontal agreements. To reflect the Commission's positive approach to these agreements, a regulation (Regulation (EC) No 2790/1999 on the application of Article 81(3) of the Treaty to categories of vertical agreements and concerted practices (OJ L336, 29.12.1999)) has been introduced which is designed to provide exemptions to vertical agreements that do not raise fears about anti-competitive behaviour.

This block exemption regulation is designed to provide a safe haven for all vertical agreements (other than car distribution) up to a market share of 30% subject to a limited number of conditions (see Article 4 of Regulation 2790/1999 – restrictions such as resale price maintenance, customer sharing or market partitioning). Agreements above the 30% market share threshold are not presumed to be illegal but instead require individual assessment by the companies themselves as to whether the agreements infringe the competition rules. Generally, it is the market share of the supplier of goods or services which is relevant. The 30% threshold switches to the buyer in the event that there is an exclusive supply obligation causing the supplier to sell to only one buyer inside the Community for the purpose of a specific use or for resale.

The block exemption regulation is based on the basic assumption that competition concerns arise only if there is some degree of market power at the level of the supplier or the buyer, or at both levels.

Many partnering agreements, while vertical in nature, may not be classic purchasing or distribution agreements. The following issues are likely to cause concern: non-compete obligations; exclusivity clauses; and agreements of long duration. By their nature, such issues are more likely to be present in strategic partnering than project-specific partnering.

The definition of a non-compete obligation is quite wide and includes any obligation on the buyer to purchase from the supplier more than 80% of the buyer's total purchases of such goods or services and their substitutes, based on the value of purchases during the preceding calendar year. Thus, provided that the market share threshold has not been exceeded (i.e., 30%), a partnership agreement which requires the buyer to purchase more than 80% of its yearly requirements can automatically benefit from the block exemption for a five-year period. The block exemption does not automatically exempt any agreement containing a non-compete obligation, the duration of which exceeds five years.

An indefinite partnership agreement, or one in excess of five years, would not be covered by the block exemption but the exemption would still apply to the remainder of the agreement, if that part were severable from the non-exempted obligations. Another method of dealing with the duration issue is to enter into an agreement for five years with a renewal clause, which requires the explicit consent of all parties (something that should not cause difficulty in the context of a partnering relationship anyway). In this context, it is worth noting that vertical agreements falling outside the block exemption (where for example, the supplier has a market share in excess of 30%) will not be presumed illegal but will require an individual assessment by the parties themselves. Thus, even a strategic partnering arrangement may not infringe Article 81(1) if the conditions for exemption in Article 81(3) are met.

There are four cumulative conditions for the application of Article 81(3). The vertical agreement must: (1) contribute to improving production or distribution or to promoting technical or economic progress; (2) allow customers a fair share of these benefits; (3) not impose on the undertakings concerned restraints which are not indispensable to the attainment of these benefits; and (4) not afford the possibility of eliminating competition in respect of a substantial part of the products in question.

EXAMPLE 1 – (see **Why is competition law and public procurement relevant to partnering**, above)

Here we have a vertical agreement, with an exclusivity provision and indefinite duration. In this respect, the analysis used to define the relevant market might conclude that it is for the supply of lifts to buildings and calculate Lift Co.'s share of that market. The block exemption could be relied on, provided Lift Co. has less than 30% of the relevant market for the supply of lifts. However, the indefinite duration would be an issue as an automatic exemption is limited to five years in the event that the agreement contains an exclusivity provision. A simple resolution to this issue would be to provide that the agreement would be renewed every five years on the express agreement of the parties. If Lift Co.'s market share were in fact in excess of 30%, a full assessment would have to be carried out in order to ensure that the conditions for exemption under Article 81(3) are met. In the event that there are very few players on the lift market and all of them are in the process of entering into long-term agreements, there may be concern that the market would be foreclosed to new entrants. There are provisions that allow the benefit of a block exemption to be withdrawn where parallel networks of agreements have similar effects and significantly restrict access to the market or to competition within it.

Horizontal agreements

When examining a partnering arrangement between actual or potential competitors, the competition law concerns are that, rather than competing in the marketplace, such arrangements could allow the companies to fix prices or share customers or markets between them. Such arrangements are likely to lead to customers paying higher prices or having less choice, thereby restricting competition.

Obviously, the above example is not in the spirit of a partnering arrangement and unlikely to be the purpose of the parties contemplating a partnering agreement. As with vertical arrangements, the Commission has provided a number of exemptions, which apply to horizontal agreements. These include co-operation agreements, which rarely fall within Article 81(1), such as co-operation between companies that cannot independently carry out a construction project.

Partnering arrangements aimed at specialisation agreements or research and development agreements (see Commission Regulation (EC) No 2659/2000 on the application of Article 81(3) of the Treaty to categories of research and development agreements (OJ 2000 L304/7)) are covered by existing block exemptions. Specialisation agreements are agreements whereby the parties agree, unilaterally or reciprocally, to cease production of a product and to purchase it from the other party. (See Commission Regulation (EC) No. 2658/2000 on the application of Article 81(3) of the Treaty to categories of specialisation agreements (OJ 2000 L304/3).)

The Commission's horizontal guidelines (see the Commission Guidelines on Horizontal Agreements (OJ 2001 C3/2)) cover a wide range of the most common types of horizontal agreements and complement the block exemptions on R&D and specialisation. Partnering arrangements could fall into a number of different headings within these guidelines. For example, partnering often involves subcontracting and while such agreements are generally vertical, subcontracting agreements between competitors are dealt with under the horizontal guidelines – except for those agreements which fall within the scope of the vertical restraints block exemption on the basis of Article 2(4), which will automatically be exempted (assuming of course that the other conditions are met).

However, Article 81(1) generally does not apply to co-operation between competitors if, prior to the partnering, the inputs or components have been manufactured for own consumption (captive production) and, under the new arrangement, are to be purchased from a partner by way of subcontracting or via a unilateral specialisation agreement. A different set of rules apply to subcontracting agreements which involve the transfer of knowhow to the subcontractor and Article 81(1) is generally inapplicable.

In both strategic and project-specific partnering arrangements which involve the outsourcing of an activity, the underlying reason is generally to buy in expertise which the outsourcing partner does not have or to gain efficiencies which its partner has already achieved as a result of supplying a larger market. Therefore, the application of Article 81(1) should not be an issue. The horizontal guidelines also provide guidance on the application of Article 81(1) to joint production, joint purchasing and commercialisation agreements. Parties wanting to enter to a bespoke partnering agreement could conceivably require these elements in order to create a successful partnership.

A partnering arrangement which results in the joint production of goods or the joint supply of services is likely to fall within the scope of Article 81(1) and needs to be carefully assessed. However, an anti-competitive effect is unlikely if the production is of intermediate goods which only account for a small proportion of the production of the final product and, consequently, the final costs.

A partnering arrangement which provides for joint purchasing is also likely to fall within Article 81(1) and requires an analysis of both the relevant purchasing and selling markets. If, however, the partners are not active on the same relevant markets further downstream (e.g., one buys polystyrene for use as an insulator in the building construction industry while the other uses it in the supply of packaging), Article 81(1) would rarely apply unless the parties have a very strong position in the purchasing market which could be used to harm the competitive position of other players in their respective selling markets. In most cases, it is unlikely that market power exists if they have a combined market share of below 15% on both the purchasing and selling markets.

A partnering arrangement may also amount to a commercialisation agreement as defined in the guidelines. Such agreements vary widely in scope, from joint selling on the one hand to more limited agreements which address one specific function such as joint advertising or distribution. The principle concern here is price fixing insofar as joint selling has as its object and effect the co-ordination of the pricing policy of the partners involved. Price fixing always falls within the scope of Article 81(1), regardless of the market power of the partners. The guidelines set out the Article 81(3) conditions that would have to be met for such agreements to be capable of exemption. Commercialisation agreements, which do not involve price fixing, are only subject to Article 81(1) if the partners have some degree of market power. This is unlikely to be the case if the combined market share of the partners is below 15%. Above this figure, the likely impact of the joint commercialisation agreement would have to be individually assessed.

Article 82

Article 82 condemns the abusive monopolistic behaviour of a dominant player in the market. The types of abuse by such a dominant player can be broken down into pricing (exploitative pricing practices, predatory pricing and discriminatory pricing) and non-pricing types of abuse (such as exclusivity, tie-in arrangements and refusals to supply).

In both strategic and project-specific partnering, it is of course possible that one party to the arrangement will be in a dominant position and seek to leverage its market power over the other. However, mere entry into a partnering arrangement with a dominant party does not automatically result in an abuse. In order to infringe Article 82, there must be abuse and the voluntary nature of partnership arrangements may militate against this taking place. The duration of a strategic partnering arrangement would raise Article 82 concerns particularly if the arrangement were an exclusive one. However, each case needs to be analysed in its own legal and economic context before any conclusions could be reached.

EC COMPETITION LAW – REFORM AND MODERNISATION

EC competition law is currently undergoing its most radical reform and modernisation to date, driven by the need to strengthen the enforcement of EC competition law throughout the Community and in preparation for the future accession of new members. Underlying these reforms is a more economic approach to competition issues, and the greater involvement of national competition authorities and national courts in the application of EC competition law.

In December 2002, the European Council adopted a regulation (see Council Regulation (EC) No 1/2003 of 16 December 2002 on the implementation of the rules on competition laid down in Articles 81 and 82 of the Treaty (OJ 2003 L1/1)) which, when it comes into force on 1 May 2004, will essentially abolish the notification and exemption system altogether. Until then, the existing system will continue to apply.

The Community system is based on direct applicability of the prohibition rule in Article 81(1) and a prior notification of restrictive practices for exemption under Article 81(3). While the Commission, national courts and national competition authorities can all apply Articles 81(1) and 82, the power to grant exemptions under Article 81(3) was granted exclusively to the Commission. In view of the fact that Article 81(2) renders agreements that infringe Article 81(1) void and unenforceable, this created a centralised authorisation system for all restrictive practices requiring exemption. The Commission's exemption monopoly led companies to notify huge numbers of restrictive practices. Worse still, as national courts and competition authorities have no power to apply Article 81(3) themselves, companies used the notification system not only to get legal security but also to block private action before national courts and competition authorities. However, all of this is set to change once Regulation 1/2003 comes into force, as this will allow national courts and competition authorities to apply Article 81(3) directly.

UK Competition Act 1998

The UK Competition Act 1998, the main provisions of which came into force on 1 March 2000, radically reformed the UK domestic law on restrictive agreements and anti-competitive practices. The Competition Act is broken up into a number of chapters. Chapters I and II contain prohibitions which are modelled on the provisions contained in Articles 81 and 82 of the EC Treaty but the chapters only apply to restrictive practices which affect trade in the UK or a substantial part of it.

UK law contains an important exclusion for vertical agreements from Chapter I (the equivalent of Article 81) in the Competition Act (Land and Vertical Agreements Exclusion) Order 2000.

The Order states that a vertical agreement "means an agreement between undertakings, each of which operates, for the purposes of the agreement, at a different level of the production or distribution chain and relating to the conditions under which the parties may purchase, sell or resell certain goods or services and includes provisions contained in such agreements which relate to the assignment to the buyer or use by the buyer of intellectual property rights, provided that those provisions do not constitute the primary object of the agreement and are directly related to the use, sale, or resale of goods or services by the buyer or its customers." The Chapter I exclusion does not, however, preclude the application of Article 81 of the EC Treaty if the partnering arrangement had an effect on trade between member states.

As a result of the exclusion relating to vertical agreements, most partnering arrangements may be excluded from the application of Chapter I. Where this exclusion is not available, Chapter I may still not apply as the UK de minimis rules may apply. (However, this exclusion does not apply to agreements which directly or indirectly fix prices or share markets, impose minimum resale prices or to any agreement which is part of a network of similar agreements which have a cumulative effect on the market in question.) These rules will be available if the parties combined share of the relevant market does not exceed 25%. In addition, Chapter I does not apply to an agreement which benefits from an automatic or individual exemption from the EC competition rules.

A partnering arrangement entered into by an undertaking which holds a dominant position in a market is however subject to the Chapter II prohibition (the equivalent of Article 82). Any abuses of such a dominant position is assessed in the same way as any other type of conduct under the Chapter II prohibition. Therefore, to the extent that a potential partner has market power, this will need to be taken into account in any partnering arrangement. In some cases, this might even work against the interests of the other partner, who may wish to lock his partner into a long-term supply agreement. However, undertakings that are dominant (40% plus market share) need to take care when entering into long-term supply or exclusive arrangements, as these can act to prevent new entrants and restrict competition in the market.

The adoption of the Enterprise Act in 2002 introduces criminal offences (fines and/or imprisonment) for individuals who dishonestly engage in cartel activities (price fixing, market sharing, limitation of supply or output and bid rigging) and is intended to operate as a deterrent to individuals engaging in such activities. In order to investigate the cartel offence, the OFT has increased powers to compel individuals to answer questions or provide information or documents relevant to the investigation, to search premises and take possession of documents as well as to place individuals under surveillance.

Joint ventures

A joint venture is a co-operative enterprise between two or more persons pursuing an agreed commercial goal or set of goals in certain circumstances this may relate to some partnering arrangements, in which case those entering into a partnering relationship may need to watch out for the European or UK merger regimes. The term "joint venture" covers all types of situations, ranging from fully fledged merger-like operations to co-operations limited to particular functions. EC and national competition rules apply in different ways to the various types of joint venture. Consequently, all joint ventures need to be considered on their own particular facts. The creation of a joint venture could result in the European or UK merger regimes coming in to play. These are considered below.

European Merger Control Regulation (EMCR)

A partnering arrangement would require merger control clearance from the European Commission in the event that it is considered to have a Community dimension by meeting certain turnover thresholds (see Annex 2, below). In such circumstances, a mandatory filing must be made to the European Commission within one week of a legally binding agreement or, for instance, the acquisition of controlling interest or the announcement of a public bid. The notification (Form CO) itself requires the preparation of a considerable amount of information, and failure to notify a qualifying merger leaves the parties open to the imposition of fines. The advantage of notifying at EU level is that in effect, it is a "one-stop shop", meaning that merger control rules at national level do not apply unless the Commission refers the merger back to the national authorities of the member states under Article 9(2)(a) of the EMCR.

While a partnering arrangement might be unlikely to result in a merger as commonly understood, the acquisition of sole or joint control over an undertaking (such as a special purpose partnership vehicle) or the creation of a full function joint venture could trigger the application of the EC merger control rules. Thus, an EMCR filing may be necessary even where a partnering arrangement has been put out to tender, and the notification would have to be made in accordance with the usual rules.

Joint ventures are only caught by the EMCR where they will perform, on a lasting basis, all the functions of an autonomous economic entity and which will bring about a lasting change in the structure of the undertakings concerned (see the Commission Notice on the concept of full-function joint ventures under Council Regulation (EEC) No. 4069/89 on the control of concentrations between undertakings, OJ C66/01, 1998). Normally, this means that the joint venture must operate on a market, performing the functions normally carried out by companies operating on the same market. Elements to be considered in this regard are whether the joint venture has management dedicated to its day-to-day operations and access to sufficient resources such as finance, staff and assets allowing it to conduct its business activity on a lasting basis.

A joint venture would not be considered as full function where it only takes on one specific function within the parent company's business activities without access to the market, and this may rule out the application of the EMCR to some partnering arrangements. An issue particularly relevant to project-specific partnerships is the question whether they will operate on a lasting basis. For example, this would not be the case where a joint venture is established for a short finite duration. Consequently, while project-specific partnering arrangements are unlikely to meet the "full function" requirements of the EMCR, strategic partnering, on the other hand, would require a more careful analysis in order to exclude any requirement to file a Form CO.

In general, the Commission is obliged to clear mergers notified under the EMCR unless they are likely to result in serious damage to the structure of competition in the market by creating or strengthening a dominant position. In fact, the Commission clears the vast majority of notifications made under the EMCR without any conditions attached. In order to obtain clearance, notifying parties are required to complete Form CO. In addition to requiring information on the turnover figures of the parties, ownership and control issues, the parties are obliged to identify the relevant product and geographic markets affected by the merger. Detailed information is required in the event that the "affected market" can be identified. These are where any horizontal overlaps can be identified between the parties resulting in a market share of 15% or more and, as regards vertical agreements, where any party has a 25% share of any upstream or downstream market.

In the context of a partnering arrangement, the parties are likely to be in a vertical rather than a horizontal relationship. This is on the basis that the parties are not actual or potential competitors operating in the same market (such as, for example, the supply of financial services to a local authority). In general, horizontal overlaps are more likely to give rise to competition issues than vertical ones, and this is reflected in the lower market share threshold for affected markets for horizontal overlaps (15% as opposed to 25%).

There are no fees to be paid for notifying a merger to the Commission (depending on the complexity of the case, legal costs will need to be considered). The Commission normally reaches its decision to clear notified mergers in Phase I (i.e., within a month of notification). If the Commission has serious doubts as to the compatibility of the merger with the common market (there are indications, for example, that the agreement notified will lead to the creation or strengthening of a dominant position which will significantly impede effective competition in the common market or a substantial part of it), it will open Phase II proceedings, a final decision being reached within four months.

EXAMPLE 3 – (see **Why is competition law and public procurement relevant to partnering**, above)

Once a concession has been awarded, an EMCR filing may have to be made (this depends on whether the parties meet the turnover thresholds and whether the joint venture constitutes a full function joint venture). The Commission will then analyse the proposed operation in order to determine whether it could result in the creation or strengthening of a dominant position on the common market or a substantial part of it. For example, in this case, it could come about as a result of chosen technology becoming a predominant platform for the provision of telematics services in the transport sector. In the event that one of the joint venture partners is already active on this market, there might be a concern that it could control, to a significant extent, the conditions of competition on this emerging market. If, in Phase I, the Commission has serious doubts as to whether the transaction would be compatible with the common market, it will open a Phase II investigation, which lasts up to four months. In view of the potential delay and uncertainty surrounding a Phase II investigation, it is prudent for all parties to consider the potential competition aspects of the transaction in advance. It is worth noting that the Commission is prepared to meet and discuss potential competition issues with the parties on a confidential basis, in advance of any notification.

National merger control rules

The fact that a partnering relationship does not qualify as an acquisition of sole or joint control, or a full function joint venture under the EMCR does not mean that national merger control rules are inapplicable. In more recent years, many EC member states have adopted or altered their merger control rules and accordingly their potential application may need to be considered.

The UK has recently passed the Enterprise Act, which considerably alters the UK's merger control regime. The UK's Office of Fair Trading (OFT) is required to investigate mergers, which meet either the "turnover test" or the "share of supply test". The turnover test is currently met if the gross value of the worldwide assets being acquired exceeds £70m. In the Enterprise Act the test will be met if the target company has a UK turnover of £70m or more. The share of supply test is met if the merging parties will together supply at least 25% of goods or services of a particular description, either in the UK as a whole or in a substantial part of it. This test is only met if the share of supply increases as a result of the merger.

A merger is deemed to arise where two or more enterprises cease to be distinct (not normally the situation in the context of a partnering arrangement) or where they come under common control. A merger is also deemed to occur where one enterprise acquires any of three levels of control over another enterprise:

(1) ownership of a controlling interest (de jure control);
(2) the ability to control policy (de facto control); or
(3) the ability to influence policy materially.

The OFT has indicated that the acquisition of any shareholding greater than 15% is liable to be investigated to determine whether the lowest level of control (see (3) above) has been acquired. This wide definition of control means that in most arrangements involving the creation of a joint venture, the parent companies will enjoy control for merger control purposes.

Unlike the position in many EU member states, there is no obligation to notify partnering arrangements which fall within the scope of UK merger control rules. The OFT has four months from the announcement of the deal to investigate it, or refer it to the Competition Commission. If the OFT believes that the partnering agreement may be expected to result in a substantial lessening of competition, then it must either refer it to the Competition Commission or, if appropriate, seek undertakings in lieu of a reference. The general duty to refer to the Competition Commission is subject to two main exceptions, however: if the market is of insufficient importance to justify a reference or if there are obvious benefits to customers that outweigh the adverse effect on competition.

In view of the fact that the Competition Commission can, following an investigation, prohibit a merger or impose undertakings on the parties, it is advisable to consider notifying partnering arrangements which fall within the scope of UK merger control rules. There are different methods of proceeding, depending on the requirements of the parties. A formal notification can be made which requires certain deadlines to be respected. There is also a procedure for obtaining confidential guidance, which can be used before an arrangement is made public. As this method does not allow consultation with third parties who may be affected, it is often used in advance of a formal notification, which is made once the deal has been announced.

Joint ventures between the public and private sectors

The HM Treasury Guidance prepared by Partnerships UK (*A Guidance Note for Public Sector Bodies Forming Joint Venture Companies with the Private Sector December 2001*) – the Guidance – provides a useful background to this topic. The Guidance states that public bodies wishing to enter into joint venture companies to provide services should not see competition law as a barrier, especially if their activities are aimed at increasing competition in a market. However, public bodies need to be aware of the potential competition issues that may arise.

There are a number of important watch points before the public and private sector can get together and create a successful joint venture. In entering into such an arrangement, both sides will need to be certain that the public authority has the necessary statutory powers to participate in a joint venture.

Where a public authority considers that a joint venture with a private organisation is a suitable way to provide services, then the procurement process (where relevant) should be applied as discussed elsewhere in this chapter.

The joint venture partners must be aware from the very beginning that where public and private sector funds are combined state aid issues may arise. State aid issues can arise where the public sector confers a direct or indirect financial advantage on the new venture. The key test is whether the private entity is receiving a benefit, which would not normally be received in the normal course of business. In other words the public authority must clearly be able to establish what it is getting in return when providing finance to the joint venture. Any potential state aid issues should be dealt with at the beginning of the project to avoid any costly unwind should the money provided by the public authority be classified as an illegal state aid.

The public and private partners must bear in mind the requirement to achieve value for money in the provision of services. This requirement must be kept under constant review and be a key objective for all parties to the joint venture. If during the establishment of the joint venture it becomes clear to the public authority that best value is no longer capable of being achieved by the creation of a joint venture, then the joint venture may be dissolved. The joint venture must provide for a continual review that the requirements of the authority are being achieved.

The assessment of value for money considerations should include issues such as which partner is most able to provide the required assets, how risks are to be handled and the prospects of long-term revenue generation.

CONCLUSION

Parties wishing to consider the use of partnering arrangements need to ensure the procurement aspects are fully investigated at as early a stage as possible. The complexity of the procurement route will largely turn on the nature, scale and duration of the partnering arrangement envisaged. Each potential partnering arrangement needs to be evaluated carefully to ensure that all relevant procurement considerations are taken account of.

There are significant practical differences between the goals of strategic partnering arrangements and more limited project-specific partnering arrangements. Parties will therefore need to give careful consideration to the differences before determining the particular strategy to be adopted.

Clearly the two types of partnering arrangements are very different and they bring with them different procurement choices and decisions.

The potential impact of regulatory aspects on a partnering arrangement cannot be ignored. While many partnering arrangements will fall out of the scope of such regulatory controls, just as many will be caught either under the EU procurement directives or possibly within the wide reaching EU and UK competition law. The concept of partnering is readily transferable into many construction scenarios and, as construction contracts become larger-scale and longer term, the breadth of the potential scope of partnering arrangements becomes extremely wide. We see that in the past there have been uncertainties relating to joint ventures and that care needs to be taken to ensure that special purpose vehicles are structured in the best interests of parties. The increased use of joint ventures and sometimes special purpose vehicles means that in some limited circumstances, parties will have to consider novel aspects not usually associated with construction contracts, such as EU and UK merger regulations.

In real terms, partnering arrangements, like other construction project arrangements, need to be considered carefully against the backdrop of the parties' aims and the particular requirements of the project in question. It is difficult to make generalisations about the potential impact of regulatory controls and each partnering arrangement will need to be reviewed to ensure that EU procurement rules and competition laws are not offended.

ANNEX 1

EC procurement thresholds

The EC procurement rules apply to public authorities (including government departments, local authorities and NHS authorities and trusts) and certain utility companies operating in the energy, water, transport and telecommunications sectors. The rules set out detailed procedures for the award of contracts whose value equals or exceeds specific thresholds. Details of the thresholds, applying from 1 January 2002, are given below.

Further information on the main characteristics of the EC procurement Rules is given in CUP Guide No 51.

Thresholds – public sector from 1 January 2002

	Supplies	Services	Works
Entities listed in Schedule 1 (SI 1995/201)[1]	£100,410 (SDR130,000) (EUR162,293)	£100,410[2] (SDR130,000) (EUR162,293)	£3,861,932[3] (SDR5m) (EUR6,242,028)
Other public sector contracting authorities	£154,477 (SDR200,000) (EUR249,681)	£154,477[2] (SDR200,000) (EUR249,681)	£3,861,932[3] (SDR5m) (EUR6,242,028)
Indicative notices	£464,024 (EUR750,000)	£464,024 (EUR750,000)	£3,861,932 (EUR6,242,028)

| Small lots | Not applicable | £49,496 | £618,698 |
| | | (EUR80,000) | (EUR1m) |

NOTES:
1. Schedule 1 of the Public Supply Contracts Regulations 1995 lists central government bodies subject to the WTO GPA. These thresholds will also apply to any successor bodies.
2. With the exception of the following services which have a threshold of £123,740 (EUR200,000):
    (1) Part B (residual) services
    (2) Research and development services (Category 8)
    (3) The following telecommunications services in Category 5[2] –
        (a) CPC 7524 – television and radio broadcast services
        (b) CPC 7525 – interconnection services
        (c) CPC 7526 – integrated telecommunications services
    (4) Subsidised services contracts under regulation 25 of the Public Services Contracts Regulations 1993.
3. For subsidised works contracts under regulation 23 of the Public Works Contracts Regulations 1991, the threshold is £3,093,491 (EUR5m).

Thresholds – utilities sector from 1 January 2002

	Supplies	Services	Works
Water, electricity, urban transport,[1] airports and ports sectors	£308,955 (SDR400,000) (EUR499,362)	£308,955[2] (SDR400,000) (EUR499,362)	£3,861,932 (SDR5m) (EUR6,242,028)
Oil, gas, coal and railway sectors	£247,479 (EUR400,000)	£247,479 (EUR400,000)	£3,093,491 (EUR5m)
Telecoms sector	£371,219 (EUR600,000)	£371,209 (EUR600,000)	£3,093,491 (EUR5m)
Indicative notices	£464,024 (EUR750,000)	£464,024 (EUR750,000)	As per appropriate works threshold
Small lots	Not applicable	Not applicable0	£618,698 (EUR1m)

NOTES:
1. Contracting entities in the field of urban railway, tramway, trolleybus or bus services.
2. With the exception of the following services which have a threshold of £247,479 (EUR400,000):
    (1) Part B (residual) services
    (2) Research and development services (Category 8)
    (3) The following telecommunications services in Category 5[3] –
        (a) CPC 7524 – television and radio broadcast services
        (b) CPC 7525 – interconnection services
        (c) CPC 7526 – integrated telecommunications services

Office of Government Commerce. © Crown Copyright 2001

ANNEX 2

European Merger Control thresholds

There are two sets of thresholds contained in the European Merger Control Regulation.

Set A

	Euros (million)
Combined aggregate worldwide turnover of all parties	5,000
Aggregate Community-wide turnover of each of at least two of the parties	250

Set B

	Euros (million)
Combined aggregate worldwide turnover of all parties	2,500
Combined aggregate turnover of all parties in each of at least three member states	100
Aggregate turnover of each of at least two of the parties in each of the above three member states	25
Aggregate Community-wide turnover of each of at least two of the parties	100

In each case, the European Merger Control Regulation will apply if either of the above thresholds are met unless each of the parties achieves more than two-thirds of its aggregate Community-wide turnover within one and the same member state.

For the purposes of calculating turnover in the context of an acquisition, the entire group turnover of the acquirer must be taken into account, together with the turnover of the "target" company. It is not necessary to include the entire group turnover of the vendor company. In the case of a full function joint venture, the turnover to be taken into account is the entire group turnover of each of the joint venture parents in addition to the turnover of the joint venture itself (if any).

If the Merger Control Regulation applies, (i.e., if either of the above sets of threshold criteria are met), domestic legislation will be inapplicable. The transaction will be subject to examination by the European Commission only. However, if neither set of criteria are fulfilled, the merger is not notifiable to the European Commission and, therefore, any or all of the competition authorities of the member states who are affected by the merger may need to be notified.

CHAPTER 7

CONTRACTING FOR
GOOD FAITH

Marina Milner[1]

The key to successful partnering is achieving a cultural shift from adversarial to collaborative working through managerial methods and practices. If this is done successfully, so that each party is fully and genuinely committed to both the project and the partnering ideal, then, as has often been pointed out by commentators, there should be no need for the law to be involved at all. In particular, there should be no need for contracts, because all the parties will operate in good faith and manage and resolve disputes for the greater good of the project, without recourse to the veiled threat of contractual obligation. Whether or not this can (or should) happen as a practical matter, the point does highlight the dilemma for UK law. Should it force the parties to behave like this? One way of doing so would be to employ a legal doctrine of good faith. The extent to which such a doctrine exists in the UK will be examined in the section *Good faith in the UK*, below.

In other jurisdictions, notably the United States and Germany, the concept of "good faith" has become an integral part of the legal system. The meaning of this phrase in these jurisdictions and its potential for use in the UK will be examined in the section *Good faith in other jurisdictions*, below. There has, however, been considerable hesitation in adopting such a good faith standard in the UK, for a variety of reasons. One is that it is considered too vague or subjective a standard to be enforceable. In addition, there are theoretical concerns, which address the dichotomy of interest that is present in every partnering arrangement. That is, while all partners commit to furthering the interests of the project rather than focusing on their own at the expense of the project, in order to create a legal principle that can enforce this, we need to understand the difference between the two sets of interests. In any event, UK law has not always been very adept at enforcing group or non-human rights and it is difficult to see how enforcing the "interests of the project" will be achieved. It may be that the existing legal concept of fiduciary obligation is of use here and this will be addressed in the section *The interests of the project*, below.

A further issue arises out of this, which again focuses on the status of individual rights within the partnering arrangement. That is, where contractual

1. Solicitor, Construction, Engineering & Projects, Hammonds.

rights have been agreed and which are in the interests of individual parties, such as exclusion clauses and limitations of liability, can that party insist on these rights? How generally will (or should) they be treated? Will parties be restrained by the overarching principles summed up in the phrase "good faith"? Again, we only have small hints at the answer to this so far, but the issue is addressed in the section *The interests of individuals*, below.

WHAT IS MEANT BY GOOD FAITH?

One of the difficulties with the concept of good faith is that there is no generally accepted definition of it. Attempts to establish one can, when phrased in general terms, ring alarm bells for those who warn that good faith is too vague and subjective a notion on which to base a legal doctrine. One example of a definition (admittedly taken out of its context here) is given by Sir Thomas Bingham in *Interfoto Picture Library Ltd* v. *Stiletto Visual Programmes Ltd* [1989] QB 422. Here he described the requirement of good faith as essentially one of "fair and open dealing". The difficulty is that it may be difficult to obtain agreement from all parties about what "fair dealing" is.

However, it is relatively clear from the commentaries, from case law and from the standard form partnering charters that good faith involves certain constituent elements. For example, it implies that parties will not depart from the spirit of the agreement they have entered into, even if in strict legal terms they have a right to do so – so that, say, the parties will follow agreed dispute resolution procedures before proceeding to court. Consequently, the principle applies to the interpretation of the contract as well as implying substantive obligations.

The principle also seems to include notions of co-operation for the greater good of the project rather than the self-interest of the parties – that is, with an eye to finishing the project on time, on budget and within agreed quality parameters. There may be obligations in terms of how negotiations are carried out; that communication is open and frank; that there is transparency, trust and confidence between the parties; and that parties abandon the blame culture. It may be possible to add more specific examples from any bespoke contract.

A more complex issue is how "good faith" is incorporated within a partnering arrangement. There seem to be two models. First, there is that used in the UK, where the partnering ideals are set out in a separate contract (or charter). (In this chapter, the terms are used interchangeably. See Chapter 8 for commentary on the standard form partnering contracts.) These usually comprise the aspirations of the project team, in terms similar to that set out in the previous paragraph: in this way, the charter embodies the concept of good faith, but this is kept separate from the construction contract itself. Furthermore, the charter may or may not be legally binding. Alternatively, there is the US model, which is based on the idea that there is no such thing as a partnering contract as such. Partnering simply obliges the parties to act in good faith and implies the existence of procedural rules (relating to dispute resolution, for example) to fulfil this obligation.

The two approaches are very similar and aim at the same result, but the UK model can mean the segregation of ideas of "good faith" from the project itself. In addition, confusion can easily arise using this model. Parties sometimes use the partnering charter to identify measurable performance targets and to set out gain-share and pain- share incentives. This creates difficulties if, first, the charter is stated not to be legally binding and, second, such mechanisms are not reflected in the underlying construction contract. The problem seems to lie in the assumption that "good faith", with all the elements it entails, is conceptually distinct from the detail of the building contract. The point (as it is understood in the United States) is to operate the building contract using good faith principles. Opinions may differ as to how best to achieve that aim, but if it is not the basis of each party's understanding, then the partnering arrangement can easily become unravelled.

GOOD FAITH IN THE UK

Development of good faith

It is still the case that there is no general doctrine of good faith in the UK. The most that can be said is that a principle of good faith is sometimes brought into play by the courts albeit not usually as a generalised idea but in order to deal with specific issues such as freedom to terminate a contract, or a duty to negotiate in good faith. In this way, UK law "tries to find a balance between abstaining from developing any wide principles of good faith and developing individual solutions to contractual unfairness" (see Jan Middleton, "Partnering in a Rough, Tough World", *Construction Law*, Aug/Sept 2000 6 at p. 7). The mentions that are made by the courts may, in time, develop into something that forms the basis of a doctrine, but there are significant obstacles in the way of this happening. There are deep-rooted objections to good faith, and these are recognised by the courts to varying degrees.

These objections have a long history. It is, for example, widely perceived that good faith provides a standard which is vague at best and which invites lawyers and judges to dabble in moral arguments that are subjective and irrelevant for legal purposes. Such a standard, it is argued, would undermine certainty in a contract as well as the true intentions of the parties, especially if these were poorly expressed.

However, these are objections that could be overcome or at least addressed as they have been in Germany and the United States. The UK courts already deal with difficult principles. It is surely not beyond UK lawyers to develop substance to a general concept of good faith that is not too vague and which could apply in certain well-established contexts. Similarly, the law could formally identify the main elements of a good faith principle and generate rules for the application of these elements: for example, a general proposition might be developed that a contractual term should not be exercised without regard to the overall purpose of the contract (see Reziya Harrison in Harrison and Jansen, "Good Faith in Construction Law" (1999) 15 Const LJ 346 at p. 367 and generally; also Barbara Colledge, "Good Faith in Construction Contracts – the Hidden Agenda" (1999) 15 Const LJ 288 for the notion that English construction law does already recognise the constituent elements of good faith).

In terms of undermining the parties' intentions, this could be prevented relatively easily (albeit with the more careful attention of the parties). In the case of *Regalian Properties plc* v. *London Dockland Development Corp* [1995] 1 All ER 1005, the court refused to imply any obligation of good faith in terms of negotiation, because the parties in this case had expressly stated that each was free to withdraw from negotiations at any time. To imply some limit on this, on the basis of a good faith principle, would therefore undermine the deal that the parties had made. The point here is, if the parties state clearly enough that they wish to exclude any duty, then the courts will respect that.

The problem is not really developing rules that are substantive, clear and easily understood. The problem is that the basis of a concept of good faith appears to be contrary to the basis of English contract law – ie the principle of freedom of contract which underlies both the UK economy and commercial law. It is in the nature of contractual rights under UK law that it is permissible and acceptable to act with self-interest (see further Jack Beatson "Public Law Influences in Contract Law " in Beatson and Friedman, *Good Faith and Fault in Contract Law* (1995), pp. 266–267). Applying this classical theory to its logical end means that when parties are negotiating and agreeing projects, they should be free to walk away at any time for any reason and, furthermore, that until the point of agreement, the parties are to be regarded as pitted against one another. An alternative analysis of the situation is that the parties are engaged in a collaborative process which results in a deal with which all parties are satisfied – and this, arguably, is the basis of partnering.

The courts have relatively recently reaffirmed the classical theory as the basis of English common law. As stated above, the arguments come up in terms of specific elements of good faith, for example, in the context of contractual negotiations. An example of the courts' approach is supplied by Lord Ackner in *Walford* v. *Miles* [1992] 2 AC 128 at p. 138. He said:

"… the concept of a duty to carry on negotiations in good faith is inherently repugnant to the adversarial position of the parties when involved in negotiations. Each party to the negotiations is entitled to pursue his (or her) own interest, so long as he avoids making misrepresentations. To advance that interest he must be entitled, if he thinks it appropriate, to threaten to withdraw from further negotiations or to withdraw in fact, in the hope that the opposite party may seek to reopen the negotiations by offering him improved terms."

As regards a duty to co-operate, the court in *London Borough of Merton* v. *Stanley Hugh Leach* (1985) 32 BLR 51 at p. 80 held: "the courts have not gone beyond the implication of a duty to co-operate whenever it is reasonably necessary to enable the other party to perform his obligations under a contract. The requirement of 'good faith' in systems derived from Roman law has not been imported into English law." It should be noted, however, that the case did uphold a duty on the part of the employer to take all steps reasonably necessary to enable the contractor to discharge his obligations, provided that these were steps that were within the power of the employer to take.

A further example of the classical theory is in relation to an obligation of trust and confidence: the court in *Bedfordshire CC* v. *Fitzpatrick Contractors Ltd* [1998] CILL 1433–1444 refused to imply such an obligation on the part of the contractor towards the employer in the context of a maintenance contract. The most that Mr Justice Dyson would say was that that there might be more justification for an obligation of that kind in a construction contract.

Such traditional objections are, however, being challenged in both academic and industry-specific debate; and in certain distinct areas of law the principle has been adopted by the legislature (see, for example, the Unfair Terms in Consumer Contracts Regulations 1994, referred to in the section *General common law (contract)*, below). In terms of construction partnering, it would appear that bespoke partnering agreements, as well as the standard forms, regularly use concepts that are at the heart of good faith and create specific obligations in those terms, even if they do not use the term "good faith" itself. Such terminology is used in more traditional forms of contract too, in certain specific contexts – such as, for example, where parties attempt to oblige each other to mediate in good faith.

To accept the good faith requirement that is at the heart of partnering into UK law does, however, entail a recognition that adversarial dealing "is not the only game in town" (see Roger Brownsword, " 'Good Faith in Contracts' Revisited" (1996) *Current Legal Problems*, Vol. 49, Pt. 2, 111 at p. 124) and that parties already do negotiate in their mutual interests, or in the interests of a mutual project; and that this is what is happening where partnering is involved. No system will allow you to predict accurately the result of every dispute. Given the continued use of good faith elements and the partnering concept, it may be that the traditional objections to the concept will ultimately be overcome.

Case law in the UK

Some commentators have argued that elements of a good faith standard have already been adopted into UK law. For example, Harrison states that there is already a duty to disclose latent defects that make a building unfit for its purpose; to carry out works with skill and care; and to co-operate, at least so far as necessary to allow a contractor to carry out the works (for the latter, see *Glenlion Construction Ltd* v. *Guinness Trust* (1987) 39 BLR 89 and, generally,

Harrison and Jansen, "Good Faith in Construction Law" (1999) 15 Const LJ 346 at p. 367).

Similarly, Colledge suggests that there is what she calls an 'implicit good faith' argument, which places limits on any discretionary powers contained within a contract, so that such discretion must be exercised honestly and in good faith and must not be exercised arbitrarily, capriciously or unreasonably. Examples are the duty to undertake in good time the renomination of a sub-contractor (*Percy Bilton Ltd* v. *Greater London Council* [1982] 20 BLR 1); or the duty not to prevent or hinder the contract performance (*Torquay Hotel Co Ltd* v. *Cousins* [1969] 2 Ch 106); or the obligation on an employer to take all steps reasonably necessary to enable the contractor to discharge his obligations and execute the works in a regular and orderly manner (*London Borough of Merton* v. *Stanley Hugh Leach* (1985) 32 BLR 51). See also Barbara Colledge, "Good Faith in Construction Contracts – the Hidden Agenda" (1999) 15 Const LJ 288; Brownsword, "'Good Faith in Contracts' Revisited" (1996) *Current Legal Problems*, Vol. 49, Pt. 2, 111).

These arguments hold good if we understand good faith as creating a fairly minimal legal framework: i.e., that parties should do the work they are paid to undertake, do it to a minimum standard, and not get in each other's way if they can avoid it. Even if that were enough for the purposes of partnering, there is no general acceptance that these points add up to a formal doctrine of good faith. In any event, if partnering is to work, the point is to create positive obligations and encourage proactive behaviour – such as co-operation and open communication – rather than simply prevent negative behaviour. This idea challenges traditional views about how to negotiate and execute a building project and requires a more radical legal approach.

Very little has as yet been decided before the courts, however, and it is impossible to gauge, from the one case that has emerged, how the courts are likely to react in terms of good faith obligations in construction partnering agreements. There are indications in other areas of contract law (of which construction is a subset) of a fledgling concept of good faith being developed and applied, and more guidance may be extracted from those cases. Once again it should be noted that the courts tend to focus on a specific context rather than a generalised concept. In this next section, we look first at the construction partnering case law, then at the wider contract law picture.

Construction/partnering case law

The case that has emerged in the area of partnering and good faith in the UK is that of *Birse Construction Ltd* v. *St Davids Ltd* [1999] BLR 194.

Birse carried out work for St Davids, building luxury apartments at Adventurers' Quay, Cardiff Bay. St Davids intended that the project should be entered into on a partnering basis. The parties carried on negotiations to agree a building contract on the basis of the JCT Standard Form of Building

Contract 1980 Private Edition without Quantities. The concept of partnering was observed, first in the form of the financial arrangements chosen by the parties and then in the form of a charter that was signed up at a "team building" seminar attended by the parties. It is not reported whether there was a clause in the charter stating that it was not legally binding, but its terms were aspirational in nature and the court held that it "was clearly not legally binding" (see p. 202 of the report).

Birse in the meantime was on site, and St Davids became unhappy with Birse's performance. The parties fell out and although negotiations on the JCT form had reached an advanced stage, they foundered before the contract was signed up. Practical completion of the works was certified on 1 July 1998. Birse then left site, maintaining that there was no contract. St Davids, arguing that there was such a contract, treated that decision as abandonment which constituted a specified default as referred to in clause 27 of the JCT form. Birse then claimed payment on a quantum meruit basis; St Davids responded that the matter should be referred to arbitration in accordance with the contract and so sought a stay of proceedings under s. 9 of the Arbitration Act 1996. It is this preliminary decision that is discussed here, and which commentators have picked up on, because of the comments on good faith in partnering made by the presiding judge, Judge Humphrey LLoyd.

Judge Humphrey LLoyd held that, on the facts, there was a contract. In doing so, he made a point of highlighting the fact that the parties had entered a partnering arrangement: "... the [principles set out in the] partnership charter ... although clearly not legally binding, are important for they were clearly intended to provide the standards by which the parties were to conduct themselves and against which their conduct and attitudes were to be measured..."

This suggests that the court would expect the parties to exercise openness and use clear and effective communication; and furthermore that the court would assume that this had been done (presumably in the absence of evidence to the contrary). Further, the court seems to have anticipated that the charter might have had effect on the treatment of the contract programme. Birse had put forward a programme (which was treated by this and subsequent court decisions as the final one). The court held that this had "obviously" been done "within the partnering ethos which it was expected would naturally have led to a sympathetic approach to questions of extensions of time and of deduction of damages for delay if the plaintiff had not been able to maintain the programme because of the occurrence of a relevant event ... and also for other reasons beyond its immediate control..."

It is possible to infer from this that parties to even a non-legally binding partnering agreement might be expected not to insist on what might otherwise be considered their strict legal rights; or at least not to make commercial capital out of difficulties that one party might face.

Judge Humphrey LLoyd also made a statement about the general effect of the charter:

"In my view the plaintiff is trying to capitalise on the lack of a formal written contract ... This is particularly surprising since these days one would not expect, where the parties had made mutual commitments such as those in the charter, either to be concerned about compliance with contractual procedures if otherwise there had been true compliance with the letter or the spirit of the charter. Even though the terms of the charter would not alter or affect the terms of the contract (where they are not incorporated or referred to in the contract or are not binding in law in their own right) an arbitrator (or court) would undoubtedly take such adherence to the charter into account in exercising the wide discretion to open up, review and revise, etc. which is given under the JCT Conditions." (See pp. 202 and 203 of the report.)

The court went further, stating that, where there is a partnering arrangement, the parties can be taken to have accepted that adherence to rigid attitudes regarding the formation of a contract was unnecessary; they had instead agreed to proceed on the basis of mutual co-operation and trust.

The decision is an interesting one for those who seek to find a meaning to the term "good faith". If Judge Humphrey LLoyd's decision is to be followed, it appears that the use of a partnering arrangement implies that parties should not be able to rely on strict legal rights, and that their contractual status – the allocation of risk between them – should be judged in the light of the specific principles to which the parties have signed up. In Birse, this meant (for example) mutual co-operation and trust, integrity, honesty and openness. It would also presumably have meant, although these were not cited specifically by the judge, maximising the profits of all parties and completing the project by mutual support, which would appear to impact more directly on risk allocation.

Caution should be used, however, when reading Birse. This was a fairly short judicial pronouncement at an interim stage of proceedings. The case itself was eventually remitted to the Technology and Construction Court for a full trial of the issue of whether there was a contract. There, Mr Recorder Colin Reese QC agreed with Judge Humphrey LLoyd that there was no contract, but on different grounds to those that persuaded the latter. Mr Recorder Reese did not use the existence of the charter to support his conclusion in the same way that Judge Humphrey LLoyd had and, in fact, made no comment about the charter at all. As far as the writer is aware, there are no further cases directly endorsing Judge Humphrey LLoyd's approach.

The approach of Judge Humphrey LLoyd was, however, to recognise the fact that the parties had taken extra care, over and above the usual contract terms, to create a different approach to the contract and had reflected these intentions in actions and express words (it is accepted that the court held that the charter was not legally enforceable but it is not reported whether the parties intended it to be so). The case does, therefore, give an example of how a duty of good faith may be used to enforce the intentions of the parties, in a clear and unequivocal way. Assuming that these early intentions should be respected, the judgment overcomes two of the objections commonly made against the use of a principle of good faith.

In terms of other construction case law relevant to good faith, it is worth mentioning *Balfour Beatty* v. *Docklands Light Railway* (1996) 78 BLR 42. Here, the question arose as to how far the court could open up the decisions of the employer regarding payments and extensions of time. The court accepted that it could not open up the employer's decisions: the contract provided (for example) that the amount due under the contract was the amount the employer decided was due. The Court of Appeal, in a judgment given by the Master of the Rolls, Sir Thomas Bingham, said that "it [was] not for the court to decide whether the contractor had made a good bargain or a bad one; it can only give fair effect to what the parties intended". This is familiar territory. However, the Master of the Rolls went on to say that the court:

"... would be greatly concerned at the implication of accepting [the employer's] argument if to do so would leave the contractor without any effective means of challenging partial, self-interested or unreasonable decisions ... by the employer. We would then have wished to consider whether an employer, invested (albeit by contract) with the power to rule on his own and a contractor's rights and obligations, was not subject to a duty of good faith substantially more demanding than that customarily recognised in English contract law. [The employer] has, however, accepted without reservation that [it] was not only bound to act honestly but also bound by contract to act fairly and reasonably, even where no such obligation was expressed in the contract (as in some clauses ... it was). Even on a more expansive approach to good faith, it may be that no more is required in the performance of a contract ... If the contractor can prove a breach of this duty, it will be entitled to a remedy. If it cannot, and cannot establish any other breach of contract, it will under this contract be entitled to none."

The Court of Appeal here therefore seems to indicate that good faith is active as a principle, and furthermore is actionable by aggrieved parties.

General common law (contract)

The wider sphere of general contract law gives further instances of good faith being successfully raised and argued. One example is *Timeload Ltd* v. *British Telecommunications* [1995] EMLR 459. In this case, the plaintiff was allocated a freephone number for the purposes of its business by BT. The number was 0800 192192 (192 being BT's directory enquiry number at the time). BT claimed that the number had been allocated by mistake or by reason of breach of duty by one of its employees. As a result and after the plaintiff had started marketing and promoting its services, BT terminated the agreement on one month's notice. It relied on its standard terms, which expressly gave it such a right to do so.

Timeload applied for an interlocutory injunction to prevent termination, arguing that it was an implied term of the contract that BT could terminate only for good cause and that there was no such good cause. Among arguments in support of its case, Timeload argued that BT could have suspended the service only in order to change the number under the same standard terms and that this was inconsistent with the argument that it could terminate for any reason at all. It is also argued that there were clauses under the Unfair

Contract Terms Act 1977 which imposed obligations preventing termination without cause. The injunction was granted. BT appealed on the basis that it had an unfettered right under its standard terms to terminate without cause and it had merely sought to exercise this right.

The Court of Appeal dismissed BT's appeal. Sir Thomas Bingham, in giving judgment, specifically mentioned as relevant the special power of BT as a public telecommunications operator and said that in the circumstances of this contract there were strong grounds for the view that BT should not be permitted to exercise a potentially drastic power of termination without demonstrable cause for doing so. In addition, he agreed with Timeload's argument regarding the limited application of the right to suspension as against the apparently free right to terminate. Most relevant for our purposes, however, are the court's comments regarding good faith. The principle arose in the context of the Unfair Contract Terms Act 1977. While, strictly, this case was held to fall outside the terms of the Act, the Master of the Rolls did not consider that to be the end of the matter:

"As I ventured to observe in *Interfoto Picture Library Ltd* v. *Stiletto Visual Programmes Ltd* [1989] QB 433, 439, the law of England, while so far eschewing any broad principle of good faith in the field of contract, has responded to demonstrated problems of unfairness by developing a number of piecemeal solutions directed to the particular problem before it. It seems to be at least arguable that the common law could, if the letter of the statute does not apply, treat the clear intention of the legislature expressed in the statute as a platform for invalidating or restricting the operation of an oppressive clause in a situation of the present, very special kind."

In other words, it seems that the principle of good faith could be used to extend the application of, or at least fill in perceived gaps in, legislation. This is not the same as a proposal that good faith could be used in a similar way to fill in gaps in contracts, but there has nevertheless been speculation that the idea developed here by Sir Thomas Bingham could apply, say, to an employer's right to terminate under consultants' appointments; and, potentially, to parties' rights under agreements formed under the umbrella of a partnering agreement.

Another case which has raised the profile of good faith in the UK is *Philips Electronique Grand Public SA* v. *British Sky Broadcasting* [1995] EMLR 472. In this case, Philips contracted with BSB to manufacture light reception equipment that would be compatible solely with BSB's transmission. Shortly thereafter, Sky and BSB merged to form BSkyB. Sales of BSB-compatible equipment were suspended with a decision that all systems would be compatible with Sky systems. Philips contended (among other things) that this was a breach of an implied term that BSB would not do anything of its own volition to frustrate the commercial purposes of the agreement.

The case reached the Court of Appeal, which dismissed the action against BSkyB, since the various terms that Philips wished to see implied into the agreement were either unreasonably broad or could only be effective up until the time BSB discontinued broadcasting. The court did make the following statement, however: "for the avoidance of doubt we should add that we would, if it were material, imply a term that BSB should act with good faith in the performance of this contract. But it is not material." The court at first instance had found that there was no suggestion that BSB had acted in bad faith, and furthermore that they had good commercial reasons for acting as they did. It has been argued, nevertheless, that "the court's willingness to recognise an implied obligation to perform in good faith might prove to be a doctrinal watershed" (see Roger Brownsword, "'Good Faith in Contracts' Revisited" (1996) *Current Legal Problems*, Vol. 49, Pt. II, 111 at p. 123; see also *Balfour Beatty Civil Engineering Ltd* v. *Docklands Light Railway Ltd* (1996) 78 BLR 42).

Note, however, the case of *Hadley Design Associates Ltd* v. *The Lord Mayor and Citizens of the City of Westminster* [2003] EWCH 1617, TCC (9 July 2003)). Here, Judge Richard Seymour QC assessed the arguments made by the Court of Appeal in *Timeload* and in *Balfour Beatty* for the implication of a doctrine of good faith and found that the idea not only lacked authority, but was "fraught with difficulty" and he declined to move in that direction, preferring the classical objections to such a move.

Nevertheless impetus for the gradual acceptance of a principle of good faith may be the Unfair Terms in Consumer Contracts Regulations 1994. These regulations were adopted to implement Directive 93/13/EEC. They were replaced with a further set of regulations in 1999, which were themselves slightly amended in 2001. They allow a public body with an interest in consumer protection to challenge terms in consumer contracts that are perceived as unfair. The Office of Fair Trading has been active in using the regulations. They are relevant here because they use the principle of "good faith". Under regulation 5(1), a term is unfair if, "contrary to the requirements of good faith [it] causes a significant imbalance in the parties' rights and obligations under the contract, to the detriment of the consumer".

This clause received attention in the case of *Director General of Fair Trading* v. *First National Bank* [1995] EMLR 472. Here, the court looked at the meaning of the term. It was held that it was equated with open and fair dealing: and also that it has both a procedural and a substantive element to it (see further Hugh Beale, "Legislative Control of Fairness; the Directive on Unfair Terms in Consumer Contracts" in Beatson and Friedman (1995) *Good Faith and Fault in Contract Law*, p. 231). Brownsword argues that "with the implementation of the EC Directive on Unfair Terms in Consumer Contracts, we might treat the doctrine of good faith as already part of the English law of contract, albeit with its application limited to the field of consumer contracts" (at p. 118). In any event, the interpretation by the court of the clause may go some way to answering those who object to the development of a good faith principle that it cannot be defined.

The Privy Council has also had occasion to apply principles of good faith, albeit in the other contexts, such as family law. For example, in the New Zealand case of *Haines* v. *Carter* [2002] UKPC 49, Lawtel, 8 October 2002, the Privy Council enforced an express provision of good faith in an agreement which, following mediation, set out how the parties' property was to be divided on divorce. Mr Haines argued that Ms Carter had breached that obligation of good faith in that she had failed to account or give credit for payments in excess of $2.7m that she had received from Mr Haines's companies without his knowledge. It was held that Mr Haines would be permitted to reopen the mediation if he could persuade the mediators that he was entitled to do so by reason of Ms Carter's breach of her duty of good faith. Once again, although the case and context may seem far removed from partnering, the approach of the Privy Council is in line with other judicial indications of tolerance for the principle.

Finally, it is worth noting for completeness certain case law concerning good faith obligations that has arisen in the area of alternative dispute resolution. The recent case of *Cable & Wireless plc* v. *IBM United Kingdom Ltd* [2002] 2 All ER 1041 upheld an obligation to refer disputes to mediation in good faith. Normally such obligations are unenforceable because (as was argued in this case) they amount merely to agreements either to negotiate (as in *Courtney & Fairbairn Ltd* v. *Tolaini Brothers (Hotels) Ltd* [1974] 1 WLR 297), or to strive to resolve a dispute amicably (as in *Paul Smith Ltd* v. *H&S International Holding Inc.* [1991] 2 Lloyd's Rep 127). It was held that these objections were based on the uncertainty of such obligations. In this case, the reference to mediation was not only to be made "in good faith" but also by means of a specified procedure, to be overseen by the Centre for Dispute Resolution. CEDR is well established and has a very detailed model procedure. The terms of the procedure, as well as the obligation to participate in it, were found to be sufficiently clear to overcome the objection regarding uncertainty. However, the court also stated: "No doubt, if in the present case the words of [the relevant clause] had simply provided that the parties should 'attempt in good faith to resolve the dispute or claim' that would not have been enforceable." The case cannot be seen as supporting the development of good faith as a principle, therefore.

Overall, good faith in the UK is very far from being widely accepted as a principle relevant to all cases, still less a doctrine. At most, it seems to be a concept that has become relevant in certain specific areas of law (such as unfair contract terms and family or commercial mediation). Most promisingly, the Court of Appeal seems to have picked up on it and has given indications that there is potential for broader use. However, it seems that the concept of good faith that is being developed is a narrow one, limiting opportunistic behaviour carried out in bad faith rather than promoting positive obligations to co-operate or promote the joint interests of the parties (see further Barbara Colledge "Obligations of Good Faith in Partnering of UK Construction Contracts" [2002] *International Construction Law Review* 175). It may be that the courts will be happier to enforce such positive obligations where the parties make their intentions very clear; but this remains to be seen.

GOOD FAITH IN OTHER JURISDICTIONS

Other jurisdictions use the concept of good faith to a much greater degree than the UK. Three are briefly described here: Germany, since it offers a good example from a civil law jurisdiction of a well-established doctrine; the United States, since it has a well-established doctrine which it applies to an active market in partnering; and Australia, since it offers an example of a Commonwealth jurisdiction which has nevertheless developed good faith to a greater extent than the UK.

Germany

German law recognises an established doctrine of good faith, contained in sections 157 to 242 of the German Civil Code. Section 157 provides that: "Contracts shall be interpreted according to the requirements of good faith, ordinary usage being taken into consideration." Section 242 provides in addition that: "The debtor is bound to perform according to the requirements of good faith, ordinary usage being taken into consideration."

The code therefore creates obligations for both the interpretation of contracts and their performance, and the courts have gone on to develop a positive duty of co-operation between parties. This has been used to fill gaps in the code, such as the lack of a code provision to protect a party from partial or incorrect contractual performance (see Alberto Musy "The Good Faith Principle in Contract Law and the Precontractual Duty to Disclose: Comparative Analysis of New Differences in Legal Cultures" [2001] *Global Jurist Advances*, at p. 1). In addition, good faith may be used as justification to vary a long-term contract where there has been a fundamental change of economic circumstances. An illustration of this is a case that arose after the first world war (judgment of 29 November 1914, RGZ, 103). Here, the obligations of one party under a long-term contract were adversely affected by the inflation that followed the war. On the strength of s. 157, the courts held that the parties had entered the contract on the basis that each party gave a promise that was adequate (if not equivalent) to the other party's promise. Therefore, if one party's obligation was changed by circumstances outside either party's control, so that the other party's reciprocal promise was no longer adequate, then the former party could request that its obligation be altered, or could refuse to perform that obligation.

Commentators have noted the extent to which the German courts have been persuaded to use ss. 157 and 242 of the code to ensure what is perceived to be the "proper" performance of contracts:

"The doctrine of good faith has been used as the justification for ... [an] action for breach of contract where it is used as a sword, and also as a shield to defend those affected by, inter alia, political turmoil engendering change in economic circumstance. In circumstances calling for a stopgap measure which could not be fulfilled by the legislature, the judiciary stepped in and took advantage of the flexibility offered by sections 157 and 242 of the [code], to ensure the proper or fair performance of contracts. An almost teleological approach was adopted, with the proper performance of contract as the stated aim." (See Kelda Groves, "The Doctrine of Good Faith in Four Legal Systems" (1999) 15 Const LJ 265 at p. 269.)

The United States

The United States, influenced by the German model, also has a well-established doctrine of good faith, again recognised by its legislature. It is set out in the Uniform Commercial Code (UCC), which has been adopted in various forms by almost all American state legislatures. Section 1-203 of the UCC provides that: "Every contract or duty within this Act imposes an obligation of good faith for its performance or enforcement."

Section 1-201(9) provides that good faith in general means "honesty in fact in the conduct or transaction concerned". A specific definition can, however, be imposed in certain circumstances. An example is in the area of sale of goods, where a party is subject to an obligation of good faith which is not only "honesty in fact" but also "the observance of reasonable commercial standards of fair dealing in the trade" (see section 2-103(1)(b)). This amounts to a higher duty in this specific area and is of course relevant to construction projects in terms of the provision of materials.

The *Restatement of Contracts* (2nd ed., 1979) adopts this higher level of obligation in its section 205, which states, in relation to all contracts (i.e., not just those covered by the UCC): "Every contract imposes upon each party a duty of good faith and fair dealing in its performance and its enforcement."

Furthermore, the *Official Comment to the Restatement* (2nd ed.) of *Contracts* explains that good faith varies according to its context: "Good faith performance or enforcement of a contract emphasises faithfulness to an agreed common purpose and consistency with the justified expectations of the other party; it excludes a variety of types of conduct characterised as involving 'bad faith' because they violate community standards of decency, fairness or reasonableness."

Although the adoption of this standard does not mean that there has been a steady expansion of good faith in the US – the 1980s in particular saw both the expansion and the contraction of the doctrine – it has become a natural part of the American approach to contract law. The duty of good faith extends to the enforcement of contracts as well as the performance of contractual obligations and, although the content of the duty can be varied by express terms, there have been attempts to establish it as an implied term that cannot be excluded. This has in fact led to some difficulty, since there are inevitable clashes between the express terms of a contract and what is meant by the implied term; on balance, it appears that the courts will respect the literal meaning of the contract. It has, for example, been held that where the contract is silent, principles of good faith will fill the gap. Such principles will not block the use of terms that actually appear in the contract. There is suspicion of any attempt to add an "overlay of 'just cause'" to the contract, because this would "reduce commercial certainty and breed costly litigation" (Easterbrook J, 908 F 1351 1357-1358 (7th Cir 1990) at 1358; and see generally Kelda Groves, "The Doctrine of Good Faith in Four Legal Systems" (1999) 15 Const LJ 265 at p. 270).

In this way, therefore, American jurisprudence recognises the same difficulties with which UK law is struggling, and yet such recognition has not prevented the courts from recognising and applying the good faith standard. Furthermore, the US has adopted the idea of partnering to a much greater degree than in the UK, and as we have seen, US partnering implicitly involves idea of good faith. The Associated General Contractors of America published a paper in 1991 (see "Partnering: A concept for success") that describes partnering as "not a business contract but a recognition that every business contract includes an implied covenant of good faith". This has been accepted by other commentators, one of whom put the position like this: "Partnering, simply put, is the express recognition of the implied covenant of good faith and fair dealing". (Kimberley Kunz, "Counsels' Role in Negotiating a Successful Construction Partnering Agreement", *Construction Law*, 15 November 1999, p. 19).

It may not be a coincidence that the use of partnering in the US is so much more advanced than in the UK, given the starting point that good faith has become an intrinsic part of the common law there.

Australia

In Australia, matters have not progressed to the same extent that they have in Germany and the US, but they are further on than in the UK. "While good faith is not yet an openly recognised contract law doctrine, it is very much a factor in everyday contractual transactions. To the extent that the common law of contracts, as interpreted and developed by our courts, reflects this reality, it is accurate to state that good faith is part of our law of contracts" (John Dorter, "Partnering – Thinking it Through" (1997) *Arbitration* 63(3) (Aug.), 210–211 at p. 210).

That there is support in the courts for developing the concept of good faith and implying terms to that effect into contracts is clear. An example is *Renard Constructions* v. *Minister for Public Works* (1992) NSWLR 234). Here the courts had to decide whether a discretionary power to exclude a contractor from site was subject to an implied term in fact and law to act reasonably. The court held that the expected standard was consistent with ideas of good faith and fair dealing in the performance of contracts. A duty to act reasonably would therefore be implied into the contract for various reasons: in order to give it business efficacy; because of the type of contract it was (a building contract which provided for a number of eventualities); and because "contracts generally were subject to an implied obligation that they should be performed in good faith." The court also considered that such an obligation would become more explicitly recognised by the courts in Australia.

Further cases have also set out what the substance of a duty of good faith is. In *Theiss Contractors Pty Ltd* v. *Placer (Granny Smith) Pty Ltd* [2000] WASCA 102, the Supreme Court of Western Australia gave some idea as to what good faith might mean. The partnering arrangement in that case included an express obligation to act in good faith "in all matters relating [to] both the carrying out [of] the works, derivation of rates and interpretation of this document". The court held that this involved a requirement of goodwill and co-operation on the part of both parties; and that they deal honestly with each other: "the obligation of good faith [requires] the parties to act honestly with each other and to take reasonable steps to co-operate in relation to matters where the contract does not define right and obligations or provide any mechanisms for the resolution of disputes." Considerations of transparency may also be relevant (see *P Ward* v. *Civil and Civic* [1999] NSWSC 727).

There is also recent case law, however, which shows a more cautious approach by the Australian courts towards obligations of good faith compared to that evinced in Germany and the US and to that explained by Priestly JA in *Renard*. The reservation applies to the situation in which such obligations will be recognised, and the effect of any express terms that are found. For example, in *NT Power Generation Pty Ltd* v. *Power & Water Authority* (2001) FCA 334, the Federal Court of Australia explained that there was no binding authority that there should be implied into every contract as a matter of law a term that each party to a contract will act in good faith and with fair dealing in its performance and enforcement of the contract (Mr Justice Mansfield here referred to Mr Justice Gummow in *Service Station Association Ltd* v. *Berg Bennett and Ass. Pty* (1993) 45 FCR 84 at pp. 91–98). The court did however, hold that:

> "where there is a particular contractual obligation to be carried out, the means by which it is to be carried out may be enforced by requiring that it be carried out in good faith. Where there is no particular contractual obligation to be carried out, an obligation to act 'in good faith' in a vacuum is not one which can give rise to an obligation to provide a particular additional service ([here], access to PAWA's infrastructure) upon certain terms or in a certain manner or within a certain time limit or to negotiate with respect to that service in good faith … The obligation as claimed that PAWA would deal 'fairly' with NT Power with regard to the 'performance and implementation of the licence' is far too vague."

Part of the point here seems to be that there must be clear express terms that the courts can enforce. It appears from *Thiess* v. *Placer*, for example, that the obligation will not be applied where clauses are clear and unambiguous, which is an approach similar to the American jurisprudence. Other case law suggests that if terms are too illusory, vague or uncertain they will not be upheld (see *Coal Cliff Collieries Pty Ltd* v. *Sijehama Pty Ltd* (1991) 24 NSWLR 1;

Australia Media Holdings Pty Ltd v. *Telstra Corp Ltd*, *Australia Media Holdings Pty Ltd* v. *News Corporation Ltd* (1997) 43 NSWLR 104).

Thiess also gives an illustration of how restrictive the courts can be in interpreting an express clause of good faith. Although the obligation of good faith was held to apply to the *operation* of the contract, it was further held that it could not apply to the *termination* clause of the contract since at that point, by definition, the contract ceased to be operated.

The courts in Australia have therefore made much greater progress towards enforcing ideas of good faith than those in the UK. Indeed, parties have founded misrepresentation claims on the basis of partnering contracts (see Dominic Helps, "Why Partnering is not a Duty", *Building*, 28 November 1997 at p. 37). This is not because the Australian judiciary do not appreciate or recognise the issues of subjectivity and vagueness; they deal with these by closely monitoring the circumstances in which the concept can be used. This is why caution should be exercised when looking at the Australian model: there are very real limits to the extent to which an idea of good faith can be relied on.

THE INTERESTS OF THE PROJECT

As we have seen, the idea of partnering is to put the interests of the project over the interests of each individual party contributing to the project. The corollary of this (dealt with in more detail in **The interests of individuals**, below) is that individuals should not insist on their strict legal rights where to do so would conflict with any obligations imposed by non-legally binding partnering charters. Behaving in this way might be regarded as one of the constituent elements of a doctrine of good faith, in partnering terms. Indeed such behaviour was specifically endorsed by the court in *Birse*. The difficulty is that, as we have seen, the approach of Judge Humphrey LLoyd in *Birse* has not yet been followed in other cases and it cannot yet be said unequivocally to represent the established approach of the courts. While such behaviour is undoubtedly in the spirit of partnering, therefore, we currently need to look further afield for legal concepts to enforce it.

An answer to the problem may be to create a special purpose vehicle (SPV) for the project, and impose fiduciary obligations on the participants in the project in favour of the SPV. Such obligations can arise in the context of a joint venture, where the joint venture agreement shows that the parties have put themselves in a position where they are placing reliance upon each other to act in each other's best interests. In the partnering context, this mechanism could be used to raise the status of the SPV's interests over those of each participant.

Fiduciary obligations impose on a party (the "fiduciary") a duty to act in the best interests of the party to whom the obligations are owed (the "principal"). Part of the obligation on the part of the fiduciary is to avoid putting itself in a position where self-interest conflicts with its duty to the principal; it must not misuse its position in its own selfish interests. The imposition of fiduciary obligations therefore represents serious inroads into the usual contractual and commercial position of parties to any project and it seems unlikely that this approach will be adopted. It should, however, be noted that any such obligations that are undertaken can be carefully limited in the partnering agreement, although if this is done, then care should be taken that the partnering agreement itself is legally binding.

THE INTERESTS OF INDIVIDUALS

Assuming that the relationship breaks down and the dispute resolution procedures that have been agreed for the project have failed, can each party then insist on its strict contractual rights? Good examples of significant points of tension are exclusion clauses and other limits on liability. The problem arises because, as some commentators have pointed out, however well-intentioned partnering is, when large amounts of money are involved, the system may not work to eliminate big disputes. Normal dispute resolution procedures may well be invoked. This is particularly likely where the underlying building contract does not match the charter in terms of its risk allocation (and this seems to be quite common); and where the parties were never genuinely committed to the partnering ideal from the start. The difficulty seems to be that there is little common ground between a fully fledged partnering agreement, which embodies notions of good faith, and a traditional style contract, which preserves the self-interest of each party.

Following *Birse*, the existence of the partnering charter (whether legally binding or not) may change normal contractual relations by means of the imposition of obligations which override strict legal rights. We have already noted the uncertainty of the enforceability of this principle, however, and it may be that parties will still be able to enforce specific legal rights despite the existence of the partnering charter: the position remains unclear.

Some commentators have, however, pointed out that the partnering approach may in fact create the potential for exposure to further claims, particularly in the areas of waiver, estoppel, misrepresentation and confidentiality. For example, partnering assumes that, and works best when, the participants enter into the relationship on the basis of full and frank disclosure. This brings the associated risk that confidential information may be disclosed. This can be overcome by means of a confidentiality clause. However, more serious concerns arise in relation to waiver, estoppel and misrepresentation.

During the partnering process, parties will make statements in order to secure contracts, again on an open and frank basis. Such representations may not be consistent with the provisions of the contract but the parties may rely on them nevertheless. This can minimise disputes and increase efficiency and effectiveness while the project proceeds. If, however, disputes do arise, then parties may find themselves facing claims for waiver, estoppel or misrepresentation. If all parties have entered the partnering process in the spirit in which it should have been suggested, then all such statements will have been made in good faith. The risk is that parties do not take into account sufficiently seriously the impact of those early statements. If relationships do begin to falter and parties begin to look to their own interests again over and above those of the project, then it may be that such claims could be framed. However, given the relatively early stage that partnering has reached in the UK, this may be more of a concern for the future.

CONCLUSION

The UK considered introducing a statutory obligation to act in good faith in 1995 – as recommended by Latham. The government chose not to do so, however. Other jurisdictions have, however, adopted the standard and, as we have seen, it has not been ignored by UK judges in various contexts, including construction. Furthermore, parties and the standard forms continue to use the concept, which suggests that there is an understanding in the industry that it forms an essential part of the partnering approach. This is confirmed by the legal approach to good faith and partnering in the US in particular. Where the parties' intentions and expectations are clear, it may be time for good faith to be more widely accepted and utilised.

The difficulty is how to achieve this. Partnering is an example of what is called by some commentators "long-term contractual behaviour". Campbell and Harris argue that the "classical" approaches to contracting, such as insisting on the self-interest of the individual in the particular project at hand, to the exclusion of the long-term relationships of the parties and future project, is outdated and inefficient. Charters can act as the framework for future relations, so that specific risk-allocation on specific projects can be left to the relevant building contract itself. They can also establish how parties can work through difficulties if they arise on a specific project. Co-operation, it is argued, is the key to such long-term relationships (see David Campbell and Donald Harris, "Flexibility in Long-Term Contractual Relationships: the Role of Co-operation" in *Journal of Law & Society* (1993) Vol. 20, No. 2, p. 166). I would add that good faith has to be a key principle underlying the concept of co-operation.

The problem is that this cannot be achieved simply by writing it down: "Without a shift in attitude, formal provision for flexibility is fruitless ... One needs the attitude to make the writing have any meaning (though the writing then reinforces the attitude) ..." (Campbell and Harris at p. 173).

The need for such change is something that the construction industry has heard before, but appears to find difficult to accommodate. Given the ever-increasing internationalisation of the UK construction industry, it may be that the law should now take the initiative and give willing parties the tools to reinforce a more co-operative approach so that partnering arrangements and agreements undertaken – it is hard to escape the expression – in good faith, may be carried through and enforced even after parties have fallen out. Awaiting such developments through the common law may be slow, especially given how few cases now come before the courts in the wake of the adjudication provisions of the Housing Grants Construction and Regeneration Act 1996. The time for appropriate legislation may now have come.

CHAPTER 8

TIME, COST AND QUALITY

Jonathan Hosie,[1] *Diana Harvey*[2] *and Tara Corcoran*[3]

INTRODUCTION

"Effective partnering does not rest on contracts. Contracts can add significantly to the cost of a project and often add no value to the client. If the relationship between a constructor and employer is soundly based and the parties recognise their mutual dependence then formal contract documents should gradually become obsolete."

Sir John Egan's 1998 report to the
construction industry, Chapter 4

Sir John Egan's message is not so much that contracts are not necessary but that an over-reliance upon contractual conditions is not the way to achieve partnering effectively. Historically, standard form construction contracts tend to provide for what happens when something goes wrong. The philosophy behind the new standard forms of partnering contract is geared more towards ensuring project success.

Any commentary on standard forms of partnering contract has to recognise the embryonic state of development of such forms. As agreed definitions of collaborative working evolve, so too should the commercial arrangements that support such processes. The forms of contract that are considered in this Chapter form part of those commercial arrangements and are likely to evolve in response to wider industry use and greater understanding of their constraints.

In its report *Accelerating Change*, published on 12 September 2002, the Strategic Forum set the target that by the end of 2004, 20% by value of construction projects let in the UK would be delivered by "integrated teams" (*Accelerating Change*, Chapter 3). This is recognised as a reference to "partnering" albeit the industry appears to be moving away from the term largely because "partnering" has been misused and misapplied. Partnering means different things to different people. Other terms are emerging, such as integrated team working or collaborative working. The term "partnering" is adopted in this book simply because of its current wide usage in the industry.

1. Partner, Construction, Engineering & Projects, Hammonds.
2. Solicitor, Construction, Engineering & Projects, Hammonds.
3. Solicitor, Construction, Engineering & Projects, Hammonds.

Other industry bodies such as Be, the pan-industry body formed by the merger in 2003 of the Design Build Foundation and the Reading Construction Forum, prefer the term "collaborative working" which they define as "working together in a seamless team for common objectives that deliver benefit to all". It is said to embrace project team and supply chain integration and to have the following critical success factors:

(a) committed leadership focused on maintaining the vision, needs, people and benefits for all;
(b) values which empower people, share learning, communicate openly and foster trust in a no-blame culture;
(c) processes and commercial arrangements which promote:
   - early involvement by the supply chain of designers, suppliers, specialist installers, constructors and other relevant parties;
   - selection by value (rather than sequential lowest tendering);
   - performance measurement enabling continuous improvement;
   - common business processes and tools shared by the integrated team;
   - long-term supply chain in relationships founded on continuous improvement; and
   - key to effective partnering is the establishment of clear commercial arrangements that support the above factors.

A contract is no more than a framework onto which parties map their objectives, their respective inputs and agreed risk allocation. Partnering contracts play an important role in assisting parties who wish to work collaboratively, helping them to formulate their objectives, inputs and risk allocation against a blueprint of collaboration, integration of skills and resources and procedures that are designed to enhance value. By their nature, such forms of contract tend to be design and construct forms although the way in which the design and construction processes are integrated distinguishes them from historical standard design and build forms such as those produced by the JCT or ICE.

Contractual or non-contractual

A distinction is to be drawn between those partnering forms which are intended to regulate parties' behaviour through a contractual framework and those which place a non-contractual partnering framework over the top of another contract and thereby seek to influence rather than mandate certain behaviours. Examples of this latter form of approach include the JCT Partnering Charter and ECC Partnering Option X12, both of which are described further below.

In these forms of procurement, an existing standard form construction contract (e.g., based on standard JCT or ECC conditions) regulates the legal rights and obligations of the parties, who are nevertheless expected to act in a "partnering" way by virtue of both agreeing to adopt the processes and procedures laid down in a non-contractually binding partnering charter. A more contractual route to partnering is seen in the other standard form conditions also examined in this Chapter. These other standard forms seek to achieve partnering in a way intended to be legally enforceable. As market experience of partnering increases, our view is that parties' advisers (and funders) should become more comfortable with the fully contractual partnering route. Time will tell.

Scope of study

In this Chapter, we have chosen to limit our review to a selected list of some of the emerging standard form conditions of contract that have been developed to support partnering, namely:

(a) PPC 2000;
(b) NHS LIFT Strategic Partnering Agreement;
(c) Defence Estates' Prime Contract (Regional and Stand Alone Capital Projects);
(d) Be Collaborative Contract;
(e) M4i Virtual Company Model Form (the M4i Consultation Draft);
(f) ECC Partnering Option X12;
(g) JCT Non-Binding Partnering Charter for Single Projects.

It is acknowledged that the list is not exhaustive. For instance, we have not reviewed GC/Works/1 (1998), edition 4 which has a number of features that would be recognised as reflecting a partnering approach by the parties. Further, other forms of partnering contract are likely to be published in due course. For instance, in May 2003 the JCT commissioned the drafting of a Partnering Framework Agreement to be used in conjunction an underlying construction contract. The JCT intend the Framework to be useable as either non-binding or binding and in either case to promote the concept of partnering. Publication of that form is not expected until sometime in late 2004.

Returning to the opening quotation from Sir John Egan, it will be appreciated that the contractual framework which sets out and supports the commercial arrangements is part, but not the whole, of the process. Partnering embraces a number of aspirational aspects, not all of which are susceptible to legal requirements of certainty. As an example, is an obligation "to act in a spirit of mutual trust" sufficiently certain so as to be enforced under English law? Nevertheless, the law (and in particular the law of contract) plays an important part in both the procurement and structuring of a partnering project.

There is a legal support for the view that parties are bound contractually to work collaboratively. (See for example, Dr A McInnis, in his paper on Relational Contracting delivered to the Society of Construction Law on 1 April 2003, available at *www.scl.org.co.uk*.) Such terms may be implied as negative obligations (e.g., not to hinder or prevent) or as positive obligations (e.g., to act in co-operation with others). Equally, such behaviours may be imposed as a promissory estoppel (reflecting the presumed shared intention of the parties). This is a developing area of the common law. There is a respectable case for saying that the common law presumes some degree of co-operation towards the achievement of mutual objectives in commercial dealings.

Of course, the boundaries of such concepts have yet to be determined. However, in the interim one sees express terms in standard form partnering contracts that set out how parties are expected to behave and relate to each other in the performance of their contractual duties. Each of the standard form partnering contracts examined in this Chapter contain examples of such terms.

We will review each of our chosen standard forms briefly and then examine how they deal with the key cornerstones of any construction contract: time, cost and quality.

CRITICAL FEATURES OF THE STANDARD FORMS

PPC 2000

PPC 2000 (amended in June 2003) is the first multi-party standard form partnering contract to be published by a professional body. Launched in September 2000 by the Association of Consulting Architects, PPC 2000 introduces a contractually binding partnering agreement that seeks to integrate the entire project team but under a single multi-party approach. It is also intended to cover the entire duration of the design and construction process, from inception including the feasibility and design phases through to completion of the works. The "partnering team members" will include the client, the contractor, all consultants and key selected specialists or suppliers. The associated contract SPC 2000 is designed to enable the partnering team members to the PPC 2000 to enter into back-to-back arrangements with their subcontractors referred to as "Specialists". The structure of SPC 2000 reflects that of PPC 2000.

PPC 2000 has enjoyed wide use since publication, particularly in the housing sector where Housing Associations have been driven by Housing Corporation requirements to embrace the Egan philosophy in their procurement of projects.

It should be noted that PPC 2000 refers to the contractor as "the constructor". This expression is therefore used throughout the section on PPC 2000.

NHS LIFT: The Strategic Partnering Agreement

NHS LIFT (NHS Local Improvement Finance Trust) is a public private partnership (PPP) initiative aimed at stimulating investment in modern integrated primary and other community based healthcare services, such as health centres and GP surgeries. To avoid the historical fragmentation of responsibilities in the provision of primary healthcare, one of the key objectives of the approach under LIFT is to bring together the various local stakeholders, interests and users that comprise the local health economy.

LIFT will be delivered regionally by local health authorities, primary care trusts and other local stakeholders, which will form partnerships using strategic partnership agreements with private sector consortiums for the provision of batches of facilities in their areas. The partnership at local level (Liftco) will be a joint venture company between the local health stakeholders, Partnerships for Health and the private sector consortium.

The Strategic Partnering Agreement will, in broad terms, establish a basis for determining which new investments and services are to proceed, how they will be delivered and paid for, how value for money will be secured and define the basis on which pricing of new developments will be agreed. Liftco will then enter into supply-chain agreements to carry out the construction work for the batched facilities. The new standard form of LIFT Strategic Partnering Agreement therefore provides the framework for the implementation and operation of the partnership. Amongst other things, its terms cover partnering principles and the achievement of mutual objectives.

Interestingly, LIFT recognises that certain partnering terms are "aspirational and not intended to give rise to legally binding rights and obligations between the parties". In the case of the LIFT Strategic Partnering Agreement, these non-binding terms include the purpose and aim of the Agreement itself ("to establish a long-term partnering between Liftco and the Participants"), as well as other requirements such as "to focus on achieving the best value for money operational performance within agreed timescales" (clause 2.4.2.) and "to develop openness and trust in a transparent information and data sharing environment" (clause 2.4.8) and so forth. Such terms indicate expected behaviours required of the parties, which anticipate that specific measures will be implemented in the course of the project to help achieve delivery of the aspirations.

Prime Contracting

The Prime Contracting initiative is an approach adopted by Defence Estates who manage the Ministry of Defence real estate portfolio and was developed in response to the recommendations made by Latham (*Constructing the Team*) and Egan (*Rethinking Construction*) for the procurement of its capital and maintenance construction works. Although the "Core Conditions" do not embrace all the principles of partnering, the central objectives of prime contracting are single point responsibility and supply chain management. The "prime contractor" is defined as "having overall responsibility for the management and delivery of a project, including co-ordinating and integrating the activities of a number of sub-contractors to meet the overall specification efficiently, economically and on time".

Whilst prime contracts do not amount to a strategic alliance between the client and the prime contractor, partnering concepts are certainly involved at the supply chain level with a strong emphasis on integrated design and construct solutions and a focus on driving down cost (in both capital and operational budgets) whilst ring-fencing the prime contractor's entitlement to overheads and profit. Incentivisation is built in through use of a Maximum Price Target Cost mechanism.

There are two types of prime contract. The first is a regional contract for the operation and maintenance of the entire estate within a region (the Regional Prime Contract). The second type is a stand-alone contract for the design and construction of large projects with a planned through-life cost model, which must be complied with throughout a compliance period (the Stand Alone Capital Projects Prime Contract). The intention of the initiative is to foster a more collaborative and less adversarial relationship between Defence Estates and the prime contractor and to deliver better value for both client and supply side.

Unlike some of the other standard forms discussed in this Chapter (i.e., PPC 2000, the M4i Consultation Draft, or the Be Collaborative Contract), prime contracting does not make the client (Defence Estates) part of the project delivery team. This is a purposeful distinction, driven by Defence Estates' position as a "hands off, eyes on" customer that needs to keep at arms length from the construction supply chain. Instead, Defence Estates expect the prime contractor to have single point responsibility for delivering the requirements set out in the prime contract, albeit the prime contractor is expected to partner with its supply chain.

Like other partnering forms, prime contracting includes an explicit approach to risk identification, evaluation and management.

The Be Collaborative Contract

This form was developed originally under the auspices of The Reading Construction Forum. At the date of publication of this book, the Be Collaborative Contract (BCC) is being trialled on a number of projects. BCC comprises a Purchase Order (PO) and a set of standard conditions (the Terms). This standard form is intended for use as a design and construct form. Unlike the public sector standard forms discussed in this Chapter (notably Prime Contracts and the LIFT Strategic Partnering Agreement), there is no intent within the form to deal expressly with operational performance of the asset once construction completion is achieved.

However, in common with LIFT, ECC Option X12 and the JCT Partnering Charter, BCC recognises the use of non-contractually binding statements of aspiration. Thus, under BCC the parties are expected to enter into a "project protocol" which not only sets out what the parties hope to achieve from their collaboration but also sets out the means by which such aspiration may be achieved. That protocol is not intended, however, to be contractually binding.

An important feature of the BCC is the inclusion within the contract of a risk register. Such registers are commonly used on large projects and PFI/PPP schemes as well as in the standard form prime contract. The project team is required to be consulted on issues that cannot be resolved between constructing parties, so as to make objective recommendations as to their resolution. The parties are required to give serious consideration to such recommendations. Whilst risk allocation remains unchanged throughout the life of the contract (unless both parties agree otherwise), the risk register (including cost and time consequences) should be regularly updated.

The M4i Consultation Draft

In the style of PPC 2000, this form of partnering contract envisages a multi-party binding partnering contract encompassing the entire project team, potentially also extending to insurers. The M4i Consultation Draft comprises a set of general conditions and a series of schedules which are intended to set out the project requirements, programme constraints and details of agreed rates and team members. The general conditions are accompanied by guidance notes, which will not form part of the contract. Alongside the partners, being the principal members of the team, there may also be "cluster partners", i.e., selected subcontractors and suppliers that form part of a team for delivery of a particular aspect of the works, the example cited in the guidance notes being those that will come under the cluster leadership of the mechanical and electrical specialist.

The structure under which the partners will operate is by the formation of a "virtual company"; the guidance notes stress that this is not intended to be a legal entity but purely a structure within which the partners will work. The methodology of this approach is for the partners to second into a virtual team selected representatives, each bringing their own skills and inputs. The environment is one where inputs are integrated in a collaborative way, for an agreed common purpose. The concept is similar to that adopted by British Airports Authority plc, where a project team albeit drawn from representatives of the client and the supply side work as an integrated team out of one office, wears one uniform to deliver the same one project.

The cost of the works is determined on the basis of cost reimbursement (on an open-book basis) with salary costs similarly reimbursed in respect of seconded staff plus an agreed and ring-fenced percentage for overheads and profit. This structure is designed to enhance the principle of integrated team working; an enabling tool which will facilitate all the partners to "buy into" the concept of a single unit striving for the same goals. The latest draft was produced by M4i in April 2002, Revision 11.

ECC Partnering Option X12

The Engineering & Construction Contract core conditions were first published in 1993. They reflect an approach and contain a number of features that are consistent with a partnering approach to procurement. In this sense, advocates of the ECC form claim that it is the earliest of standard form partnering contracts.

The ECC expressly introduces the concept of partnering by the act of the parties including Option X12 into the contract. Within the ECC framework, the partnering Option X12 is selected for use with an "Own Contract", namely another contractually binding contract between the parties. The ECC Option X12 does not expressly create legally enforceable obligations or contractual relations between partners, other than those between parties to the Own Contract. It is intended more as a guide to collaborative project management, with references to "Partnering Information" including any requirements on the use of common information systems, as well as participation in workshops, arrangements for joint design development, value engineering, value management, risk management and the like.

JCT Practice Note 4: Non-Binding Partnering Charter for Single Projects

The JCT adopts a relatively simple approach. It is a guidance/practice note plus a two- page Partnering Charter, which is non-binding in its nature and available for multi-party use. Like the ECC Option X12, it is designed to operate alongside the use of an existing JCT Standard Form of Contract and aims to promote good teamwork within that context.

The Charter contains only two brief statements; the first being how the parties are to conduct the dealings between themselves, and the second being the four objectives to be achieved by the team under the headings of (1) "Delivery", (2) "People", (3) "Team working" and (4) "Commercial".

As to how the signatories to the Charter are to act, this includes statements of aspiration (acting in a way to avoid disputes by adopting a "no-blame culture") as well as more explicit terms such as to act "in a co-operative way" and "fairly towards each other". However, such terms are nonetheless not intended to create legally enforceable obligations as between the signatories to the Charter.

As to the four stated objectives in the Charter, these are to be measured against performance indicators to be established. An agreement to agree is, in English law, void for uncertainty unless the parameters of the agreement are set out with sufficient precision so as to enable the court to say what the terms of the agreement should be. Such concerns do not, of course, concern a non-contractual Charter. Thus, the signatories are left to agree as loosely or precisely as they wish; ultimately no party can enforce its "rights" under the Charter because it has no such rights.

TIME, COST AND QUALITY IN THE STANDARD FORMS

Drafting contracts for partnering projects

The issue facing the industry is that with a new culture of co-operation and transparency (partnering), can one draft a contract to reflect this change particularly for an industry known for its adversarial behaviour which for many years created a history of substantial disputes, be it of litigation or arbitration? Before one seeks to answer this question it is worth considering the subject matter of many of these disputes. They tended to divide into three potential areas of risk.

The first issue is one of time. An employer agrees with a contractor that a project was to be completed by Christmas but completion is delayed until Easter. The client has therefore not had the use of the building for approximately four months. The client potentially has a loss of use claim which the construction industry tends to regard as a liquidated damages claim for delay.

The second issue is one of cost. To use a car analogy, the client paid a Rolls-Royce price for a Ford car. If the client had asked for a Rolls-Royce and received a Rolls-Royce for a Rolls-Royce price there would be no complaint, but sadly this did not occur.

The third issue is one of quality. An employer agrees with a contractor a specification of work. The contractor, for a number of reasons, fails to provide the end product to meet the specification. This is the quality issue. To continue with the car analogy, the client was promised a Rolls-Royce but instead got a Ford.

Taking therefore the three issues of time, cost and quality, one can (and indeed the construction industry has a habit of doing this) create a cocktail of problems. In other words, the client ordered a Rolls-Royce, received a Ford, paid a Rolls-Royce price and it was four months late.

It is perhaps worth considering whether the partnering culture of co-operation and transparency can overcome this cocktail of disaster leading to claims and disputes. After all, a Ford is a Ford and either one knows how to build one within a certain period of time or not. However, if it is intended to build a Ford car by a particular date, the partnering ethos of supply chain management and integrated teams ought to assist and be a move in the right direction. It must be sensible, by way of example, for the engine maker to liase with the bodywork designer. In construction terms, it must be sensible for all those involved in the construction process to adopt a more integrated approach where they are committed to talking to each other, sharing views and disclosing know-how for the ultimate benefit of the client and the end product, namely a completed building/structure etc.

The principles of partnering referred to throughout this book ought to assist in ensuring that there are fewer problems when it comes to the issue of time, cost and quality. These three issues more than any others dominate the mass of case law that the industry has generated over the last 25 years.

If one accepts that the partnering culture is of benefit, how will the client want that culture reflected in some form of written document? Are the words to have binding effect or are they to stand simply as statements of aspiration? As commented upon earlier, some parties feel more comfortable with a non-binding charter sitting on top of a formal construction contract. Others go for a full-blown partnering contract with all terms (however aspirational) expressed in a form that is intended to create legally enforceable rights and obligations. Having outlined in brief terms the origin, purpose and some key features of the standard forms discussed in this Chapter, we set out below how each of the forms address the perennial issues of time, cost and quality.

Each of these issues impact on each other but it is within the framework of other partnering terms and mechanisms that the impact of such issues is managed. It is this particular pro-active management of risk that distinguishes the standard form partnering contracts from historical, non-partnering forms of procurement.

As a preface to looking at how the various contracts deal with the issues of time, cost and quality, the next section will look briefly at some general points associated with each one.

Management of time in partnering contracts

Time is always a necessary feature of any construction contract. One needs a commencement date, duration and completion date. The contractual partnering forms dealt with in this Chapter acknowledge this but some include the explicit recognition that a collaborative approach requires engagement of the supply chain and client early on to agree time-related issues. Thus, two-stage processes will often be seen whereby the team initially embarks on a scoping and costing phase, one of the outputs of which is a programme setting out when and in what stages the works are to be undertaken. The parties then commit to deliver the works to this programme or to use the programme as a management tool against which to monitor progress.

It is axiomatic that "time is money" on a construction project. Some projects value time over other considerations, e.g., cash generating casinos are reported to be able to justify considerable resources to complete on time to deliver the end product, with the cost of construction being a secondary concern. However, can parties control better delivery to programme with collaborative, partnering forms rather than historial standard form construction contracts?

To answer this question, one needs to appreciate the manageable reasons for delay on a project and ask whether the partnering standard forms provide a robust regime to manage those risks. Accurate and timely design information, co-ordination of the supply chain and managing the interface of works packages all, typically, provide opportunities for delay. It is considered that those forms which have an explicit risk management system are more likely to be able to manage such risks. On the other hand, it is suggested that terms which require parties to act in good faith and trust each other do not (by themselves) ensure the achievement of any particular tangible outcome.

Cost and incentives

Paragraph 34 of the practice note accompanying the JCT Partnering Charter makes the undoubtedly true suggestion that, whilst costs (and who these are allocated to) should not be one of the key aspects underpinning a partnering relationship, unless these issues are addressed "at the outset in an non-confrontational way there is potential for major problems to arise". A partnering contract should be structured so that it encourages long-term relationships throughout the supply chain where there are mutual benefits, including financial ones, for all the parties in sustaining these relationships. In other words, it should ideally be structured so there is an element of shared financial motivation. Ensuring such shared financial motivation requires a careful consideration of the basis upon which the supply chain members are paid for their contributions to the project, or projects, which fall within the scope of the partnering arrangements.

A recommendation of the Latham Report was that a modern form of a construction contract should contain a mechanism for the allocating of risk between the parties to the party best able to mange, estimate and carry the risk. It follows that a prerequisite of any properly structured partnering arrangement is for project risks to be able to be identified and the cost consequences of these risks occurring allocated between the parties in a way that encourages rather than discourages collaborative working.

A partnering contract should contain payment terms that are fair and do not penalise any party. The Latham Report made various suggestions and recommendations as to the form payment provisions in a modern construction contract should take, acknowledging that certain features of the payment terms common in historical construction contracts formed an impediment to more collaborative relationships, particularly between main contractors and sub-contractors. Particular recommendations were the provisions of alternatives to monthly valuations, advanced mobilisation payments in appropriate situations, the right to interest on late payments and clear time scales for payment. Subsequent legislation, in the form of the Housing Grants, Construction and Regeneration Act 1996 (the "Construction Act") and the Late Payment of Commercial Debts (Interest) Act 1998 have done much to make the implementation of these recommendations mandatory.

In Sir John Egan's final report before stepping down as Chair of the Strategic Forum, *Accelerating Change*, the industry as a whole was encouraged to develop a culture of performance measurement against industry standard key performance indicators (KPIs) with continuous improvement measured against these KPIs. Undoubtedly, appropriate incentives to reward good performance, penalise poor performance and encourage ongoing performance improvements are a crucial element of any partnering contract. A partnering contract should, at its most basic, provide a description of what good and poor levels of performance are (project-specific KPIs), how actual performance will be measured against these KPIs and what the consequences to the parties of good and poor performance are going to be.

A performance incentive common across the construction industry is the deducting of a monetary amount (the retention) from payments made under the contract to provide an incentive to the contractor to correct defects in the work. The Latham Report suggested it would be better to either keep these amounts in the secure trust fund or to put in place retention bonds, which could reduce in value against milestones. *Accelerating Change* went somewhat further still by encouraging insurance backed supply and fix collateral warranties instead of the use of retentions.

Quality

Whilst never a minor concern on any client's agenda, there has been a perceptible escalation in client expectation of quality standards in the last decade, as the industry has sought to address its past failures. The momentum behind this drive to achieve significantly higher standards has been coincidental and consistent with the various government commissioned reports on the construction industry. These have already been extensively discussed in the preceding chapters and include: *Construction Best Practice* (DETR); the Latham Report *Constructing the Team* (1994); and the Egan Report *Rethinking Construction* (1998). In the Egan Report, a "quality driven agenda" is described as fundamental to the process of change within the industry. The report states that "Quality means not only zero defects but right first time, delivery on time and to budget, innovating for the benefit of the client and stripping out waste, whether it be in design, materials or construction on site. It also means aftersales care and reduced cost in use. Quality means the total package – exceeding customer expectations and providing real service" (Chapter 2). Against the background of numerous long-established standard construction contracts which are perceived as having singularly failed to promote quality standards as a key objective, the vehicle by which quality can be delivered has now been identified as the industry's adoption of partnering. Indeed, one of the core objectives of partnering is to facilitate delivery to the client of a quality product.

The concept of quality is therefore evolving from the delivery of an end product, which complies with the client's immediate requirements and from which the parties involved in its delivery then walk away, to the provision of a wider service that recognises the client's future requirements regarding the on-going functionality of the structure and the contingent liabilities that will necessarily arise in the course of the structure's life span. These contingent liabilities relate to the costs of operation, maintenance, repair and alteration.

In addition to the subjective requirements of the particular project, it is clear from the various reports critiquing the industry that there are objective aspects to a quality product or service that will be relevant across the board, regardless of the project specific requirements. The hallmark of a process that is therefore likely to successfully deliver a quality service is one which allies itself to certain key principles that will influence all stages of the development, from the production of the outline design through to the evaluation of factors such as on-going maintenance. These principles include sustainability, value for money and the incorporation of innovative practices and techniques.

In *Rethinking Construction*, Egan made clear the issues that are now setting the agenda for the evaluation of a quality product or service, namely:

"(a) clients want greater value from their buildings by achieving a clearer focus on meeting functional business needs;
 (b) clients' immediate priorities are to reduce capital costs and improve the quality of new buildings;
 (c) clients believe that a longer-term, more important issue is reducing running-costs and improving the standard of existing buildings;
 (d) clients believe that significant value improvement and cost reduction can be gained by the integration of design and construction."

If these quality expectations are to be met, the partnering arrangements must put in place a quality management strategy. The key to the successful implementation of a quality improvement initiative lies in effective contract administration, characterised by a number of critical features. First, there must be a clear expression of the principles that are to facilitate the collaboration, which might be described as the methodology for "teamwork best practice" . An example is a commitment to open communication between the parties. It is essential that the partners "buy into" these principles from the outset. Second, the partnering arrangements need to provide for the bringing together of a small multidisciplinary team through which the collaborative dealings of the partners can be put into practical effect and monitored. The third feature is the provision of an administrative framework to enable the partners, and perhaps specifically the designated team, to procure the achievement of the objectives.

It has already been said that there is a tension between the aspirations of partnering and the established principles of English contract law, in particular that the nature of the obligations to be imposed on the parties, and the benefits to which the parties become entitled need to incorporate sufficient certainty as to be enforceable. It may be argued that the intangible nature of the wider expectations of quality set out above are therefore incompatible with contracts as construed by English law. Despite the difficulty that this presents, the published forms have largely attempted to encapsulate the essence of Egan and Latham, and in conjunction with achieving the agreed specified outcome for the particular project, have set wider goals for the parties.

PPC 2000: HOW DOES IT DEAL WITH TIME, COST AND QUALITY?

PPC 2000: Time

PPC 2000 comprises of a Project Partnering Agreement (PPA) which is signed up to by the Partnering Team (which will include the constructor, named consultants and specialists "working in mutual co-operation to fulfil their agreed roles and responsibilities and apply their agreed expertise in relation to the Project, in accordance with and subject to the Partnering Terms ...". The PPA lists the partnering documents as comprising a number of documents including those dealing with project brief, price framework and KPIs. In addition, the partnering documents expressly include "the Partnering Timetable".

The procurement method envisaged by PPC 2000 is essentially a two-stage process. Stage 1 of the exercise is to define the scope, required resources and programme for the works together with a price and Stage 2 involves the signing up by the partnering team to deliver to the identified deliverables in Stage 1, albeit set as targets. Indeed, the definition of partnering timetable makes it clear that this is relevant only to Stage 1 of the procurement process, i.e., governing the activities of the partnering team members in relation to the project prior to the date of the Commencement Agreement. Clause 2.5 of PPC 2000 confirms that all partnering documents are to be treated as complementary but there is a priority order listed in clause 2.6. Discrepancies between the partnering documents are required to be aired and the parties are expected to put forward proposals to resolve "without adversely affecting the agreed cost or time for completion or quality of the Project".

The core group (an identified group of representatives from the partnering team) are required to meet regularly to review and stimulate progress of the project and implementation of the partnering contract. Albeit not expressed as such, it is thought this will include the agreement of measures necessary to maintain progress against any agreed programme.

It is also relevant to recall that in all activities, the partnering team members are required to act reasonably and without delay (clause 1.7).

The key to the management of programme risks under PPC 2000 is the fact that this is a multi-party contract and the partnering team includes the client. In terms of managing time risk, PPC 2000 obliges partnering team members to consider and develop common tools and processes as shall benefit the project including any specific arrangements set out in the project brief or project proposals. In practice, this could include the sharing of programming networks and databases and other collaborative communication tools to enable teams from different organisations to collaborate over a shared network, facilitating an exchange of design, construction and programme information (clause 3.10). As a project management tool, it is argued that such networks facilitate the sharing of design, supply and construction expertise thereby minimising the scope for poor co-ordination and clashes at the interface of design and construction activities that have historically beset construction projects.

Further, partnering team members are required to keep records of their activities as required by the partnering documents. Such records would include progress records.

In essence, the extension of time provisions under PPC 2000 follow a fairly traditional format. A list of events is set out which entitle the constructor to claim an extension to the extent they "adversely affect the Date for Completion" (clause 18.3). It is considered that the decided court cases based upon the extension of time workings and risk allocation of the JCT standard forms of contract would apply to extension of time issues under PPC 2000. (See *Henry Boot Construction (UK) Ltd* v. *Malmaison Hotel (Manchester) Ltd* (1999) 70 Con LR 32; *Royal Brompton Hospital National Health Authority* v. *Frederick Alexander Hammond*, 76 Con LR 148). Thus, if the constructor is in culpable delay itself, the occurrence of an event listed in clause 18.3, which would otherwise adversely affect the date for completion, will nevertheless entitle the constructor to an extension of time.

Subject to this, under PPC 2000 there are a number of conditions precedent to the constructor obtaining any extension of time. The first is that it uses its "best endeavours" to minimise any delay to the project caused by any of the events requiring the constructor to have taken steps to avoid or reduce delay (e.g., clauses 18.3(iii) and 18.3(vi), relating to delay in receipt of third party consents or, delays by statutory bodies or utilities).

It is also noteworthy that, in clause 18.6, PPC prescribes that the constructor may recover the cost of "unavoidable additional work or expenditure" incurred by certain events and, by virtue of clauses 18.4 and 18.5, may also recover the cost of time-based overheads (to be identified in the price framework). PPC 2000 also seeks to impose an exclusive remedies provision:

"the Constructor shall not be entitled to claim additional payment of any kind, other than those payments described in Clause 18.5 [time-based site overheads] and this Clause 18.6 [unavoidable additional work or expenditure for certain events], by reason of any event described in Clause 18.3". (clause 18.6(iii))

Thus, under PPC 2000 it is thought that in cases of concurrent delay, the constructor gets both time and money but only to the extent of time-based site overheads identified in the price framework and then only for certain events. For instance, delays caused by third party consents, exceptionally adverse weather, utility delays or damage due to insured perils will not entitle the constructor to additional monies.

Whether the exclusive remedies provision in clause 18.6(iii) is effective to exclude damages claims at common law for breach of contract is a moot point. The clause does not expressly exclude common law rights, and House of Lords authority confirms that clear words are required to achieve this (*Gilbert-Ash (Northern) Ltd* v. *Modern Engineering (Bristol) Ltd* [1973] 3 All ER 195).

Moreover, there is no carve out in respect of possible claims based upon fraud and certain first instance authority suggests this could render such a clause unenforceable. (*Thomas Witter Ltd* v. *TBP Indistries Ltd* [1996] 2 All ER 573.)

PPC 2000: Cost and incentives

The price the client pays is established by two separate methods. Initially, in the period prior to possession of the site, the constructor is paid on a fixed price activity basis for any activities undertaken and separately, on such basis as is agreed, for any services delivered. Thereafter, the constructor is paid amounts on an interim basis up to an agreed maximum price as consideration for carrying out and completing the project, such agreed maximum price to be both:

"within any Budget set out in the Price Framework and otherwise as low as achievable consistent with best value" (clause 12.3)

The price framework will set out fixed amounts for the constructor's profit, central office overheads and site overheads which will form part of the agreed maximum price. The agreed maximum price will also include the prices of any supply chain member (known in the PPC 2000 as a specialist) or constructor direct labour package over which the client has had pricing approval, either by approving the appropriate business case or by requiring the constructor to go out to competitive tender.

Ordinarily, the specialists are appointed and paid directly by the constructor. However, the client retains significant control over the value for money of specialists costs, as these form part of the agreed maximum price and the relationship with the specialists should be "open-book to the maximum achievable extent" with full records being kept of payments (clause 10.1(i)).

Responsibility for payment of the consultants rests entirely with the client, unless a consultant is given the status of a specialist, but PPC 2000 gives no specific guidance on what an appropriate basis for pricing the consultant's contribution to the project.

In accordance with clause 12.9, the constructor is to notify the client of "All and any proposed risk contingencies" but only those approved by the client, taking advice from suitable partnering team members, and in respect of which proposals to eliminate, reduce, insure, share or proportion the risk in question have been approved are to be incorporated into the price framework and hence into the agreed maximum price. In addition, when certain specified events occur the constructor may be entitled to an increase in its time based site overheads, at the rate set out in the price framework, and/or a "fair and reasonable increase in the Agreed Maximum Price" due to "unavoidable additional work or expenditure" (clause 18.6). These entitlements will only arise if the constructor uses its best endeavours to minimise increased cost to the project.

Whilst there is no explicit obligation on the client to pay a fair price, "fairness" is one of partnering team's objectives. However, this should be read alongside the provisions enabling the core group of partners to investigate savings against the agreed maximum price and make appropriate recommendations to the client. There are also obligations on the partnering team members to keep records and permit the inspection of these records by other partnering team members, although these records are not specifically required to be kept on an open-book basis. The partnering team members are obliged to operate an early warning system in respect of all aspects of their performance under the contract.

PPC 2000 contains fairly industry standard payment terms including provision for interest on late payments (clause 20). Considerable freedom is given to the client as to how interim payments are to be valued. Of particular note are provisions which enable the partners to share the benefit of any volume supply agreements which any one partner may have, if such is felt to be of benefit to the project. However, any third party benefits, offered or received by any partner in relation to the project, if not otherwise approved by PPC 2000, will require client approval. There is no concept of either a retention system or a trust fund.

PPC 2000 requires each partnering team member to implement the recommendations in the Egan Report (*Rethinking Construction*) and to pursue the targets stated in the contractual KPIs for those aspects of performance which are set out in clause 4.2. These aspects of performance closely reflect those in the Egan Report but the partners are free to tailor their actual performance targets and KPIs to the specific requirements of the project and their relationship to one another. The performance of each partnering team member is to be kept under regular review by the core group, by reference to the KPIs, and the team members are to provide information, on an open book basis, to the client on progress against the KPIs.

There is a mechanism to adjust payments to the constructor/consultants in line with the achievement of a specified date for completion and/or the attainment of any target set out in a KPI (clause 13). In addition, the contract contains space for the partners to set out any shared savings arrangements and/or value added incentives they wish to apply and there is a mechanism to adjust payments to the partners in accordance with such arrangements. In both instances, the detail of how any such financial incentives should operate is left for the partners to develop themselves.

PPC 2000 specifically obliges the partnering team members to work together and individually:

"to maximise through measurable continuous improvement the potential for the project to achieve the objectives set out in Clause 4". (clause 23.3)

Such continuous improvement is to be measured against the continuous improvement criteria in the KPIs. Finally, following completion of the project the partners are required to attend a meeting to review actual improvement against the KPIs and to consider the scope for further improvement on future projects.

PPC 2000: Quality

PPC 2000 contains a number of expressions of teamwork best practice. These include clause 1.3 which provides that the partners are to work together in "a spirit of trust, fairness, and mutual co-operation for the benefit of the Project". Further, in all matters concerning the partnering contract, the partners are "to act reasonably and without delay" (clause 1.7). Throughout the project, there is to be a transparent and co-operative exchange of information and the partners are to organise and integrate activities as a collaborative team (clause 3.1).

The overall objectives set for the partners are set out in clause 4 and specific quality objectives appear in clause 16. These include the reduction of capital and operating costs, the reduction of defects, the adoption of innovative practices, the increase of the project's expected life-span and improved sustainability. By reference to the KPIs, discussed further below, the partners are to work together and individually to maximise through continuous and measurable improvement, the potential for the project to achieve these objectives and to provide best value for the client (clause 23.3).

Reference has already been made to the core group, responsible for keeping the implementation of the project under continual review. This includes the responsibility to review the partners' performance by reference to the set contractual targets (clause 23.1) and the investigation of any proposals made for the purposes of achieving continuous improvement (clause 23.4).

In line with what will be the project specific requirements, PPC 2000 envisages that a separate quality management system will be developed, the substance of which is not dictated by the terms of the contract and will remain to be agreed between the parties (clause 16.3). Perhaps the most critical requirement of any quality improvement regime is the means by which the performance of the parties can be measured against agreed targets. In clause 23, these targets are set by reference to KPIs, which are likely to include nationally known KPIs, as well as specifically tailored and project specific KPI targets. (There is similar provision in ECC Option X12 and the BCC.) By reference to clause 4.2, KPIs encompass targets over a number of areas including improved quality, sustainability and value enhancing matters. Agreement of the KPIs is one of the preconditions to the commencement of the project on the site (clause 23.1) and also provides a link between payment and the achievement of KPIs.

As regards minimising the risks that could undermine the achievement of the quality objectives, there is an "early warning system" under which the partners are to notify each other of any matter that is likely to adversely affect the project, and this notification is to be accompanied by that partnering team member's proposals for the avoidance or correction of the matter in question (clause 3.7). The partners are also called upon to develop a risk management strategy, which will identify the risks involved in the delivery of the project and the anticipated costs associated with those risks (clause 18.1). The analysis involved in these exercises may include proposals as to ways in which those risks can be eliminated or reduced and the apportioning of the risk according to the party best able to manage it.

The regime set out in this contract has sought to reflect the objective "aspirational" aspects now associated with a quality service and the core features of an effective administrative framework (performance evaluation, risk management and problem solving).

NHS LIFT STRATEGIC PARTNERING AGREEMENT: HOW DOES IT DEAL WITH TIME, COST AND QUALITY?

NHS LIFT: Time

Under the standard form of Strategic Partnering Agreement (SPA), Liftco undertakes to the other Participants that in relation to "New Projects" (i.e., new facilities required to provide healthcare services), Liftco will "procure the design and construction of those projects and delivery of Lease Plus Services under the terms of a Lease Plus Agreement with the relevant Tenants".

LIFT assumes that certain of the Participants (i.e., healthcare providers such as Primary Care Trusts or Strategic Health Authorities) will transfer ownership of their real estate assets to Liftco who then procures that the accommodation is leased back to the Participant, or another healthcare provider, under the terms of a Lease Plus Agreement (LPA). In terms of Liftco's or its subsidiary's obligations to complete New Projects by any specific date, this will be set out in the LPA.

However, the SPA contains certain over-arching terms that will impact as to extensions of time on New Projects. Thus, Liftco expressly acknowledges and confirms under the terms of the SPA that

"it has conducted its own analysis and review of the Information and, before execution of the Project Documents, has satisfied or will satisfy itself as to the accuracy, completeness and fitness for purpose of all such Information upon which it places reliance; and

it shall not be entitled to make any claim against the Participants or any of their agents, servants or advisers, whether in damages or for extensions of time or additional payments under the Project Documents, on the grounds of any misunderstanding or misapprehension in respect of the Information or on the grounds that incorrect or insufficient information relating thereto or to any Site was given to it by any person whether or not in the employ of the Participants, nor shall it be relieved from any risks or obligations imposed on or undertaken by it under the Project Documents on any such ground." (See SPA Clauses 15.8.1 and 15.8.2.)

Moreover, by reference to Clause 28.1, Liftco is responsible for performance of its designers, contractors and suppliers ("Supply Chain Members") and there is a statement of intent (not a direct obligation as such) under clause 8.6 of the SPA whereby the parties (i.e., Liftco and the other Participants) "agree that it is fundamental to the successful operation of this Agreement that Liftco devotes sufficient resource and expertise to providing the Partnering Services in a competent and timely manner and otherwise in accordance with the standards set out in Clause 8.2 and Schedule 17 (Partnering Services)". What happens if sufficient, competent and timely resources are not applied is an issue that is only partially answered in the SPA. However, and as noted earlier, further detail is to be found in the Lease Plus Agreement.

Under the LPA, Liftco's subsidiary (Fundco) has an incentive to complete its design and construction works without delay as Fundco receives no lease payment until the premises are complete. Subject to that commercial consideration, the LPA provides for Fundco to obtain an extension of time for certain defined events. These events are fairly narrowly defined.

Fundco is to prepare and maintain a "Project Programme" which should detail the duration and sequence of design and construction activities. The programme may be varied, provided this does not affect the completion date, thus giving Fundco some flexibility as to how it wishes to organise its resources. Fundco is not obliged in terms to follow its programme but it is expected to monitor progress against it and advise the Tenant (GP's etc.) of any changes to it or delays to the works.

Liquidated damages for delay to the completion date are provided for under the LPA, but only as an option. The term of the lease starts to run from financial close of the transaction and thus any delays to completion of the works simply erodes the term of the lease (and the period over which Fundco is to be paid). The LPA therefore recommends that the liquidated damage clause only be used where specific circumstances require certainty over the completion date, e.g., the Tenant has given notice to quit other premises. It may be commented that the imposition of liquidated damages is a historically used device in construction contracts to compensate for the cost of delay but it is a somewhat blunt tool in terms of managing the risk of delay.

NHS LIFT: Cost and incentives

As noted above, the SPA cannot be read in isolation from the other contracts which form the NHS LIFT suite of documents, as only when these are read as a whole is it possible to appreciate the full relationship between the parties and the entirety of their obligations to one another. Under the SPA Liftco provides the Participants with what are termed Partnering Services, such as estate planning and management, on an exclusive basis for the entire duration of the SPA. However, Liftco's subsidiaries also provide Tenants with serviced accommodation, under various Lease Plus Agreements (LPAs), in return for which these subsidiaries (Fundco's) are remunerated by the receipt of a monthly lease payment from the Tenants. There is a management agreement in place between Liftco and Fundco to enable some of these payments to be passed back to Liftco.

The provision of such serviced accommodation breaks down into the design, construction, finance, operation and maintenance of the accommodation. However, the lease payment is similar to a PFI style service charge in being a total amount for the project forming the subject matter of the LPA rather than including identifiable streams for the design and construction of the asset. The lease payment will also include an amount in respect of a proportion of the Partnering Services, even though the Tenants are not the direct recipients of such services, being part of the general business overheads of Liftco and Fundco. This pricing method requires a sophisticated approach to risk management and pricing by Liftco and is backed by obligations on Fundco to keep records on an open-book basis for both themselves and their Supply Chain Members.

Only if a proposed New Project is rejected or if the Participants are defaulting under the SPA is there a mechanism for Liftco to recover directly from the Participants, under the SPA, its otherwise unrecoverable Partnering Services Costs. If the SPA terminates due to the fault of the Participants, Liftco is entitled to recover amounts for lost profit from the Participants.

Payment of amounts to Fundco will be governed by the terms of the LPAs.

The standard form of LPA will contain extremely detailed PFI style performance measurement regimes. The LPA anticipates that performance of Fundco is regularly measured against KPIs (phrased in PFI-style terminology as Unavailability and Service Failures) and deductions made from the monthly lease payment for sub-standard performance. The SPA envisages there will be particular KPIs for the Partnering Services, against aspects of performance such as defects, safety or user satisfaction. Furthermore, the SPA sets out various non-binding aspirations for Liftco and the Participants relating to, amongst other matters, continuous, measurable and measured improvement and the establishment of open book relationships throughout the Supply Chain.

NHS LIFT: Quality

In the Strategic Partnering Agreement, the conditions identify "the high level principles which underpin the delivery of the parties' obligations" under the agreement (clause 2.3). These principles include the setting in place of "business and cultural processes" (clause 2.4) to enable the parties not only to agree and meet performance objectives, but also to better them. As part of an integrated approach to health and social care, the parties are to "co-ordinate and combine their expertise, manpower and resources" and "to develop openness and trust in a transparent information and data sharing environment." However, the contract also acknowledges "the partnering ethos, principles and objectives … are aspirational and not intended to give rise to legally binding rights and obligations between the parties" (clause 2.9). Each party under-takes to co-operate in good faith with the others to facilitate the proper per-formance of the agreement. However, this is again qualified by reference to the freedom of the parties to arrange their affairs in whatever manner consid-ered appropriate to perform their obligations under the agreement. Equally none of the parties are obliged to incur any additional cost or to suffer any loss of profit in excess of that which would be ordinarily required for the proper performance of the obligations under the SPA (clause 53).

The parties are to be managed by a Strategic Partnering Board (SPB), comprised of representatives of the Participants, a representative of the Liftco board and a number of representatives of the stakeholders in the local primary and community based health and social care community (clause 14). The function of the SPB is to provide strategic input, concentrating on the finan-cial and operating aspects. Unlike PPC 2000, decision-making is by majority vote.

The parties' commitment to continuous and measurable improvement is to be evaluated by reference to quantitative and qualitative targets which are to be "specific, challenging, add value and eliminate waste" (clause 2.7). The value for money of all new products is to be demonstrated via alternative methods based on market testing.

PRIME CONTRACTING: HOW DOES IT DEAL WITH TIME, COST AND QUALITY?

Prime contracting: Time

The prime contract requires for the contractor to provide a detailed pro-gramme that permits effective monitoring of progress but there is no positive express obligation to work to that programme (in common with most stan-dard form construction contracts). The programme is required to be of the critical path type, with networks of linked activities. This enables monitoring and assessment of events impacting the completion date. Whilst drafted before the advent of the Society of Construction Law's Delay Protocol, it can be said that the prime contract provisions as to programming would likely find approval within the SCL sub-committee who drafted the Protocol.

The contractor is allowed extensions of time for certain events (including "any delay, impediment, act of prevention or default by the Authority") but to the extent the contractor is in culpable delay, the Authority can withhold liquidated damages from any milestone payments otherwise due or can demand payment. Such damages will usually be subject to a maximum aggregate sum.

Although the prime contract does not constitute a partnering arrangement as between contractor and the Authority, there are mechanisms for the man-agement of time risk as between the parties to the prime contract. Such man-

agement takes the form of monitoring progress against the master programme. The Authority can require the contractor to revise his programme
to show how it will ensure execution of the works in a regular and diligent
way but there is no express power, as such, for the Authority to instruct the
contractor to accelerate its performance. Ultimately, the blunt instrument of
liquidated damages is used to discourage delay.

It is important to stress, however, that the contractor has single-point
responsibility to the Authority and is required to manage effectively its supply
chain of designers, suppliers and specialists so as to discharge its responsibilities. In practice, it is the integration of the supply chain parties and efficient
resource planning that enables the contractor to deliver to its master programme (and other deliverables). Such integration is achieved in prime contracting by the contractor entering into partnering arrangements with its supply chain. Such arrangements may include an integrated project agreement
between the first tier of the supply chain under which they collectively undertake to work together in a collaborative way to achieve the outputs required by
the prime contract. These arrangements are bespoke and beyond the scope of
this Chapter.

Prime Contracting: Cost and incentives

The prime contractor is paid for the works (design and construction) and
services (operational and maintenance services) provided to the client on a
maximum price target cost basis. Mobilisation payments fall outside of the
maximum price target cost regime.

Maximum price target cost requires the establishment, by the parties, of a
maximum price the client will pay, above which the contractor takes the risk
of all price overruns. There will also be various target costs for individual
aspects of the contract and a target profit amount. If the actual costs are less
than the target costs there will be a "gain" amount paid to the prime contractor whilst if actual costs are greater than the target costs the prime contractor
will suffer an amount of "pain".

The prime contractor's payments to its supply chain form actual costs of the
prime contractor and records of such amounts, if over a specified financial
limit, are required to be kept on an open-book accounting basis. Various other
provisions require the keeping of other detailed records relating to the contract
and provide for the audit and inspection of these. There are no specific duties
on the prime contractor to provide an early warning to the client of cost overruns and the making of retentions from interim payments is not envisaged.

Certain risks are termed accepted risks and if these occur the prime contractor is entitled to an adjustment to the maximum price target cost pricing
provisions. Other risks are termed contingent risks and an estimated target
cost for the effects of the risk occurring is to be agreed in advance between the
parties.

The prime contractor is entitled to the interim payments as against agreed milestones and fairly industry standard payment terms apply. Interest on late payments is payable at the rate set out in the Late Payment of Commercial Debts (Interest) Act 1998.

These are certain incentives placed on the prime contractor to reduce costs built into the pricing mechanism. In addition, the contract envisages there being a form of performance recovery system whereby the prime contractor's performance is measured. If the performance is not acceptable the prime contractor will then be allocated points, which will ultimately convert into monetary deductions from the milestone payments. However, the drafting is indicative only and it is assumed this concept will be developed by the parties on a project specific basis.

In addition, the contract envisages the prime contractor installing an information technology system to assess service delivery against performance indicators and to provide detailed performance reports. The prime contractor is also to produce and keep regularly updated, a continuous improvement plan against which actual performance should be reported. These performance reports may result in the client proposing service delivery changes that in turn may result in changes to the maximum price target cost pricing provisions.

Prime contracting: Quality

The prime contracting regime stands in contrast to the published partnering forms as the arrangement between the prime contractor and the MoD is one of supply chain management with a single point of responsibility in the prime contractor. Although there will be an integrated project team there is no decision-making core group. In both contracts, the prime contractor is to manage and operate a supply chain management plan and to provide information as to the best practice procedure that each member of the supply team has agreed to comply with.

The prime contractor must be proactive in developing policies and procedures to improve the operation and maintenance of the facility as regards the upgrading of performance and the addition of value. Under the Regional Prime Contract, the prime contractor is to provide to the MoD a "continuous improvement plan" (clause 2.28) which is to be reviewed, as a minimum, on an annual basis. Measurement of performance is by reference to a performance management report, which will summarise the progress that has been made by comparison with both KPIs and the proposals made in the continuous improvement plan. This exercise will take place at regular intervals to be agreed between the MoD and the prime contractor. In the Stand Alone Capital Projects Prime Contract, clause 7 requires the prime contractor to prepare a project execution plan, the contents of which are to include a quality management system and information on risk and value management.

Be COLLABORATIVE CONTRACT: HOW DOES IT DEAL WITH TIME, COST AND QUALITY?

BCC: Time

The BCC refers to production of a project programme (clause 3.14) and envisages this to be a project management tool against which to monitor progress. The project programme is to be prepared by either the purchaser or the supplier (the choice of option is identified in the purchase order). Similarly, the supplier may be designated as responsible for arranging regular progress meetings (clause 3.15). Where the supplier prepares the project programme, it is required to update it regularly and to "co-ordinate" (clause 3.14 of the Terms).

Thus, BCC envisages the parties to the contract ventilating before other parties engaged by the purchaser or supplier to provide design or construction services or supply equipment or materials, so far as relevant to the time issues in question. This provision may well require very different behaviours from parties than has previously been the case in construction contracts.

The BCC is accompanied by a *Guide* to its use. The *Guide* states that

"The Risk Allocation Schedule provides not only for the allocation of the cost consequences but also for the allocation of the time consequences of an identified risk. If considered too complicated, the columns in the Risk Allocation Schedule relating to the division of responsibility for the time consequences of an identified risk can simply be left blank. It is suggested that the pre-allocation of particular time consequences for the occurrence of particular risks may be particularly relevant where the Date of Completion of the Project is critical: for example, completing works to an educational establishment before the start of term time. Alternatively, the parties may decide, for example, that the time consequences of the occurrence of a specified risk may be shared equally. In such a case, if the delay to the Date or Dates for Completion resulting from the occurrence of the risk is two weeks, the Supplier will be entitled to an extension of time equal to half this amount, namely to one week." (See paragraph 5.8.5 of the *Guide to Use*.)

It should also be noted that under the BCC, the supplier will only be entitled to claim an extension of time if the cost of dealing with the identified risk, e.g., adverse ground conditions exceeds the supplier's share of the risk allowances in the risk allocation schedule. Otherwise, the adverse ground conditions do not qualify as a relief event.

The occurrence or likely occurrence of any relief event is to be notified immediately by whichever party first becomes aware of it to the other. It will be interesting as to what the courts may conclude as to the timing definition of "immediately"; if the courts adopt a similar approach to limitation periods, under the various Limitation Acts it is likely to err on the side of generosity by delaying the moment of awareness.

Once notice of a delay event is given, the supplier must then provide a statement setting out (in as much detail as is reasonably practicable) the effect that the supplier considers the relief event will have on the cost of performing the services and/or the date or dates for completion.

If the parties cannot reach agreement on the effects of the occurrence of the relief event, they will be determined in accordance with the dispute resolution procedure. Note, however, that if the purchaser decides that the effect of any relief event is too uncertain to be forecast with reasonable accuracy, it must agree with the supplier the assumptions to be made to enable the estimate of the effect of the relief event to be made (clause 4.11 of the Terms). If these assumptions subsequently prove to have been wrong, the purchaser and the supplier are obliged to agree the corrections needed to be made to the original estimate. Again, any failure to reach agreement will be resolved in accordance with the dispute resolution procedure.

BCC: Cost and incentives

The contract provides for a choice of two alternative pricing mechanisms, either pricing by target cost (with or without a guaranteed maximum price) or by contract sum (paid against activities/milestones). The *Guide* acknowledges that target cost pricing is closer to the principles of collaborative working but that as the contract is capable of use right across the supply chain it may be both easier and more usual to have a fixed sum in a simple sub-contract or in a consultant's appointment.

If the target cost option is used the supplier is paid its actual costs, up to any agreed guaranteed maximum cost, on a monthly basis. The supplier is under an obligation to record these costs on an open book basis and to make monthly cost breakdowns available to the purchaser. The contract requires the parties to agree the parameters for the breakdown of costs and the keeping of records prior to the first payment. Profits and central office overheads will not form part of the actual costs but will form part of an agreed supplier's margin, which will be paid to the supplier at such intervals as are set out in the purchase order. There are pain/gain sharing arrangements if the actual costs are greater than/less than the target.

There is a sophisticated process of initial risk assessment by the parties the results of which are to be set out in a risk register, which is regularly updated. In addition, the parties are to complete a risk allocation schedule, which allocates the time and cost consequences of certain risks occurring between the parties. If there is an allowance made for a particular risk in the target cost/contract sum then if this risk occurs, and the resulting costs are greater than the allowance made, then the overspend will be allocated between the parties in accordance with the risk allocation schedule.

Whichever option is chosen there are similar Housing Grants Act compliant payment terms with provision for interest on late payments. There is no ability to make a retention from payments made under the contract.

Part of the overriding principle of collaboration, in clause 1.1, is the agreement by the parties that they will both give and welcome feedback on performance. Clause 5 obliges the purchaser to monitor the supplier's performance against the KPIs set out in the purchase order and there is provision for regular performance reviews. However, there is no specific link between good or poor performance and the amounts which are paid to the supplier, nor is there any concept of continuous improvement over the life of the contract. Financial performance incentives are of the traditional time related variety, with provision for liquidated damages for delayed completion and an early completion bonus for early completion

BCC: Quality

As stated in the opening review of this contract, the parties will draw up a project protocol, which will detail aims and objectives both in respect of the project and the development of the parties' working relationships. Paragraph 2.4.2 of the accompanying *Guide* explains that this protocol is to supplement the standard contact provisions so that it becomes an expression of the parties' project specific commitments. This protocol will not be contractually binding.

The position taken by the BCC on teamwork practice is elevated into an "Overriding Principle", with the *Guide* drawing an analogy with the "overriding objective" found in the Civil Procedure Rules of the English courts. Interestingly, clause 1.7 of the Terms states that where the parties resort to the dispute resolution mechanism, "any court or adjudicator or other forum ... shall take account of the Overriding Principle and of the parties' adherence to it when making any award".

The administrative team is to be a project team, to comprise the client and all other participants that the client considers necessary for the successful delivery of the project. Although the project team is to guide delivery of the project, unlike the ECC Option, it cannot issue instructions to other project participants, or indeed take any decisions that are binding on them (paragraph 2.3.2 of the *Guide*). Accordingly, the project team's remit extends to two specific functions. First, in the event of an occurrence that may affect the performance of the project participants, the project team will consider how the issue should be dealt with and all the parties are called upon to give serious consideration to any resulting recommendations that it may produce. Second, the project team forms the first tier of the dispute resolution process.

The issue of risk management is dealt with in considerable detail (paragraphs 5.6 and 5.7 of the *Guide*) and this aspect has already been commented upon under the sections relating to time and cost. The *Guide* emphasises the importance of a "robust system of risk identification and management", and certainly the scheme devised under the BCC appears to satisfy this objective.

MOVEMENT FOR INNOVATION "TRUST AND MONEY" VIRTUAL COMPANY MODEL: HOW DOES IT DEAL WITH TIME, COST AND QUALITY?

Movement for Innovation: Time

The starting point for assessing delivery under the M4i Consultation Draft is the "functional brief". This document describes what it is the client wants. This may include a requirement for delivery to a certain timetable or completion date.

The form allows a degree of flexibility in defining the parties' "objectives", by providing a list applicable to either the construction or operational phase of the project and allowing the parties to rank these in order of priority. For instance, "Certainty of Completion" may be ranked number one whereas "Lowest Capital Cost" may be less of a driver.

Under the M4i Consultation Draft, the parties (termed "partners") agree to "use their best endeavours to deliver the Functional Brief in accordance with the Objectives". Under English law, the term "best endeavours" has attracted some judicial attention. It is usually compared to "reasonable endeavours" and is regarded as meaning a higher duty than that, even extending to the expenditure of money so as to achieve the end desired, albeit not to the point of bankrupting the payer. However, in standard form construction contracts, parties often use the term "best endeavours" to mean trying to achieve something but not to he extent of spending money on such attempts.

Whether this issue will be determined in the context of extension of time clauses in new form partnering contracts such as the M4i Consultation Draft, remains a question. However, the risk has to be considered (in the case of the M4i Consultation Draft) against the agreed risk share provisions. Under the M4i Consultation Draft, the parties (i.e., the client and the supply chain) agree at the outset to share the financial risks of completing the project to programme in pre-determined percentages, irrespective of individual culpability. This form of risk sharing is said to promote team work in that it discourages risk transfer and blame and replaces this with a common purpose whereby all parties are motivated to help solve problems that could affect them all.

Another central idea to the M4i Consultation Draft is the creation of the project team. Clause 8 states: "The Partners and Cluster Partners shall second to the Virtual Company such staff as shall be required to constitute an integrated Project Team and to deliver the Functional Brief in accordance with the Objectives. Each Partner shall provide all necessary 'overhead' support to its secondees." The responsibilities of the project team (and, ergo, the duties of the parties from whom the team members are seconded) include "controlling ... programme in accordance with ... project consents and timetables" and "instituting an early warning system for delays ...".

To assist in the management of the project, the form provides for the establishment of a "virtual company board", which typically would comprise representatives from the client, architect, construction manager, structural engineer, concrete/steel frame specialist, cladding specialist and so forth. There is also provision for insurers to be represented, as appropriate. The role of the board is to maintain the organisation of the project team and approve the appointment of "cluster partners" (i.e., specialists brought into the project from time-to-time, consistent with their required inputs, e.g., ductwork and controls specialists under the "sponsorship" of the M&E contractor). The board also approves the appointment of the "project team leader" whose responsibilities include "ensuring that the project and delivery timetables are adhered to and that programmes at every level are kept up to date".

More particularly, the project team leader is responsible for "ensuring that information is freely exchanged in a timely and co-ordinated manner with the project team, particularly design and production information". In practice, such information exchange can most easily be achieved by the deployment of a project extranet, allowing each of the project team members to collaborate over a shared and common platform that records inputs and incorporates ideas into the design. The use of such tools serves an important role in helping to keep to the project timetable and avoid delays.

Like all forms of partnering procurement, ultimately the M4i Consultation Draft is about trying to organise a team of designers, suppliers, specialists and contractors so that the functional brief can be delivered to the client's requirements, i.e., on time, to budget and at the required quality. Each contracting party is obliged "to adhere to the project timetable". What happens if the client sign-off of design team details for construction purposes occurs such that the timetable (and completion date) is likely to be delayed?

One has to appreciate that, under the M4i Consultation Draft, each of the parties is expected to enter into a separate supply or works contract with third parties for the supply and execution of the works. Such contracts are likely to allow each of the parties remedies against the third parties in the event that culpable delay is caused. However, as between the parties to the M4i Consultation Draft, the risk of delay (and its cost) is shared in the percentages set out in the contract, irrespective of individual fault. That provision is, however, expressed to be without prejudice to the client's right to bring a claim against the other parties "for the purpose of pursuing a claim against a supplier or works contractor for defects of other breaches" such as a failure to complete on time.

Movement for innovation: Cost and incentives

Payment is made by the client (known as the customer) for the contributions of the partners to the project under three broad headings. First, partners are obliged to second staff to the virtual company and are paid the actual payroll costs of these seconded staff, plus an agreed multiplier on such costs to cover supporting overheads and profit. Secondly, the partners will be paid the actual costs incurred for goods, materials, equipment, services and works, either their own costs or those of their sub-contractors, used in the project. Finally, the partners will be paid a share of the financial rewards, if any, of the project.

The partners can agree that the profit and overheads element a partner may be recover from the customer should be capped, and above this amount the other partners will contribute to any cost overruns in accordance with their share of the project rewards up to a further overall cap on liability.

There are obligations on the partners to maintain an open book policy.

There are not currently any detailed payment terms in the virtual company contract.

The virtual company model seeks to incentivise the partners and to align their financial interests by sharing the financial rewards of the project between the partners in specified proportions, which will be set out in the contract and which are intended to reflect the relative contributions of the partners to the achievement of the objectives of the project. These shares are fixed unless there are changes to the functional brief for the project or the partner's objectives or unless a partner defaults and is removed from the virtual company in circumstances where no alternative partner is introduced, thus requiring a pro rata realignment of shares.

How the financial rewards are calculated will be set out in a formula attached as a schedule to the contract. However, given the win-win philosophy of the virtual company these rewards should not be capped.

The virtual company envisages that there may be clusters of sub-partners who will work alongside the main partner in delivering the objectives under the contract. The main partner's share of the project rewards will be shared with these cluster partners.

The concepts of KPIs and continuous improvement are not explicitly addressed in the contract, however, the whole structure of the virtual company incentivises performance by the more direct method of reward sharing.

Movement for innovation: Quality

Under clause 3 of the M4i Consultation Draft, the partners will set out in the body of the contract, the express objectives that have been discussed and agreed between them. The guidance notes explain that there will be corresponding construction and operational objectives and these will include "quality/sustainability" in the construction context allied to the operational objective of operational utility. A further construction objective is "lowest capital cost" with the corresponding operational objective of cost in use.

Taking an analogous approach to the other published partnering forms, the paradigm of good faith in dealings between the partners also appears under the M4i Consultation Draft, with the partners additionally agreeing to full co-operation with each other and to maintain an open-book policy (clause 4). The partners will moreover agree to adhere to a partnering charter to be incorporated into the contract and which will, according to the guidance notes, encompass their project specific needs.

The two operative levels of administration have been described under the section relating to time. The project team will have the immediate responsibility for risk management, ensuring that environmental and quality control policies are in place and maintained and encouraging and facilitating innovation and the reduction of waste (clause 8). The project team leader has the specific responsibility of encouraging the contract's principles as to best team working practice: co-operation, free exchange of information and the like. The project team leader is also to ensure that environmental and quality control policies are adhered to and to keep the virtual company board informed of opportunities to improve value or reduce cost (clause 14).

Whilst the M4i Consultation Draft clearly anticipates that quality control mechanisms are to be put in place, the draft does not detail the indicators against which the partners' performance is to be monitored against the contractual objectives. It is possible that this is an issue that the project specific partnering charter will encompass.

ECC OPTION X12: HOW DOES IT DEAL WITH TIME, COST AND QUALITY?

ECC: Time

As noted earlier in this Chapter, ECC Option X12 is intended for use alongside an ECC standard form contract. In partnering projects, this is most likely to be the ECC core conditions with one of the main options being Option C, target contract with activity schedule. The core conditions of the ECC form contain extensive provisions as to the establishment of a programme of activities although (in common with most standard forms) the programme is not a contract document. Instead, it is intended as a management tool to help plan progress and signal early warnings of events likely to impact the completion date.

The programming details required by the ECC core conditions promote effective programme management albeit on projects with large numbers of compensation events, practitioners report that the requirement to constantly re-programme can be onerous one.

The mechanics of the extension of time provisions of the ECC core conditions are dealt with in other publications, notably in Dr Arthur McInnis' book on the NEC, and we do not propose to repeat them here. However, in passing it should be noted that ECC provides a series of secondary option clauses that parties may choose to adopt, including Option L (sectional completion), Option Q (bonus for early completion) and Option R (delay damages). All of these may be relevant to consider in terms of how ECC manages time risk issues.

ECC Option X12 allows the extension of time to be considered more fairly in the light of all circumstances, without such an onerous time limits as in PPC 2000. However, both contracts also provide that the Partners should work together to resolve such difficulties which includes warning the other partners when their own performance may prevent the clients' objectives being met.

The danger with this type of provision is that by "admitting" this type of failure, a team partner may void his own professional indemnity policy, thereby losing the benefit of a source of funds that could have been used by way of financial compensation. This provision is clearly significant in a partnering arrangement and it will be interesting to see how the industry and, more importantly, underwriters respond.

ECC: Cost and incentives

As Option X12 forms part of a bilateral ECC contract the pricing method will be governed by the main option used in the EEC, Subcontract or Professional Services Contract, in question. This provides scope for the parties to customise the pricing method used to the project or to the individual role of the partner within the project. For example, if the EEC Option A is used the contractor will receive a lump sum price, paid against particular activities, and if Option C is used for the sub-contract the sub-contractor will be paid on a cost reimbursable basis up to an activity based target price.

In all the main options where costs are reimbursed on an actual cost basis, to enable transparency as to these costs, there is an obligation to keep records (although not specifically on an open-book basis) and to allow the project manager to inspect these records. Not only does the EEC contain an early warning clause amongst its core clauses, which obliges the contractor to provide an early warning of price increases, clause X12.3 provides additional obligations on the partners to work together and provide early warnings to each other.

Price will vary in accordance with the standard risk sharing mechanisms found in the ECC suite of contracts which are primarily based around the concept of compensation events valued on an actual cost basis.

The payment terms will be as per the core clauses of the EEC. These are, broadly speaking, compatible with the Latham Report recommendations. The use of the secondary options allows for the contract either to provide for retentions (Option P), or for a trust fund to be set up (Option V).

Option X12 envisages that performance targets will be set for the project and aspects of performance will be measured against project KPIs which will be set out in the schedule of partners. These KPIs may apply to any one or more partners and any partner's performance may be measured against any number of individual KPIs. The schedule of partners contains space for the partners to set out their own provisions for measurement of the KPIs and the amount of each partner's payment, if any, which attaches to achievement of, or improvement on, any stated target. If two or more partners share a KPI their performance achievement, and any bonuses attaching to this, inevitably stand or fall together. There is, however, no automatic passing of targets down the supply chain. The actual payment of such bonuses will be made under the terms of the particular ECC contract.

Other incentives to good performance are built into the inherent structure of the ECC suite of contacts and the parties are free to incorporate any one or more of the secondary options, such as Option Q (bonus for early completion) or Option R (delay damages), which they choose. In addition, certain of the main options will incentivise the contractor to reduce costs more than others. In particular, Option E imposes no inherent incentive on the contractor to minimise costs, indeed if the fee is linked to a percentage of costs this mechanism could perversely encourage the contractor to increase costs.

ECC: Quality

The ECC Option calls upon the partners to work together "in a spirit of mutual trust and co-operation" (clause X12.3). This obligation appears separately in the respective underlying contracts. The ECC Option does not contain generalised statements as to overriding quality objectives. However, it incorporates a "schedule of partners" which anticipates that the partners will each provide their proposals under the heading of "Contribution and objective". The "client's objective" is also recorded separately within the body of the Option.

The ECC Option provides that the core group will be responsible for the implementation of the project (clause X12.1(3). Although this group will necessarily be made up of representatives of the client and the partners, as in the case of PPC 2000 it is not required that all the partners will be represented in the group. The core group is not only invested with the decision-making function on behalf of the partners, (which will then be issued as instructions to the respective partners in the context of their own contract) but also with the power to issue instructions to change the partnering information (clause X12.3(6).

JCT PARTNERING CHARTER: HOW DOES IT DEAL WITH TIME, COST AND QUALITY?

JCT Partnering Charter: Time

The JCT Practice Note 4 remains silent on time. This is hardly surprising given that it is non-binding. It therefore falls back on relevant events (some which carry money and some which do not) which are normally found in the underlying JCT standard contracts with which the JCT partnering charter is designed to work.

Current practice in some parts of the industry tend to support the use of a hard-edge construction contract hedged by an aspirational partnering charter. Whilst the latter has no contractual force, commercially it tends to promote certain behaviours and cultural changes. Thus, formal claims are discouraged and parties often seek a more consensual resolution of issues that arise. The danger, however, is when the consequences to the client of issues impacting exceeds expectations, parties may tend to fall back on the hard-edges terms of the underlying contract. Uncertainties can then arise as to the contractor's entitlement time or other claims if it has not previously served formal notices of claim. One example of a non-contractual "partnering" arrangement going wrong is to be found in *Birse Construction Ltd* v. *St Davids Ltd* [1999] BLR 194 (see Chapter 7).

Notwithstanding these difficulties, the use of non-contractual aspirational charters and other terms appears to be a "comfortable" compromise for parties who still require a hard edged contract (perhaps to satisfy financiers' or internal audit requirements) yet are keen to have some partnering relationship in place. Philosophically, lawyers tend to regard such arrangements as uncertain and tending to add cost rather than value because of likelihood of costly legal disputes created by uncertain contractual arrangements.

JCT Partnering Charter: Cost and incentives

The price paid to the contractor and the risk allocation between the contractor and the client will follow the structure of the underlying JCT standard form of building contract used in the project. For example, if the JCT standard form used is the 1998 edition with contractor's design, the contractor will be paid the tendered contract sum as varied in accordance with the standard contractual provisions. Such a contract would not envisage any overriding principle of fairness as to the price paid to the contractor nor would it contain any specific open book, early warning provisions or terms obliging the contractor to manage its supply chain in a collaborative manner

The partnering charter does part company with the more historical JCT philosophy of the underlying standard forms which have adopted a robust approach to risk allocation. This regime appears to be ameliorated under the terms of the charter which provides that the whole partnering team should work together "to produce a completed project…within an agreed budget/ price" by "acting in an open and trusting manner" and "fairly towards each other". However, and as noted earlier, the partnering charter is non-binding and aspirational only.

Payment will be made to the contractor in accordance with the terms of the underlying standard form of building contract. These will be Construction Act compliant, include provision for interest on late payments and provide for retentions to be made from interim payments.

The partnering charter sets out various objectives, grouped under four broad headings, attainment of which are to be measured against performance indicators which are to be agreed upon by the partnering team. As the part-nering charter is intended to be non-binding, the consequences of achieving or failing to achieve these objectives will not result in any direct financial rewards or penalties for the partners. There is no specific mention of contin-uous improvement in the JCT partnering charter itself, as distinct from the accompanying Practice Note

JCT Partnering Charter: Quality

In paragraph 4 of the general introduction to the JCT Charter, partnering is described as being "Above all...about quality management" and that a key aspect that underpins partnering is continuous improvement. Accordingly, in the objectives expressed under the category of "delivery", the stated aims are for right first time with zero defects, the utilisation of the best and safest prac-tice, the encouragement of innovation and the efficient use of resources and the maximisation of the efficiency of the contributors to the project.

The objectives that are to be achieved by the signatories are to be "meas-ured against performance indicators to be established". However, there is no systematic regime whereby attainment or failure can be measured in any of these categories. Although the JCT Charter is based on the same premise as the ECC Option X12, it does not set out a formal structure of management that might compromise the existing structure in the underlying JCT Standard Form Contract. The Charter merely states that the process must involve all participants and emphasises that "everyone from senior management to oper-atives on site is engaged in the process".

CONCLUSION

In 1963 the JCT produced their well-respected main contract between an Employer and a main contractor. It contained amongst many provisions a fair-ly straightforward set of provisions dealing with time, cost and quality. Over the last 40 years, the contractual matrix has become, particularly where part-nering or strategic partnering is involved, much more complicated. There are, by way of example, many more parties involved in the construction process. The legal drafting of construction contracts has perhaps been reticent if not slow to respond to these changes and the move towards a less adversarial cul-ture in the form of partnering. As this book highlights, the legal process does not lead a cultural change, it reflects it.

The construction industry is undergoing enormous change. The rise and rise of partnering and the public sector promotion of partnering presents the industry with new challenges and potential pitfalls. The draftsmen of partner-ing contracts, particularly when dealing with the three most critical and sen-sitive issues, namely time, cost and quality, have in the view of the authors of this Chapter missed the point. Is the role of contracts to reflect established commercial behaviour or to provide a best-practice role model in advance of the industry having evolved to satisfy that requirement? The real issue, in our view, is to tackle procurement procedures (i.e., tender on best value, not lowest cost), to select the delivery team (i.e., designers, suppliers, constructors) concurrently rather than sequentially, and to implement collaborative working techniques such as robust early warning provisions and open-book communications covering design, scope and cost development. In contrast, the draftsmen of the partnering contracts have in many cases produced wonderful words, which lack the legal discipline and structure of earlier standard forms and seek to impose behaviours which are not always consistent with market practice. However, this is not surprising given the diverse and complex nature of partnering which is still in its infancy.

Equally, it should be recognised that whilst any contract (be it reflective of a partnering arrangement or not) is expected to represent an agreed code of conduct between the contracting parties, self interest is never far from the surface. As Tillotson says (in *Contract Law in Perspective* (1995, 3rd edition)): "If one gets to the bottom of things, one will see that all harmony of interests conceals a conflict which is latent or simply adjourned." A recognition of that state of affairs is a healthy requirement in the drafting of any partnering contract.

This comes back to the point that contracts are frameworks onto which parties map their objectives, their respective inputs and agreed risk allocation. In this sense, contracts confirm the commercial relationship and reflect the agreed processes and procedures of the parties rather than impose (by themselves) new ways of working. As noted at the outset of this Chapter, partnering standard forms are in their infancy. We expect the forms discussed in this Chapter to evolve (and further standard forms to be published) as collaborative working practices become more prevalent and common features emerge. The *Strategic Forum's Tool Kit,* published in 2003, will help. The Tool Kit explains how supply chain and clients work together collaboratively in order to meet the Strategic Forum's targets of having 20% in value of projects delivered through integrated teams by the end of 2004, with this target rising to 50% by the end of 2007. The assistance gained from the Tool Kit, however, is not so much that it contains any contract terms but that it is intended to represent a set of common processes and tools for the parties to adopt in working collaboratively. By adopting and implementing those behaviours, it is expected that common issues (e.g., as to time, cost and quality) will be addressed in a consistent and collaborative manner. With this behavioural and procedural infrastructure in place, contracts can then be formulated (and perhaps some of the currently published standard forms revised) to support the parties' agreements. Contracts, in the views of the authors of this Chapter, should support established commercial objectives rather than set their own objectives ahead of where the industry currently is at any given point in time.

Another issue for the industry to be wary of concerns the potential for parties to regard collaborative working as an easy option and the adoption of a standard form partnering contract as a panacea. The reverse is in fact true. Collaborative working requires careful pre-planning and close management of all the various inputs (design, manufacturing know-how, installation expertise, cost and value management, hands-on project management, explicit risk management and so forth). Parties entering into partnering agreements who focus simply on cultural behaviour changes rather than managing risks may find that rose-tinted glasses obscure their vision. When some of their aspirations start to unravel because the risks that impact time, cost or quality issues have not been addressed in a robust manner, the project and participants suffer.

It is also worth recalling that the construction industry doews not operate in a vacuum but exists to serve its customers. The businesses and operations of those customers are required to be ever more efficient, whether to meet both private or public sector investments and value returns. Just-in-time production, concurrent design, supply chain management and best value are neither inventions of the construction industry nor are they confined to the construction industry. The industry's customers expect improvements in their own businesses and are looking increasingly to construction to demonstrate similar improvements in delivery. Standard form partnering contracts have their part to play in delivering these improvements but cannot deliver it by themselves.

Moreover, the processes and products that underpin partnering in the UK construction industry are not confined to the UK but have a global application. The globalisation of partnering already has a firm basis. The alliancing approach pioneered in the oil and gas sector is practised in other jurisdictions beyond the UK and has been applied in other sectors, such as transport. Moreover, the Tang Report (produced by the Construction Industry Review Committee in Hong Kong in 2001) echoes many of the ideas and recommendations of Egan.

The current Chief Executive of Constructing Excellence, Professor Dennis Lenard, has emphasised the UK construction industry's potential to become a world leader, pointing to the UK Construction Best Practice and PPP initiatives as having taken the industry about 40% of the way. The globalisation potential of partnering presents an exciting opportunity for the first generation of partnering standard forms. Will the UK again lead the way with its partnering standard forms forming the basis of procurement procedures in the global construction market in the same way that the ICE standard form was adopted as the model for the FIDIC forms for international contracting?

Finally, we will await with interest how the judiciary continues to respond to the industry's cultural change. In our view, the battleground of change will tend to centre upon legal certainty of the written word of the contract as against the day to day intent of the parties. There is no doubt that the culture change in the industry will assist in the goals of partnering being achieved. It must be sensible to create a more integrated approach through supply chain management to achieve better value for money and a quality product completed on time. It must also be in the industry's interest to communicate in a more open and transparent way. It must be in the industry's interest to avoid, if not eliminate, confrontation. However, this remains an industry where cash is very much king. When the cash starts to run out, those involved tend to fall out, notwithstanding what may be the good intentions of partnering. In the long-term, the cultural change of partnering will change the approach and attitude of the parties involved and in particular to the industry's most sensitive issues of time, cost and quality. In the meantime, the cynical die-hards may maintain that partnering contracts are simply moving the deckchairs on the *Titanic*.

CHAPTER 9

INTELLECTUAL PROPERTY RIGHTS

Mike Butler[1]

INTRODUCTION

Intellectual property consists of a range of distinct but related rights. The most well known of these rights are copyright, design rights (registered and unregistered), patents and trade marks. In addition, there are a number of other rights, including rights in confidential information, the law of passing-off and a new right which protects databases.

In the context of the construction industry, copyright is the most important right. Copyright will subsist in architects' drawings, engineers' designs, and software created in the design process, together with models and mark-ups. On the one hand, copyright is a very powerful right as it is able to grant monopoly rights from one dimension to the next; a building made in three dimensions will infringe the copyright in the original two-dimensional drawings unless the appropriate authorisations have been obtained. On the other hand, copyright serves only to protect against copying; it does not protect against the "borrowing" of ideas. The limits of copyright are examined in this chapter.

Understanding the scope of the intellectual property right, however, is only part of the equation. Intellectual property rights are, as they state, "property rights" and, like property, can be sold and leased (licensed). Any partnering arrangement needs to take into account how these property rights will be regulated as between the parties (particularly on termination of the arrangement).

This chapter examines the following issues:
- the first section looks in detail at copyright and considers two construction related case studies;
- the next four sections look more briefly at the other forms of intellectual property rights: design rights, patents, trade marks and confidential information;
- the next two sections look at ownership issues around intellectual property and how licensing can be used to achieve the same ends as ownership; and

1. Solicitor, Commercial and Intellectual Property, Hammonds.

- the eighth section examines specific terms used in partnering and other construction arrangements.

COPYRIGHT

Introduction

Unlike some of the other rights discussed in this chapter, copyright arises automatically and is a non-registrable right. As such, there is no register of copyright works (as there is, for instance, for patents or trade marks) and the owner of copyright need take no formal steps whatsoever in order to maintain the right.

Definition

Copyright is the right to prevent unauthorised copying of a "work". The current legislation applicable in the UK is the Copyright, Designs and Patents Act 1988 (CDPA).

Subject-matter

Copyright will automatically subsist in works that:

(1) are original;
(2) fall within the scope of the CDPA;
(3) are recorded in permanent form; and
(4) meet the qualifying criteria as regards author or country of publication.

Taking each of these individually:

(1) "Original" merely means that the work is the product of the creator's own effort and skill – essentially, that the work is not itself a copy. The test for originality is generally not regarded as being particularly onerous.

(2) The CDPA covers, amongst other things, "literary works" and "artistic works". Examples of literary works include "a computer program" and "a database", whilst artistic works include "graphic works" and "works of architecture being a building or a model for a building" and "works of artistic craftsmanship". The CDPA further defines graphic works as a "drawing, diagram, map, chart or plan" and buildings as "any fixed structure and a part of a building or fixed structure". This means that an architect's drawings are designs for an artistic work and fall within the scope of copyright protection.

(3) Copyright does not protect a mere idea. Consequently, no protection will arise for a "thought" until that thought has been set down in a permanent physical form. The distinction between what is an "idea" (which is not protectable) and what is the expression of that idea is not always an easy one – see page 196 for a discussion of a case (*Jones*) which demonstrates this issue.

(4) The author of the work in question must either fall into the category of a British national, a UK resident or a UK company. Alternatively, copyright protection is also afforded to works that were first published in various designated countries. The list includes the UK, the European Economic Area and many other countries with which the UK has a treaty obligation. As the UK is a signatory of various international copyright treaties, it is highly unlikely that a work will not qualify.

Consequently, assuming that all of the above criteria are met, not only do computer programs, databases, model buildings, drawings, diagrams, maps, charts and plans, all of which form the very basic tools of any construction project, qualify for copyright protection, but so does the final building itself.

For completeness, it is noted that the originality test for computer programs has recently changed to a requirement for "intellectual creation".

Ownership

Section 11(1) of the CDPA provides that the "author" of a work is the first owner of the copyright. The author is the person who creates the work. However, if the work was created by an employee in the course of his or her employment, then the employer is the owner. The important point to note is that commissioned works do not fall within the employer/employer rule and hence the copyright will remain with the author.

In simple terms, copyright will lie with either the author, the employer of the author, or the party performing the commission. The architect will be the owner of the copyright in his or her drawings and, interestingly, the owner of the copyright of the building. In complex projects, multiple architects or engineers may have been used for individual components and each of the individual authors will own the copyright in their drawings and the copyright in the part of the final building that is represented by these drawings. A single building can then encompass many independent copyrights.

Duration

The duration of copyright varies depending upon the nature of the copyright work. In respect of the copyright works detailed (ie literary and artistic works), the right lasts for 70 years from the end of the year in which the author dies. This means that it is possible that copyright may still subsist in buildings erected over 100 years ago.

Scope

As the owner of copyright in a work, the owner has the exclusive right to do, or to authorise others to do, certain prescribed acts (termed "restricted acts"), as defined in s. 16 of the CDPA.

These are:

(1) to copy the work;
(2) to issue copies of the work to the public;
(3) to rent or lend the work and/or copies of the work to the public; and
(4) to adapt the work or to do any of the above acts in relation to adaptation.

While the owner of the copyright can, of course, perform any or all of these acts, third parties may do so only with consent from the copyright owner, ie by the grant of a licence.

Infringement

In general terms, copyright protects against "copying". Copying of a work includes making a three-dimensional representation of a two-dimensional work (and vice versa). Therefore, constructing a building from an architect's design, without his or her consent, is an infringement of the copyright in that design.

The copyright in a work will be infringed by a party who, without the consent of the owner, undertakes any of the acts detailed in s. 16 of the CDPA in relation to:

(1) either the whole or a substantial part of the work; and
(2) either indirectly or directly.

Taking these two elements in turn:

(1) "Substantial part" has been the subject of much comment and discussion. The difficulty arises where some, but not all, of the work has been copied. Although a court would always look at the facts in each individual case, the general principle that has emerged is that the test is one of quality and not quantity. The copying of a small portion of a building may amount to infringement if that portion is important or significant to the design.

(2) While the meaning of "directly" is obvious, "indirectly" is intended to cover the situation whereby a copy is made of a work by means other than directly copying that work itself. For instance, copying a copy of the work or reproducing a work from a description may still amount to infringement even though the copy is made without direct sight of the work. Consequently, if an architect is given a detailed description of another building and asked to produce a similar design then the resulting design may still infringe the copyright in the original work.

Case studies

In *Cala Homes (South) Ltd* v. *Alfred McAlpine Homes East Ltd (No. 1)* [1995] FSR 818; *(No. 2)* [1996] FSR 36, the important players were Cala, a well-known company involved in the designing and building of houses, D, the design director of one of Cala's associated companies, and McAlpine, a company involved in the same line of business as Cala. By 1985, D had produced many designs for different styles of houses (the 1985 Designs) which where built around the UK by Cala. In 1987, Cala made the decision to standardise its range of designs and D set about producing a set of designs for this range, called the Standard House Range Designs (SHR Designs). However, D was unable to complete the task on his own and instructed an external firm of draughtsmen (HH). HH used the 1985 Designs as a base and produced many of the drawings for the SHR Designs. However, HH were given explicit instructions as to what changes to make to the designs by D.

In 1991, one of Cala's directors (R), left and moved to McAlpine where he was asked to undertake a review of their house range and produce a more standardised set of designs. R also instructed HH to help in the design process. HH's first draft of the new range for R was produced in the form of manuscript amendments to the SHR Designs. Eventually the drawings were completed and McAlpine built houses to the designs.

Upon learning of McAlpine's designs, Cala sued for copyright infringement on the basis that the McAlpine designs amounted to substantial reproductions of the '85 Designs.

The questions that arose before the court were:

(1) Did copyright subsist in the 1985 Designs? The court considered the requirements for copyright to subsist and decided that copyright did subsist in the 1985 Designs.

(2) Did HH or D (or indeed both) own the copyright in the SHR Designs? Whilst HH had actually drawn the SHR Designs, D had had extensive input as to their preparation. In effect, HH had acted more like "scribes", preparing the designs to D's instructions. Cala argued that copyright in the SHR Designs belonged to both D and HH as joint authors. It was of course in McAlpine's interest to show copyright vesting in HH exclusively and they argued that the standard RIBA (Royal Institute of British Architects) terms applied and that therefore copyright remained with the architect. On the facts, the judge found that, due to the provision of a high level of instruction and supervision by D, the copyright was held to reside with both HH and D as joint authors. Consequently, Cala, as D's employer was deemed to own the copyright in the SHR Designs jointly with HH.

(3) Had McAlpine copied the SHR Designs and therefore infringed copyright? The court found that McAlpine had substantially reproduced the 1985 Designs in the SHR Designs and infringed the copyright of Cala.

The *Cala* case shows that, even though HH had physically produced the SHR Designs, the amount of skill and labour (the "sweat of the brow" that copyright aims to protect) input by D meant that he, too, owned the copyright. Further, in *Cala*, the judge accepted that, where a series of drawings exist, with each one differing only slightly from the others, then it is not always possible to determine which was the original. In this case, copying one of the series still constituted infringement.

In *Jones* v. *London Borough of Tower Hamlets (No. 1)* [1996] 19 (11) IPD 19103, *(No. 2)* [2001] RPC 23, Jones (J) was instructed by a developer (A) to design a housing development in Bow. The housing market suddenly contracted and A was thrown into financial difficulty after partially building only one block of houses. Due to its financial position, A did not pay J. The local authority (TH) took over the development, had a further series of designs drawn up and eventually built a series of houses. J brought proceedings against TH alleging that it had copied his drawings, in particular the bathroom partition and "total design concept". TH claimed that any similarities were due to the physical limitations on the configuration of the site and not due to copying. During the case, the judge actually visited the site and, although similarities were evident and it did have the same "look and feel", he was satisfied that TH was correct in its assertion that such similarities were dictated by the site itself. The court stated that the "total design concept" or "general feel" of a project was not something that was capable of protection by copyright and therefore found against J in respect of this claim.

However, the court also found that the specific feature in the houses of the bathroom partition was such an ingenious and unique feature that it could not have been pure chance that J and TH had hit upon the same idea. It therefore found that TH had copied this aspect of the design. Interestingly, the court believed that TH had not consciously copied the design but had, having viewed J's designs earlier, subconsciously reproduced the design from memory.

The case is interesting as it shows that copyright protection lies in specifics (e.g., a design for a bathroom partition) rather than general features as to look and feel. Moreover, it demonstrates the limited nature of copyright protection: good ideas as such are generally not protectable.

Moral rights

In addition to copyright, the designers of buildings have additional rights known as "moral rights" which are related to but distinct from copyright. A moral right is a personal right of the actual person who created the work and cannot be transferred (assigned) to any other person. For example, a designer who creates a design will always own the moral right in the design but the copyright may have been transferred to the person commissioning the design.

(1) *Paternity right*: The paternity right is the right of the author to be identified as such when the work is published. In the context of artistic works (including works of architecture), the author has the right to be identified whenever the work is exhibited in public. Further, in respect of works of architecture, the author has the right to be identified whenever copies of the work or photographs of it are issued to the public. Finally, in the context of buildings, the author has the right to be identified on the building when constructed or, where more than one building is constructed, the right to be identified on the first one. Identification in this sense means clear and reasonably prominent wording stating who the author is.

The author of a work needs to have asserted his or her paternity right, that is, brought it to the attention of the third party, before he or she can enforce it.

(2) *Integrity right*: The integrity right is the right to prevent a work being subject to derogatory treatment. In essence, this means the right to object to an alteration or adaptation of the work that amounts to a distortion or mutilation of the work. In the world of construction, this right is limited to models of buildings and is infringed by the issue to the public of graphic works representing, or photographs of, a derogatory treatment of the building. In the case of the building itself, the right of the author is limited to demanding that the identification be removed.

Practical steps for protection

There are two practical steps that copyright owners should undertake to protect their copyright works.

First, the work should always carry a copyright notice in the form of "© Smith and Sons 2003", where the year denotes the year of first publication. While this is not legally required in most countries, including the UK, a notice of this sort will help to place third parties on notice that the work is subject to copyright protection.

Secondly, in order to enforce copyright, it will be necessary to prove ownership. As copyright is not registrable, there is no registration certificate to prove ownership and some other form of evidence must be obtained. It is important to retain documentary evidence either in the form of an assignment (see *Employee v. Contractor* on page 206) or original dated material, which is sufficient to show the identity of the true owner.

Database right

It was noted in the introduction that there is a new right which protects databases. This right is a separate right from copyright, although it shares some of its characteristics. This is a complex area of law, which needs to be borne in mind if the creation of databases features in any partnering arrangement.

UK DESIGN RIGHT (UNREGISTERED)

Introduction

Design right, as the name suggests, protects designs of articles provided that they are original and not commonplace. Although the terminology is confusingly similar, a design (or unregistered design right, as it is often called) is a separate and distinct right from that gained via registered design right; this is discussed briefly below. The principle behind unregistered design rights is to give industrial designs – for example, designs of tools – legal protection but not as much protection as is given to copyright works.

Definition

Design right is the exclusive right to prevent the unauthorised manufacture of articles to that design. Design right may also be used to prevent the sale of infringing designs, their possession for commercial purposes, or their importation into the UK .

Subject-matter

Design right will automatically subsist in designs that:

(1) are original;
(2) are not excluded by the CDPA;
(3) meet the qualifying criteria as regards the designer, employer or first marketer; and
(4) have been recorded in a design document.

Taking each of these individually:

(1) Original bears the same meaning as for copyright ie that the work is not itself a copy.

(2) The CDPA specifically excludes the following:

(a) a method or principle of construction (CDPA, s. 213 (3)(a));
(b) features of shape or configuration of an article which enable the article to be connected to, or placed in, around or against, another article so that either may perform its function.
(c) features of shape or configuration of an article which are dependent upon the appearance of another article of which the article is intended to form an integral part;

(3) In order to qualify for design right protection, the design must meet certain criteria. In essence, the designer must be a citizen of the EU or another country to which the CDPA has been extended; or the employer or commissioner (including a company) must be such a citizen. If neither of these applies, then a design may still qualify for protection if it is first marketed by a qualifying individual in a qualifying country. A qualifying individual is a citizen of a qualifying country which includes the EU.

(4) Design right cannot subsist until the design has been recorded in a design document or an article has been made to the design.

Ownership

Section 214 of the CDPA says that the designer is the person who creates the design. In the case of computer-generated designs, the designer is the person who undertakes the arrangements necessary for the creation of the design.

The designer is the owner of the design right, except where the design is created in the course of employment, or under a commission, in which case the employer or the commissioner, as appropriate, is the owner of the design right (CDPA, s. 215). Consequently, the position with design right is the opposite of that for copyright, because the design right in commissioned designs automatically flows to the commissioner.

Scope and infringement

The owner of design right has the exclusive right to produce the design for commercial purposes by either:

(1) making articles to that design; or
(2) by making a design document recording the design for the purpose of enabling such articles to be made.

Design right is infringed by a person who, without the licence of the design right owner, does, or authorises another to do, anything which is the exclusive right of the owner. The reproduction of such articles is defined as meaning copying the design so as to make articles exactly or substantially to that design.

Duration

Design right is a relatively short-lived right. The right exists for either 15 years from the end of the calendar year in which the design was first recorded in a design document (or an article was made to the design), or ten years from the end of the calendar year in which the first articles were made available for sale, whichever is the shorter period.

Practical steps for protection

As with copyright, design right arises automatically and there is no register or public record of ownership. Designers should, therefore, keep detailed records and evidence which is sufficient to prove ownership. It is recommended that the designer should sign and date design documents and also keep records of the design process. The date of first marketing should also be noted as this date is the key to determining the date from which design right exists. Although there is no official requirement or format for marking articles, it is advisable for all such goods to be marked with the words "design right", the name of the design right owner and the year of first marketing.

Interrelationship between design right and copyright

UK design right and copyright cannot subsist simultaneously in the same article or design. In effect, copyright will override and replace design right and vice versa.

Section 51 of the CDPA restricts copyright to those articles which fall within the definition of "artistic works". If an article is an artistic work, it will be subject to copyright protection – as will be the design of an article which, once designed, is an artistic work. As mentioned previously, this includes works of architecture and buildings. Accordingly, an architect's drawings will be protected by copyright and not design right.

If an article, once designed, is not an artistic work, design right will be appropriate. This could apply (for example) to a chair or desk that is not, for the purposes of CDPA, a work of artistic craftsmanship.

COMMUNITY DESIGN RIGHTS

Definition

The law relating to designs has recently undergone a marked change in the UK. A European directive seeks to harmonise UK design law with that of the European Union and a European regulation has introduced an entirely new community registered design right. The community registered design right is expected to be in force in 2003.

Community design right (in the case of unregistered designs) runs parallel to the UK unregistered regime, allowing two sets of rules to apply to certain designs. A design is protected by the right to the extent that it is new and has individual character.

It is felt that copyright will continue to be the most important right for the construction industry.

Requirements

To qualify for protection as a registered right, the design must:

(1) be new; although this is a world-wide test, it excludes disclosures that "could not reasonably have become known in the normal course of business to the circles specialised in the sector concerned operating within the community";

(2) have individual character; ie the overall impression it produces on the informed user must differ from the overall impression produced on a user by any design which has been made available to the public before; and

(3) not be excluded from protection; any designs that are dictated by technical function are not registrable.

Ownership

The author is the owner of the design, save for where he or she is employed or working under commission, when the design is owned by the employer or commissioner respectively (the same position as for unregistered design right).

Rights acquired

The owner of a registered design has the broad right to prevent the unauthorised use of the design.

Duration

A registered design is registered for a five-year period and a further four extensions of five years are available, giving a total of 25 years of protection.

PATENTS AND TRADE MARKS

Introduction

The area of patent law is complex and, while it is not impossible to imagine a patentable invention arising out of a construction project, it is likely to be infrequent. This subsection is therefore only a brief overview of the relevant points.

Both physical articles and methods/techniques are capable of gaining patent protection. Patents could be sought, for example, in respect of a new method of inserting foundations as well as in respect of inventions.

Anyone believing that they have a patentable invention or technique:

- *should not* publicise the invention. A patent by its very nature is a "new" invention; it must not therefore be known to anyone other than the inventor; and
- should immediately seek the specialist help of a patent lawyer or patent agent.

Definition and scope

Patents protect new inventions and methods/techniques. A patent is a monopoly right; it gives the owner exclusive rights to exploit the invention and to prevent others from doing so. The current law relating to patents in the UK is set out in the Patents Act 1977.

Requirements

There are four requirements that an invention must fulfil to gain protection as a patent:

(1) the invention must be new, i.e., the invention must not have been known beforehand: the information within the patent must not form part of any published material anywhere in the world;

(2) it must involve an inventive step; this step must not be obvious to a person with ordinary skill in the particular area;

(3) it must be capable of industrial application; ie in the broadest sense, it must be capable of being made or used in industry; and

(4) it must not be excluded; the Patents Act 1977 sets out certain categories that are explicitly excluded, for instance mathematical methods, computer programs and methods for the treatment of humans or animals by surgery.

Ownership

The inventor will normally be the owner of the patent. However, in common with many intellectual property rights, the employer may be the owner of the patent if the invention was made during the course of the inventor's employment.

Application procedure and rights acquired

Patent rights may only be obtained via registration. Advice from a qualified patent attorney is crucial.

A patent is a national right and it enables the proprietor to stop third parties making, importing, selling or keeping the object that is the subject of the patent.

A patent lasts, subject to the payment of renewal fees, 20 years from the date of application.

Trade marks and passing-off

Trade marks are brands under which businesses offer services or goods. Each party to a construction project will undoubtedly already have its own trade marks and these will be unaffected by the partnering process. Trade marks are a registered right which can last indefinitely. This is a vast area of the law and is beyond the scope of this chapter.

There is perhaps one possible scenario whereby the project partners may wish to consider trade marks and that is if they decide to manage the construction project under a new joint "umbrella" brand name. If so, it is strongly recommended that the parties seek expert guidance from either a trade mark lawyer or trade mark attorney.

The opening of this chapter also referred to the right of passing-off. This is a right (given by the courts) to protect the goodwill in brands, names and other types of material which distinguish a business (e.g., packaging) even if no registered trade mark exists. Again, this is beyond the scope of this chapter.

CONFIDENTIAL INFORMATION

Introduction

The purpose of patents is to reward an inventor for publishing the invention by allowing him or her a certain fixed period of exclusive use. However, most technically valuable information will not qualify for patent protection. In these circumstances, the law of confidence is used to give some protection to information which the owner wishes to keep secret.

The law of confidence is the one area of intellectual property law where ideas may be protected. But this will only be for as long as the information is secret. Breaches of rights of confidence are difficult to prove so it is prudent to obtain extra contractual protection; this is explored below.

Types of information that may be confidential

Broadly speaking, two types of confidential information are recognised: commercial information (customer details, pricing strategies, etc) and technical information (recipes, know-how, formulae, etc).

Requirements

Rights in confidential information are fragile and will only be upheld where the confidentiality of the information has been maintained. This means that information in the public domain is not protected. For example, confidential techniques may have been used to produce a product but, once that product is in the marketplace, it is legitimate for people to reverse-engineer the product to understand the techniques behind it.

The case of *Coco* v. *A N Clark (Engineers)* [1969] RPC 41 sets out the three criteria necessary to assert a right of confidence:

(1) the information must have the necessary quality of confidence attached to it (i.e., it must have some value and importance);
(2) the information must be passed to a third party in circumstances imparting an obligation of confidence; and
(3) the confidential information have been used in an unauthorised manner to the detriment of the party that disclosed the information.

If we examine each of these in turn:

(1) *Necessary quality of confidence*: There is no requirement that, in order to be treated as confidential, information must pass tests as to novelty or level of inventiveness. It is sufficient that the initial idea or inspiration is identifiable, original and of potential commercial application. This will include information gleaned from publicly available information but interpreted or combined in such a way as to produce a result that could only be obtained by a third

party carrying out exactly the same process. Trivial information and information within the public domain will not be protected.

(2) *Obligation of confidence*: Information will only be protected if the person receiving it is made aware that it is confidential. However, it is not necessary to state explicitly that the information is confidential. If the information is handed over in such a manner that the reasonable man would realise that the information was confidential, then it will be protected notwithstanding the fact that no explicit promise or statement was made.

An example of where the law implies the obligation of confidence is the relationship of employer and employee. An employee owes a duty to his or her employer to act at all times in the employer's best interests; information which the employee learns or creates during the course of his or her employment will be protected. Upon leaving employment, the duties owed to the ex-employer are considerably more limited. (*Faccenda Chicken Ltd* v. *Fowler* [1986] 1 All ER 617). In short, only information which may be regarded as a trade secret (for example, details of technical processes) will be protected after termination of employment.

(3) Used in an unauthorised manner: Any use or disclosure of the information for purposes outside the scope for which the information was originally intended may be deemed an unauthorised use.

Ownership

Confidential information is owned by the person who has or acquires the knowledge without use or disclosure obligations. It is important to realise that rights in confidential information are not monopolistic and, if a third party acquires or generates the same confidential knowledge independently, then that party will also have ownership together with equivalent rights of use and disclosure.

Duration

Confidential information has no limit in time. The right will exist so long as the information remains confidential. The rights will be lost once the information becomes public.

Non-disclosure agreements

Having to rely on uncertain rights to protect valuable information is far from ideal. The vast majority of disclosures of confidential information take place within the context of a written contract. These are often called non-disclosure agreements (NDAs). The purpose of these agreements is to remove uncertainty and to seek to define the rights, remedies, nature of the information, and limitations on its further use and disclosure, in order that both parties have no doubt as to their rights/obligations.

An NDA should always, as a bare minimum, cover the following three points:

(1) The definition of the confidential information: Clearly defining the information sits at the very heart of the NDA and is in effect the keystone of the arrangement. The disclosing party will always seek a broad definition, while the recipient will want a very narrow definition. For the recipient, it is equally important to include clear statements as to what does not constitute confidential information, for instance "information currently in the recipient's knowledge".

(2) The rights and restrictions upon the receiving party: Once the receiving party has the information, it must be left in no doubt as to what it may do with it. It is therefore in the interests of both parties to set out clearly what use may be made of the information and what, if any, further disclosures may be made. For instance: can a company disclose the information to its fellow group companies?

(3) The purposes for which the information has been disclosed: The reason for the disclosure is important as it gives the context of and the reason for the agreement. The rights, restrictions and nature of the information may then all be interpreted in the context of the purpose for which the information has been disclosed. Both parties should seek a tight and specific definition.

In practical terms, it is recommended that, wherever confidential information is to be disclosed or exchanged, the parties should enter into an NDA. If, however, there are real concerns that the information will not be protected, the ultimate practical protection is not to disclose it at all.

OWNERSHIP

Introduction

The parties involved in a project will, if the project is to be successful, work closely and collaboratively. Increasingly (aided by electronic tools such as web-based technology), design work is an iterative process, with multiple creators from different organisations. In intellectual property terms, these designs will create a flurry of rights: copyrights, design rights, confidential information and even patents.

The collaborative nature of design is specifically acknowledged in the ACA Project Partnering Contract (PPC 2000). Clause 8.2 provides:

"...each Design Team member shall contribute those aspects of the design of the Project that fall within its role, expertise and responsibilities as stated in the Partnering Documents. The Design Team shall work together and individually in the development of an integrated design, supply and construction process for the Project..."

However, where intellectual property rights are created jointly, the law is far from clear as to how those rights can be exploited by each of the parties. In the absence of an express written agreement detailing each of the parties' rights, there will be confusion (and potential legal action), particularly at the termination of a relationship.

Employee v Contractor

As noted above, the treatment of ownership of copyright is fundamentally different depending on whether the rights are created by an employee or by a contractor or consultant. The effect of the law is often at odds with commercial practice. While for architects the position is likely to be subject to the Royal Institute of British Architects' terms and conditions (see further, below), for other types of consultants, the law is clearly in their favour. A common complaint of commissioning parties is "I paid for it therefore I own it". This is not the case. The commissioning party needs either to have:

(1) obtained an assignment – this is effectively a sale of the copyright. To be effective this needs to be in writing and signed by the assignor (i.e., the consultant); or

(2) obtained a licence from the consultant – see further below.

Joint authorship and ownership

In the case of *Cala Homes*, noted above, the judge held that the draftsman and original designer were joint authors. However, any parties to a partnering arrangement who seek to rely on the law relating to joint authorship tread a dangerous path. This is illustrated by the case of *Robin Ray* v. *Classic FM Plc* [1998] FSR 622.

The claimant in this case was Mr Robin Ray, who acted as a consultant to Classic FM. Mr Ray used his expertise in the creation of a database which was used to determine which music should be played on the radio station. One of Mr Ray's tasks was to develop appropriate "fields" for use within the database. The copyright works in dispute in the case were five documents in which Mr Ray had gradually refined the fields to be used, and the catalogues of information provided by Mr Ray. Each of these works was included in the database produced and the database was the joint creation of Mr Ray and Classic FM.

The judge held that there was nothing in the collaboration between the parties whereby Classic FM contributed sufficient work (equivalent to "penmanship") to amount to a joint authorship of the works in question. Although Classic FM had done considerable work in setting the parameters within which the fields would be defined, this did not of itself give rise to co-authorship.

In any event, even if the judge had found that the parties were joint authors, this would still beg the question as to what rights each party had in relation to the exploitation of the works in question. In this particular case, the judge restricted the licence implied to Classic FM to the minimum necessary to give effect to the expected use contemplated by the parties when they entered into their relationship. This effectively restricted Classic FM to selling licences in the UK and not using the database worked on by Mr Ray to sell to foreign radio stations.

It would not be unreasonable to think that the joint owners of intellectual property would be free to do with that intellectual property as and what they saw fit. Unfortunately, this is not the case and English law is far from clear on the extent to which joint owners (in the absence of agreement) can use intellectual property which is jointly held. For example, if parties to a partnering arrangement agree to own jointly all the design work created, the position at law will be unclear as to the rights of each party to exploit that design work, both with respect to the project itself and in relation to any new projects an individual party may wish to undertake.

Section 173(2) of the CDPA provides that any reference in the CDPA to the copyright owner is a reference to all copyright owners. The consequence of this provision is that, in order for a co-owner to use or exploit the copyright in a work, there must be unanimous consent between all the co-owners. This means that a co-owner of copyright may not even copy the work (let alone license it) without the permission of all co-owners. The position in English law contrasts starkly with the US position, where co-owners of copyright are free to use and exploit jointly-owned works, provided they account to each other for appropriate shares of the profits.

Even more confusingly, the position on co-ownership is not the same for all types of intellectual property rights. For example, s. 36(3) of the Patents Act 1977 provides that a co-owned patent may not be licensed without the consent of all the co-owners. But, on the other hand, each co-owner is free to use the invention for his or her own benefit without the need to obtain consent from the other co-owners (Patents Act 1977, s. 36(2)). Accordingly, the legal regime which applies to patents is less restricted than that which applies to copyright.

Any co-ownership must therefore be regulated by appropriate contractual licence terms to avoid confusion. This can be demonstrated by the case of *Drummond Murray* v. (*1*) *Yorkshire Fund Managers*, (*2*) *Michael Hartley* [1998] 2 All ER 1015.

In this case, a team of six individuals came together with a view to purchasing the assets of a company in receivership. They approached Yorkshire Fund Managers for additional finance and, in the course of meeting Yorkshire Fund Managers, disclosed certain confidential information to them (in particular the business plan). Mr Murray (the claimant) was one of the team of six but was regarded by Yorkshire Fund Managers as being unsuitable. An employee of Yorkshire Fund Managers proposed to the other five team members that he should replace Mr Murray and they agreed; the new team (i.e., with the new employee) modified their investment proposals and finance was provided.

It was agreed in the case that there was no contract between the parties and there was no other form of legal relationship (such as a partnership) which could govern their rights in the information. The nub of the case was whether the other five members of the team could effectively authorise the use of the confidential information by the Yorkshire Fund Manager's employee without requiring the consent of Mr Murray.

In this particular case, the court adopted the view that there were no real limits on what each member of the team could do with the confidential information and that, accordingly, they had been free to use this information without the consent of all the parties involved. The case has been criticised as going beyond existing views in this area and allowing co-owners of confidential information to ride roughshod over the wishes of other co-owners in order to achieve commercial ends. In practical terms, what the case indicates is the difficulties of co-ownership and the need to regulate the position by the use of written agreements. In particular, anyone bringing valuable ideas to a partnering arrangement (ideas are not protectable by any other means other than confidential information), should agree appropriate non-disclosure agreements which prevent members of the partnership from using the information to his or her detriment or effectively removing him or her from the partnership.

LICENSING

Introduction

We have seen above that merely agreeing to be co-owners of intellectual property will be insufficient for the proper regulation of each co-owner's ability to use these rights outside the scope of the project. In order to ensure that each party in a partnering arrangement has fully secured ongoing rights to use intellectual property, it is important that the parties enter into licences to avoid later dispute as to their entitlement to use the intellectual property created in the course of the project. In most cases, these licences (often referred to as cross licences) can be as effective as ownership of the intellectual property rights themselves.

What is a licence?

A licence is a permission to perform some act that would otherwise be unlawful. For example, to copy a drawing without the licence of the architect is an infringement of the copyright. Fundamentally, a licence is a type of permission.

There is no requirement for a licence to be in writing. However, it would be very difficult to enforce (as a matter of evidence) a licence which is not in writing and therefore any licence of intellectual property rights should always be reduced to writing.

Terms applicable to licences

Invariably, there are a number of attributes which are common in licences. These attributes define the rights granted to the licensee and need to be looked at closely to ensure that the necessary rights have been secured. These common attributes include:

(1) *non-exclusive/exclusive*: an exclusive licence means that only the licensee can exercise the rights granted. For example, an author of books will commonly grant to a publisher the exclusive right to publish the work in all media. This means that, even though the author retains ownership of the copyright, the copyright in the work could not be licensed to another publisher to publish the work. If a licence does not state whether it is exclusive or non-exclusive, the general principle is that the licence will be non-exclusive.

(2) *duration*: the general principle is that a licence is revocable at any time by the licensor (i.e., the owner) on reasonable notice. Accordingly, in a partnership arrangement, if there is a wish to have the right to use the intellectual property post-termination for an indefinite period, it is important that the licence should state this. This can be achieved easily by using the words "irrevocable" and/or "perpetual" (preferably both).

(3) *payment*: the licence may attach details of the payment required for the on-going use of the intellectual property rights licensed. Where no payment is required, the custom is to use the words "royalty-free".

(4) *territory*: licences may be limited as to the territory in which the rights may be exercised.

(5) *scope*: the licence will invariably be limited as to the nature of the way in which the rights licensed may be utilised. This is clearly a key feature in any partnering agreement whereby licensed rights are generally limited to use in connection with the completion of the project (see further under *Industry terms* on page 210). The scope of any licence needs to be considered particularly in the context of any termination of a relationship – for example: will a party have an on-going right to use jointly created intellectual property to complete the design without the co-owners? Will each of the co-owners be able to use the jointly created intellectual property for other projects?

(6) *subject matter*: the licence will define what rights are being licensed. There is a common distinction made between the pre-existing rights a party brings to a project (background intellectual property) and rights created in the course of the project (foreground intellectual property). Different licence terms will attach to each of these types of rights.

Express v implied licences

A written licence (customarily included within a contract covering all aspects of the parties' relationship) is an express licence and will be interpreted in accordance with what is written down. However, even when no written document exists, the law will imply licences where this is necessary to make sense of the commercial relationship.

For example, in cases where there is no contractual term which addresses copyright, the legal position is that, once the architect instructs a quantity surveyor or engineer and provides them with the drawings, the court will imply a licence in favour of the owner of a building to construct the building using the drawings (see *Blair* v. *Osborne & Tompkins* [1971] 2 QB 78).

Implied licences, by their nature, are rife with uncertainty. For example, even though, in the situation above, there is an implied licence for the owner to construct the building using the drawings, is there also an implied term that this licence may be revoked if the architect has not been paid his fees? This was considered in the case of *Ng* v. *Clyde Securities* (1976) 1 NSWLR 443 in which the judge said:

"In my view, it is not reasonable to imply a term that the licence, once granted and acted upon, may be revoked in the event of subsequent non-payment. This is particularly so when, as here, a licence for immediate use of the copyright is granted in return for promises of payments at the dates of future events contingent on its use. The withdrawal of the licence would not merely affect the future activities of the licensee but, by preventing the completion of a building, would render valueless what might be an enormous past investment in the building."

The position above has now been clarified by the RIBA terms and conditions (see further under *Industry terms,* below) but the judgment above indicates the uncertainty of relying on implied licences.

INDUSTRY TERMS

Introduction

The concept of partnering in the context of intellectual property rights needs to be balanced with the fact that the rights created in any project are a form of property and need to be dealt with accordingly. In particular, it is not sufficient simply to rely on co-ownership to protect one's interests. The exact extent of any licence granted under a partnering arrangement needs to be looked at closely.

PPC 2000

Clause 9.2 of PPC 2000 provides:

"Each Partnering Team member shall retain Intellectual Property Rights in all designs and other documents that it prepares in relation to the Project, and as beneficial owner grants to the Client and the other Partnering Team members an irrevocable, non-exclusive, royalty-free licence to copy and use all such designs and documents for any purpose relating to completion of the Project and (only in regard to the Client) the Operation of the Project, in all cases with the right to transfer and sub-license such rights for the same purposes, and shall ensure that such licence shall have the support of such rights from third parties as are necessary to allow the grant of such licence."

Partners seeking to rely on this clause will need to think carefully as to whether it is sufficient for their purposes. The licence granted is both limited in its subject matter (it relates only to documents prepared by one partnering team member in relation to the project) and as to its scope (these documents can only be used in relation to the completion of the project). Where partners have engaged in a truly collaborative project where it is not possible to identify who has prepared specific documents (on the basis that they have been prepared by a range of partners) and there are opportunities for exploitation of these rights beyond the project, then PPC 2000 will not be sufficient.

RIBA terms

The Standard Form of Agreement for the Appointment of an Architect (SFA/99) as published by RIBA contains specific provisions dealing with a client's entitlement to use drawings created by the architect. This express copyright licence is set out at clause 6 as follows:

"The Architect owns the copyright in the work produced by him in performing the services and generally asserts the right to be identified as the author of the artistic work/work of architecture comprising the project.

The Client shall have a licence to copy and use and allow other consultants and contractors providing services to the project to use and copy drawings, documents and bespoke software produced by the Architect in performing the services hereinafter called 'the material', for purposes related to the project on the site or part of the site to which the design relates.

Such purposes shall include its operation, maintenance, repair, reinstatement, alteration, extending, promotion, leasing and/or sale, but shall exclude the reproduction of the Architect's design for any part of any extension of the project and/or for any other project unless a licence fee in respect of any identified part of the Architect's design is stated in schedule 3.

Provided that:

(a) the Architect shall not be liable if the material is modified other than by or with the consent of the architect, or used for any purpose other than that for which it was prepared, or used for any unauthorised purpose;

(b) in the event of any permitted use occurring after the date of the last service performed under the agreement and prior to practical completion of the construction of the project, the client shall:

   (i) where the Architect has not completed detailed proposals (work stage D), obtain the Architect's consent, which consent shall not be unreasonably withheld; and/or

   (ii) pay to the Architect a reasonable licence fee where no licence fee is specified in schedule 3;

(c) in the event of the Client being in default of payment of any fees or other amounts due, the Architect may suspend further use of the licence on giving seven days' notice of the intention of doing so. Use of the licence may be resumed on receipt of outstanding amounts."

In essence, the RIBA forms of appointment are stating that the client can only reproduce the architect's design by executing the project if the architect has completed a scheme design and any fees due to it have been paid. Arguments may arise as to what entitlement the client has to use the architect's drawings if it no longer wishes to use the architect following completion of work stage D (scheme design which encompasses application for planning permission). The industry has tended to proceed on the basis of the belief that, if planning permission has been obtained on the basis of an architect's drawings, the project cannot proceed without infringing that architect's copyright (unless obviously a licence has been obtained). However, as noted above in the case of *Jones*, if all the client is doing is taking the ideas within the drawings, then there is no copying of the drawing and no infringement of copyright.

A further issue arises as to the architect's position should his client become bankrupt or liquidated with his fees unpaid. In these circumstances, the issue is whether the purchaser of the site can use the architect's plans to complete the building. If the RIBA terms of appointment have been entered into (or a court implies that they apply as a result of the normal terms of engagement of the parties), then the architect will be able to rely on clause 6.2(3) to revoke the licence for non-payment of fees. In contrast, if the RIBA terms do not apply, it is possible that the purchaser will have an implied licence and the architect's remedy will be simply to claim against the client for damages (as an unsecured creditor).

Where the architect's fees have been paid, there are numerous cases which state that there is an implied licence given to the original client's successors (e.g., on a sale or liquidation) to use the architect's plans in connection with the project. Otherwise, architects would have particularly strong rights to stultify projects notwithstanding they have been paid.

It should also be noted that the ACE Conditions of Engagement (1998, 2nd edition) provide for similar types of provisions with respect to the copyright owned by the consulting engineer. Again, the consulting engineer retains ownership of the copyright in the drawings and grants a licence for a range of purposes in connection with the project. The consulting engineer can terminate this licence on seven days' notice if the fees due under the agreement have not been paid.

Before concluding it is worth touching briefly on the other forms of partnering agreements which have been discussed elsewhere in this book. These are not examined in any detail since, unlike PPC 2000, the majority of these contracts are not generally considered to be multi-party partnering contracts, but operate as bilateral contracts working under a partnering umbrella. Consequently, they do not take the debate concerning the extent of intellectual property provisions in partnering type arrangements that much further.

The JCT Partnering Charter and the ECC Partnering Option X12 unsurprisingly do not contain specific provisions dealing with intellectual property rights (although the ECC Partnering Option does acknowledge that there may be joint design development in the definition of Partnering Information) since they are intended to operate within a specific contractual framework. The provisions dealing with the design obligations and intellectual property will be contained in the underlying construction contracts, such as clauses 21 and 22 of the ECC core clauses.

In the case of the Be Collaborative Contract, each supplier will enter into its own Purchase Order, with the related Collaborative Construction Terms in addition to a project protocol. As is to be expected of any form of construction contract, the Terms do contain express provisions dealing with copyright and patents (clauses 7.14 and 7.15). These clauses provide for the supplier to grant "an irrevocable, assignable, royalty free licence to use, copy and reproduce all designs and related documents prepared in connection with the Services" and for the supplier to indemnify the purchaser against patent infringements.

Although the M4i Consultation Draft is intended to be a multi-party partnering contract, as yet the Draft contains no specific reference to intellectual property rights. Clause 9 lists, amongst the responsibilities of the project team members, the "preparation of designs and drawings", but the details of this obligation has yet to appear.

KEY MESSAGES

There is a range of practical steps which should be implemented to afford protection to intellectual property, a number of which have been touched on in this chapter. In the context of partnering, there is a number of key messages as follows:

(1) co-ownership is fraught with difficulty under English law. Those agreeing to own rights jointly must also ensure that appropriate licences are put in place to secure on-going rights outside the project;

(2) the standard partnering terms (e.g., PPC 2000) are useful but do not secure all the rights required. In particular, it is necessary to include specific licensing terms to cover any right to use intellectual property once the partnering relationship has finished;

(3) the RIBA terms give architects fairly strong rights in relation to non-payment of fees and this needs to be borne in mind if they are used in the context of a partnering arrangement; and

(4) co-ownership of confidential information is a particularly vexed area and should always be regulated by written agreement.

CHAPTER 10

INSURANCE IN A CHANGING INDUSTRY

Katie Graham[1]

INTRODUCTION

The Latham and Egan reports, the handbook of supply chain management *Building Down Barriers*, the advance of project partnering and strategic alliances, the introduction of PPC 2000 and the wealth of literature which has been published as a result, have all paved the way for a new or at least an improved approach within the construction industry to the procurement of projects. There has been a determined move away from the traditionally adversarial approach in many substantial projects although such changes are clearly taking time to materialise. It is necessary for all the team players concerned, including the client "end user" to fully understand and "buy in" to this collaborative process, if it is to succeed in delivering overall best value.

The role of insurance has also had to change or at least adapt as dramatically to facilitate the advances described above. The scale of such change has been further affected by the wider impact on the insurance market as a whole following the terrorist events of 11 September 2001.

The purpose of this chapter is to:
- consider the relationship between the allocation of risk and insurance;
- discuss the various products currently available in the insurance market;
- consider the products which have been recently developed or which are in the process of being developed to facilitate the collaborative approaches in accordance with partnering and strategic alliancing arrangements;
- examine how insurance arrangements are dealt with in the context of the new PPC 2000 contract, the new Be Collaborative Contract, the M4i Model Form of Multi-Party Partnering Contract (M4i Consultation Draft), a generic Prime Contract and the new JCT Major Project Form (MPF) 2003 Edition;
- consider the impact of adjudication on insurance as a result of Part II of the Housing Grants Construction and Regeneration Act 1996 (which came into force on 1 May 1998);
- briefly review the overall impact of the events of 11 September 2001, over two years on.

---

1. Solicitor, Hammonds.

THE PURPOSE OF INSURANCE

General

It is widely accepted within the construction industry that projects are sensitive to an extremely large matrix of hazards and risks. The allocation of risks amongst the parties to the construction process has a direct bearing on the costs of the project. Unexpected conditions or events may cause the costs and time to increase. Robert J. Smith in his article "Risk Identification and Allocation: Saving Money by Improving Contracts and Contracting Parties" [1995] ICLR 40, considers contractual misallocation of risk to be the leading cause of construction disputes in the USA. According to William Young and Chandra Bhuta in their article "Effective Risk Apportioning in Contracts" [1996] 47 *Australian Construction Law Newsletter*, much the same appears to be the case in Australia.

Risk and insurance

Although risk and insurance are inter-related, there is a clear distinction between risk clauses and insurance clauses in construction contracts. An insurance clause is a clause which describes the risk to be insured and the person who must arrange the insurance. A risk clause is a clause which allocates responsibility for risk.

Although the contractor is ultimately responsible to the employer for loss or damage to the works (including sub-contract works) insurance of the works is generally in joint names with the employer. Strictly, the employer and contractor are co-insured, not joint names because they have different interests in the works. However, the effect is that each party is treated as being the policy holder and is therefore entitled to an indemnity from insurers and, significantly, not affected by a breach of an insurance policy condition by the other party. Taking out a joint named policy gives those parties named full entitlement to the policy as if each had taken out a separate policy.

The other way in which the benefit of a policy can be extended to other parties is when insurers agree to a waiver of subrogated rights. Normally, if an insurer has indemnified the insured in respect of a loss, the insurer then has the legal rights of the insured and can take proceedings in the insured's name to recover from any party legally liable. In the context of a building contract, this could be a sub-contractor, supplier or an individual employee or director of the contractor or the employer. However, if an insurance policy contains a waiver of insurers' subrogated rights then insurers agree not to seek to recover loss from any party to whom the waiver has been extended. Thus, in a policy containing a waiver of subrogation rights against a sub-contractor, the insurers would agree not to sue a sub-contractor to recover a loss suffered by one of the joint names. The sub-contractor does not become an insured party under the insurance policy and would not be able to make a claim himself; he is simply protected from being sued.

Standard forms vary in the extent to which they identify and deal with particular risks. Generally matters to be considered include:

- damage to the works prior to take-over;
- damage to the works after take-over;
- faulty materials and workmanship;
- thefts and vandalism;
- design defects;
- damage to the insured's property;
- damage to third party property;
- consequential losses from damages;
- injuries to the contractor's employees;
- injuries to the employer's employees; and
- injuries to third parties.

Allocation of risks

The philosophy which underlies most standard forms is that risks should be allocated to the party best able to control them. Thus take-over of the works by the employer is usually seen as a watershed in respect of the works. Up to that time the contractor has care of the works and is generally responsible for damage, whereas afterwards the employer becomes responsible – subject to the proviso that the contractor is responsible for any damage he causes whilst remedying defects.

Responsibility for damage or injury to third parties usually follows the cause but damage to the employer's property is the employer's risk in some contracts.

The contractor is almost invariably responsible for the quality of work and carries the risks of faulty workmanship and materials. Responsibility for defective design generally falls on the party which undertook the design but that is not always the case.

Excepted risks

Excepted risks, or the employer's risks as they are called in some contracts, are those risks which are expressly excluded from the contractor's responsibility.

Broadly the excepted risks fall into three categories:

- fault or negligence of the employer;
- matters under the control of the employer;
- matters not the fault of either party.

The logic of the first two categories is obvious enough; the argument of the third category, where it applies, is that the employer is the party better able to carry the risk.

Limitation on liability

Some contracts place limitations on liability of the contractor to the employer for his acts and defaults. Such limitations, however, apply only between the contractor and the employer and they do not protect the contractor against third party claims.

Typical insurance provisions

Construction contracts invariably impose insurance requirements on one or both parties to ensure that funds are available to meet claims and to facilitate the completion of the works. Some forms specify only the insurances which the contractor must carry. Other forms place obligations to insure on both parties.

The most common insurance provisions of construction contracts are:
- the contractor is responsible for care of the works until completion;
- the contractor must insure the works to their full replacement costs;
- the contractor must indemnify the employer against claims for injury to persons or damage to property;
- the contractor must insure against that liability;
- the contractor must insure against damage to the contract works themselves including site materials;
- the contractor must insure against third party claims or public liability insurance.

These areas are generally regarded as high risk areas where substantial claims may cause financial hardship resulting in delays to the contract. However, prudence or the demands of banks financing projects may dictate that wider insurances are purchased such as, environmental insurance and project delay insurance by way of examples. These insurances are dealt with in more detail on pages 224 and 227.

Policy wording

The wording of the actual insurance policy will also typically contain details of the minimum levels of cover, exclusions, levels of excesses/deductibles and a claims notification period which should be followed in the event of a claim. It is also worth noting that most insurances are liability based and are designed to protect the insured against legal liability – without a legal liability the insurers will not be prepared to indemnify the insured.

PRODUCTS CURRENTLY AVAILABLE AND IN GENERAL USE WITHIN THE INSURANCE MARKET

Professional indemnity insurance

Employers who engage consultants as designers almost invariably require that they carry professional indemnity insurance.

As the name of this insurance implies, it is to cover design liability for breaches of contract or negligence to clients and third parties in performing professional obligations. It is normally carried by professionals (and is compulsory for many members of professional institutions) such as architects, engineers, surveyors and project managers. However, if a contractor is carrying out design as part of his contractual obligations, he could obtain professional indemnity insurance to cover his design responsibilities.

Professional indemnity insurance is relatively expensive and some contractors or sub-contractors would not normally carry it. The employer therefore needs to consider whether or not it is actually needed.

An option often offered by contractors, particularly sub-contractors who carry out design, is product liability insurance. This insurance covers physical damage, personal injury or death caused by a defective product, e.g., cladding. However, it does not cover damage to the "product" itself, nor does it cover pure economic loss. It is generally an extension to a public liability policy, rather than a professional indemnity policy. It is therefore much narrower in scope than professional indemnity insurance.

For cover where consultants are the designers there are two main problems. Material damage and public liability policies are written on an "occurrence basis". The policy in force at the time of the damage is the policy which will be effective. As the contractor is only liable for damages during the course of the works (or when he is returning to carry out defects) and only liable for personal injury, death and damage to other property caused during the works, there is only a need for him to carry contractor's "all risks" insurance and public liability insurance during the period of the contract works.

Professional indemnity insurance however is written on a "claims made" basis, i.e., the policy in force at the time a claim is made is the policy which will be effective regardless of when the design was actually carried out. In respect of professional liability for design (and possibly also professional management), the claim could arise at any time in the six or 12 years of the professional/contractor's liability period. This means that professional indemnity cover needs to continue for the period of six or 12 years after the contract has ended for the employer to get full security from the existence of the professional liability insurance. This raises administrative problems in checking that the professional/contractor is continuing to comply with his insurance obligations. Normally also, there has to be provision for circumstances where the cost of professional liability insurance becomes prohibitive.

Most professional liability policies include a "series provision" which means that claims arising out of one event are treated as one claim and insurers only provide one limit of indemnity. *Mabey & Johnson Ltd* v. *Ecclesiastical Insurance Office plc* (unreported, QBD, Commercial Court 20/07/00) considered the position where there was no express "series" provision. Mabey & Johnson had built a steelwork bridge in Ethiopia which collapsed. They had also used the same structure in bridges in Peru and elsewhere, so the question arose whether claims in respect of each bridge would be one claim because they were a series of claims arising out of one event. Insurers argued either that (a) it was a necessary part of any policy providing a limit of indemnity in respect of each and every claim that claims arising out of one event would be treated as one claim, or (b) that a "series" provision was implied by custom and practice. The Commercial Court rejected both arguments; a series provision cannot be implied into an insurance policy.

Secondly, there is the problem that the legal responsibility of a professional designer is limited at common law to the exercise of reasonable skill and care and his professional indemnity cover is usually similarly limited. The issue of fitness for purpose in the context of a professional indemnity policy is discussed separately below under *Fitness for purpose* on page 221.

Notwithstanding the vagaries of the market and the type of cover available, it is sensible to seek confirmation from insurers that a particular contract is actually covered. This is surprisingly difficult to obtain in practice. Brokers and insurers will comment on the document but will rarely formally confirm cover. The attitude seems to be that they will wait until a claim arrives before committing themselves. In practice, the relevant consultant or contractor must satisfy themselves that the document is more or less in keeping with usual practice and not outside the policy.

Contractors' design

Contractors who undertake design in addition to their more traditional role of builder only can insure against negligence of their own designers. The cover is usually defined as being in respect of a negligent act, error or omission of the contractor in performance of his professional activities.

The need for such insurance arises because a contractor's "all risk policy" usually excludes design entirely or limits the indemnity to damage caused by negligent design to third party property or construction works other than those designed.

An ordinary professional indemnity policy does not cover the contractor against the problem of discovery of the design default before completion. At that stage there is no claim against the contractor as there would be against an independent designer. To overcome this, contractors usually seek a policy extension giving first party cover, i.e. cover for their own works. In effect this amounts to giving the construction department of the contractor's organisation a notional claim against the design department.

Contractor's all risks insurance

This type of insurance covers against any physical loss or damage to work executed and site materials, i.e., it is not limited to specific perils such as fire, flood or explosion. No policy, however, covers everything and exclusions will apply such as wear and tear or defects in design although in the case of the latter of these the consequences of defects in design can be covered.

Public liability insurance

The object of the public liability insurance is to protect the insured against his legal liability for bodily injury to third parties or loss of or damage to their property where such injury or damage occurs during the period of insurance in connection with the business insured by the policy.

FURTHER PRODUCTS ACCOMMODATING RISK IN PARTNERING ARRANGEMENTS AND STRATEGIC ALLIANCES

Fitness for purpose

The PPC 2000 and Prime Contracting Initiatives by way of examples impose on contractors and their supply chains the added obligation to provide an end product which is required to be "fit for its intended purpose". This requirement has in the past caused contractors and their supply chains concern due to the difficulties in obtaining this particular insurance cover. Although certain insurers have been willing to provide a specific "fitness for purpose" insurance cover in such circumstances (for an added premium), this cover is generally only provided as an extension to an existing professional indemnity insurance cover and insurers specifically request that these policies are subject to the said purpose being "identified in the Project Brief" (PPC 2000) or "Output Specification/Strategic Brief" (Prime Contracting).

Since the events of 11 September 2001, the availability of fitness for purpose insurance in the market cannot be guaranteed. Uninsurability is discussed further under *Hardening markets* on page 236. This will have to be a factor to be borne in mind by employers when evaluating tender bids for long term and large scale projects. It follows that although fitness for purpose is to remain a risk on the contractor, he may not be able to insure against it and ultimately an employer could face the option of having to sue the contractor out of his own pocket without the protection of an insurance fund in the event that the end product does not meet the purpose or purposes specified in the contract requirements.

Latent defects insurance

Latent (or inherent) defects or decennial insurance provides the insured, namely the owner/tenant/mortgagee of the property, with 10-year cover for the cost of repairing damage due to latent defects or, if the building is unusable, the cost of rendering it stable, which can be bought for a one-off premium.

Latent defects are the problem which is causing the focus of attention onto warranties, professional indemnity insurance and remedies under the law.

These problems have been foreseen for many years. In 1984, the National Economic Development Office set up a committee to consider the implications of latent defects, with the task of assessing and seeking ways of improving economic performance. The NEDO "BUILD" Report was published in October 1988 and received widespread publicity. Its main conclusion was to recommend Building Users' Insurance against latent defects as the most satisfactory solution for all concerned; employer, developer, funder and tenant, together with the producers, both professionals and contractors. The essential elements of the recommended cover, as valid today as in 1988, can be summarised as follows:

(a) Non-cancellable material damage insurance: This cover is on a material damage basis and therefore does not rely upon proof of negligence or liability, merely that the damage falls within the policy cover.

(b) Protection for a period of 10 years from practical completion.

(c) Cover initially limited to the structure, including foundations and weather-proofing: Calls for much wider protection were considered unrealistic compared with the cover the market was willing to provide.

(d) Policy negotiated by the developer or building owner during the preliminary design stage: This is necessary to ensure that the insurers' monitoring agency, generally consultant engineers, have an opportunity to check the design as well as monitoring the construction process in order to issue a certificate of acceptance required by the underwriters.

(e) The Policy is transferable to successive owners and also allows tenants to be indemnified: This is essential to aid marketing.

(f) A waiver of subrogation rights against all those producing the building: This is the essence of BUILD; a no fault policy where the policy protects everybody.

(g) A single premium to cover insurance and the technical control.

(h) Inflation safeguards must be built in: This can be achieved by either increasing the sum insured by a pre-set annual percentage or allowing an option for increasing the sum insured during the period of cover.

(i) Realistic deductibles: These should be set at a level sufficient to impose discipline on both developers and producers. Ideally the apportionment between all participants could be agreed at the time of appointment rather than waiting until a claim arises.

(j) Risk assessment and verification to be undertaken by independent consultants appointed by the insurer.

The Latham Report, *Constructing the Team*, published in the summer of 1994, broadly accepted the recommendations of the BUILD Report. They formed part of the proposals for new construction legislation – The Latham Package. In spite of intensive lobbying, not least of all by the insurers, a lack of Government support meant that the Housing Grants, Construction and Regeneration Act 1996 did not include a provision for compulsory latent defects insurance. There were certainly too many unresolved issues to justify compulsion, although there was considerable support from the consultants and contractors, for whom it would have been an attractive solution to some of their risk exposure.

Unfortunately, despite the recent increase in support by the UK market, what is currently available in this market as latent defects insurance does not yet offer anything like a complete alternative to the various indemnity insurances available and which are outlined in this section. First and foremost, the employer has to pay extra to ensure that the consultants/contractors are not pursued by the insurer exercising their right of subrogation after they have paid a claim. Also, the excess under the policy is usually substantial and the employer will have to seek to recover this from the consultant/contractor.

A typical latent defects insurance policy only covers damage or instability - it will not help if there are financial losses or the equipment simply does not work or does not perform as expected. It will not reimburse the employer where work has to be re-done during the project because of errors in design or where there are delays in completion. This type of insurance is, however, a step in the right direction – the insurer is likely to still be there in six years time regardless of the fate of others in the meantime and the insurer will not be able to say that it does not want to be in that market any more. It is also arguable that an increase in latent defects cover will result in a decline in professional indemnity claims with the "knock on" effect of reducing premiums.

M&E latent defects

One of the major complaints which has been made by clients and their professional advisers alike over the past few years has been the failure of the standard latent defects policy to provide protection in respect of mechanical and engineering plant, where cover is, in essence, limited to defects in the structure or consequential damage to other parts of the building. Fortunately, breakthroughs are now being made and some insurers have successfully negotiated new policies with leading providers of engineering insurance and inspection services which will rectify this deficiency.

The new policy, like its structural counterpart, is for a 10-year period and is transferable to future owners, tenants and, indeed, funders. This policy is taken out on a material damage basis, paying for the repair of damage rather than in response to liability, although insurers will require subrogation rights against negligent contractors or consultants. There will be a monitoring and evaluation process during the design and construction stages and also active involvement in pre-commissioning -- the insurers want to know that the equipment works before they take over responsibility for its long-term condition. Following handover the normal statutory and other inspections will be carried out by the same insurer, who will also provide breakdown cover for the 10-year period alongside the latent defects policy. The policy will stand alone from any structural latent defects insurance and the existence of that cover is not a pre-requisite for the issue of the new engineering policy.

Environmental insurance

With the focus moving to longer-term partnerships and commercial relationships, the demand for environmental insurance cover has increased over the last 20 years and considerably in the past few years. This is separate from other liability policies and requires a detailed technical appraisal of the site to be covered. The relatively low number of policies issued to date results from a combination of high premiums and less than satisfactory cover. Both these are improving as the market and developers become aware of the requirements of their counterparts. Fuelled by the increasing reluctance of funders to be involved in contaminated sites and the need to regenerate urban areas there is no doubt that an acceptable insurance solution will emerge.

Many public liability and contractor's "all risk" policies either exclude cover for environmental damage or provide very restricted cover. This has led to the development of stand-alone policies which are often bespoke or focused on individual sites or facilities. The cover is generally for clean-up, allowing the sale of a property. There has been very little English case law on environmental insurance, although this will no doubt develop over the next few years.

Environmental liability may be to a third party, where the third party suffers damage to property or injury by a pollution incident, for example where pollution migrates from one side to another. Liability is based on the common law torts of nuisance, negligence or trespass, and on legislation relating to occupier's liability, i.e., the liability of the occupier of the site from which the pollution emanates.

The second form of liability is for clean-up costs, where a property has been damaged, or lost market value, for environmental degradation for which no one person can be held liable. It is possible to take out insurance against the expense incurred in cleaning up the site in order to comply with various environmental regulators, such as the Local Authority, Environmental Agency or the Scottish Environment Protection Agency, all of which have statutory powers to order clean-up or remediation to render a site suitable for use or sale.

Due to the difficulties in linking gradual pollution (i.e., seepage) to specific occurrences under the early policies, "claim-based" environmental policies are emerging. However, the effect of a claims-based policy is that insurance needs to be taken out every year to cover against the possible long-term effects of pollution, as claims may be made many years into the future.

Common exclusions, even now, are exclusions for gradual pollution, as opposed to accident-specific pollution. Loss or damage to the insured's own property is often not covered. Some policies may only cover named perils, for example, unintended fire or bursting of pipes, rather than giving more blanket coverage for any incident which causes pollution. Radiation is generally specifically excluded.

The types of policies available include:

(1) *Environmental impairment liability, sometimes known as pollution legal liability.* These policies cover liability to third parties for bodily injury, sickness, disease, psychiatric damage and property damage (including clean-up costs) from gradual pollution or sudden or accidental pollution incidents. These policies can be "claims made" (insurance responds only when a claim is made/submitted to the insurer during the period of insurance) or "occurrence" (claim attaches to the time the event occurred and the insurance in place at that time) worded. The duration of environmental impairment liability policies will depend on the wording of the policy ("claims made" or "occurrence" wording).

(2) *Environmental remediation insurance.* These policies may also be known as first party pollution clean-up policies. They cover the actual clean-up costs on a site, but not any claims from other parties in respect of the pollution. These policies are also unusually site-specific. Generally, the premiums are high for fairly limited cover. The insurers may require an environmental audit as a pre-condition to giving cover and liability may be excluded for any conditions which existed prior to the policy inception.

Pool Reinsurance Company Ltd schemes

Pool Reinsurance Company Ltd (Pool Re) is a mutual reinsurance company that is authorised to transact reinsurance business only for property and pecuniary classes of business. Any insurance company that is authorised either by the UK regulator or an overseas regulatory authority to transact property insurance in the UK is eligible to be a member of Pool Re. Lloyd's Syndicates are also eligible for membership. Members undertake to offer terrorism cover to clients who request it.

Insurance cover for damage arising from terrorist attacks was reviewed substantially in the early 1990s as a result of the IRA bombing campaign. The result was that insurers limited insurance cover for damage caused by fire or explosion as a result of terrorism up to a threshold of £100,000. Cover in excess of that amount was provided by Pool Re and its Pool Re scheme so ensuring that there was no coverage gap. The Pool Re scheme was backed by a government guarantee whereby the UK Government became liable as "insurer of last resort" should the pool ever be exhausted by a series of large claims.

Following the attack on the World Trade Centre in September 2001 substantial changes took place in the reinsurance market with regard to coverage for terrorism.

Post-11 September, insurers determined they were no longer in a position to continue to provide terrorist cover. Hence they applied exclusions in respect of damage caused by perils other than fire and explosion and also applied a wider definition of what constitutes an "act of terrorism" by reference to the Terrorism Act 2000. This is discussed further on pages 234–236, below. As a result of discussions which took place towards the end of 2001, HM Treasury announced its willingness to enter discussions with the insurance industry, Pool Re and other interested parties to review the operation of the scheme. In July 2002 announcements were made on the agreement that had been reached.

It was agreed that the scope of cover provided by Pool Re to its members would be extended. Rather than being restricted to "acts of terrorism" resulting in fire and/or explosion the cover is to be offered on an "all risks" basis. The existing nuclear exclusion is to be deleted and the only excluded losses after 1 January 2003 will be in respect of war risks and computer hacking and virus attack. However, it should be noted that the Pool Re scheme still refers to the narrower definition of terrorism as defined in the Reinsurance (Acts of Terrorism) Act 1993 as opposed to the wider definition in the Terrorism Act 2000.

At the same time, the practice under which Pool Re specifies the rates which are charged to the original insureds by members ceased from 1 January 2003. Insurers are now free to set their own terrorism premiums for their underlying policies according to normal commercial arrangements but Pool Re will continue to make reinsurance cover available. Members have a maximum loss retention per event combined with an annual aggregate limit which is based on the degree of their participation in the Pool Re scheme. The retention for each insurer is set annually as a proportion of an industry wide figure and advised to the member at the start of the relevant underwriting year. It is the intention that over the next four years the industry wide retention will be increased on the following scale:

Applying from	Per event	Per annum
1/1/2003	£30million	£60million
1/1/2004	£50million	£100million
1/1/2005	£75million	£150million
1/1/2006	£100million	£200million

At the same time arrangements under which Pool Re has been entitled to additional premium from members in respect of years that result in an underwriting loss and where members are entitled to premium rebates in respect of years that result in an underwriting profit will be discontinued. The payment of reinsurance commission to members has now ceased and Pool Re no longer controls the basis upon which members supply terrorism cover to their original insureds. For example, it no longer determines the intermediary commission which is to be paid by members. However, members continue to be obliged to provide terrorism cover in the terms of the scheme to those insureds who request such cover.

The amendments made to the Scheme in 2003 represent fundamental changes requiring a different approach on the part of Pool Re members as well as Treasury and Pool Re itself. The original insureds also face a new situation with regard to terrorism cover to which they will have to adapt.

2003 will be a transitional year and the way the new arrangements operate will be monitored closely by all of the interested parties.

Project delay insurance

Where projects are delayed for reasons which are not the responsibility of the contractor, the employer would not be normally be entitled to be paid liquidated and ascertained damages because the contractor would be entitled under the contract to claim additional time to complete the works.

Equally, if an insured risk occurs, such as a fire, or storm damage, the contractor is also given additional time to complete the works and liquidated and ascertained damages would not be levied against the contractor. There is available in the insurance market, a policy to cover this potential financial loss of use to the employer. The contractor is required to take out insurance which will pay damages at the equivalent rate of the liquidated and ascertained damages figure for the period of delay caused by an insurance risk event. Insurance premiums for the contractor are expensive.

An employer can himself take out insurance to cover project delays in completion of building works. Such insurance covers loss of profit during the period when the works cannot be used. Generally there is at least a 45-day non-insured period (when the employer will still rely on the liquidated and ascertained damages payable by the contractor to recover lost profits) as well as a maximum period of cover. Premiums on project delay insurance are generally lower than the contractor's premiums to cover liquidated and ascertained damages, so this is generally a more cost-effective method to cover economic loss. It is likely that an employer will require both forms of insurance to fully cover the potential economic loss of delay to the works.

Single project insurance

This type of policy of insurance has deliberately been left until last for discussion as it is one of the most important changes introduced by the insurance industry to address the need to accommodate partnering and strategic alliancing arrangements. The benefits of such a policy have been subject to some debate and further examples of its actual success on specific projects are required before the "jury" will finally decide on its true value as a means within the insurance sector of implementing the Latham and Egan objectives for collaboration and integrated team working on construction projects.

Single project insurance has developed due to the deficiencies of the more traditional insurance arrangements whereby an insurance policy taken out by any of the parties to a construction project only covered the liability for that party. Owing to the multiplicity of parties in a construction project, and because it is often very unclear as to which party's negligence or breach of contract actually caused any particular damage, much time, effort and costs have been wasted by insurers (or the parties themselves) attempting to determine which party is liable for the damage.

Arguably, one way to avoid this situation is to take out one "single project" insurance policy which covers all of the parties to a building project, and covers all the risks. Such insurance will be specific to one particular project. It is commonly taken out by the employer so that the employer has control over the amount insured and the conduct of claims. Project insurance is fully supported in the *Accelerating Change* report. The provision of such insurance is viewed as a tool to facilitate integrated working and to enable risk management issues to be fully addressed by the whole team. Integrated teams of the client, contractors, facility management contractors, design consultants, specialist contractors and key manufacturers are fundamental to the concept of partnering and to improvements in construction procurement.

Under a single project insurance, if an insured loss occurs (i.e., damage to property, liability of one party to another), the insurers simply pay as soon as it has been established that an insured loss has occurred.

As with any relatively new concept there are commentators who welcome and those who oppose the wide spread use of single project insurance. Consultants have argued, for example, that the "one-size-fits-all" approach is unfair. Clients also have expressed concerns with an untested system. Others such as Mr William J Gloyn (Chairman of Aon Ltd) have expressed concerns as to the cost-effectiveness of single project protection. He stated:

"I have to question whether the high premiums concerned make real economic sense. The practical difficulties of arranging the cover are also immense. Each professional has to provide considerable information about the whole range of his activities, not merely the project in question, including previous claims experience. It takes little imagination to appreciate the reluctance which would be encountered in this direction."

On the other hand, there is a growing belief that these policies have enormous benefit when an insured loss does occur because payment from the insurers is made much more quickly. There is no delay whilst liability for the loss is established. This enables the works to continue more quickly, and protects the cashflow of both the employer and contractor. Also, no time or money (including monies which are part of the limit of insurance cover) are expended in establishing liability. The benefits of such a policy arguably therefore outweigh the fact that the premiums may be slightly higher than if the employer decides to rely on the existing policies of the contractor and the professional team.

Although it is possible to include professional liability in a single project policy, it is fair to say that, most commonly, such single project policies generally only cover the risks in a contractor's "all risk" policy and in a public liability policy. The parties insured under a single project policy would be the employer, possibly other contractors engaged by him, the contractor and sub-contractors in any tier. Even without professional indemnity insurance cover for the consultants, there are still substantial advantages in cutting out the need to establish which party is liable for the loss.

To conclude, it is useful to look at an example of a single project insurance policy which is working on a partnering project. This example is the Terminal 5 project at Heathrow. BAA has reported that by drawing the insurance together rather than allowing the suppliers and contractors to obtain their own insurance it is both "cost effective" and "consistent with our partnering approach" because it reduces the cost of premiums by removing overlapping cover.

Sir John Egan has welcomed this move in his *Accelerating Change* report, the follow-up to *Rethinking Construction,* published in September 2002. He confirmed the hope "that fully integrated team planning will encourage the insurance industry to insure the products". Zara Lamont, chief executive of the Confederation of Construction Clients, has also backed this view. It therefore seems that single project insurance will have a greater role to play in this changing industry.

INSURANCE AND PARTNERING CONTRACTS

PPC 2000

PPC 2000 is examined in chapter 8 of this book, in relation to time, cost and quality provisions. The risk and insurance provisions within PPC 2000 are set out at clauses 18.1, 18.2 and 19. It should be noted that clause 19 also cross-refers to Parts 1 to 4 of Appendix 4, which forms part of PPC 2000.

Risk

Clause 18.1 expressly recognises the need for the partnering team to analyse and manage risks by identifying, costing, eliminating, reducing, sharing and insuring them, as appropriate. Clause 18.2 effectively states that it is the contractor who shall be responsible for managing all such risks, unless otherwise agreed elsewhere.

Insurance

Clause 19.1 goes some way to promoting single project insurance as a policy to be taken out for projects pursuant to PPC 2000 by requiring the insurance of the project and site to be taken out by "the Partnering Team member named in the Commencement Agreement, in joint names and with waivers of subrogation". This allows recovery to be "cleaner" and reduces the "blame culture" of establishing liability under standard policies. Single project insurance is discussed in detail on pages 227–228, above.

The insurance provisions under PPC 2000 are more flexible than under other standard forms. They allow for the other more progressive forms of insurance to be adopted which are better suited to longer term projects where collaboration and integrated team working is encouraged. This is preferable to insurance requirements resting with individual team members as they may feel exposed and isolated in the event that future claims arise. This can lead to expensive and protected litigation.

However, third party liability insurance is still listed as a separate insurance required to be taken out by each party's team member. Third party liability insurance (widely defined) is provided for at clause 19.3 and is required by each partnering team member to the extent such liability results from negligence, omission or default of the relevant Partnering Team member. Third party liability insurance is discussed further on page 221 (where it is referred to as public liability insurance).

Professional indemnity insurance or product liability insurance is dealt with at clause 19.4 and it should be noted that such insurance is only expressly required to be maintained while "generally available in the market place on reasonable terms and at reasonable premiums". This protects contractors and supply chains in the event that market conditions worsen to unacceptable extremes.

Environmental and latent defects insurances are provided for at clauses 19.5 and 19.6, respectively. These are fully discussed on pages 224–225 and 221–223 of this chapter.

The use of single project insurance is further encouraged by the use of clause 19.7 which provides for the project to be covered by Whole Project Insurance if so specified (Whole Project Insurance being defined as insurance covering all aspects of the project).

The remaining insurance provisions relating to the maintenance of the insurances under clause 19 and the procedures in the event of claims are set out in Part 4 of Appendix 4 to PPC 2000 (cross-referred to in clause 19.8) and are fairly standard. Item 6 of Appendix 4 however, requires permitted exclusions and deductibles to be "reasonable" and approved in advance by all relevant parties. This arguably allows considerable "front end" discussion and negotiation to take place between the parties and their insurers. This also takes insurance obligations further than under standard forms.

The Be Collaborative Contract

The Be Collaborative Contract discussed elsewhere in this book does not really take the concept of single project insurance any further forward because its insurance provisions are very brief. The relevant provisions (clause 7) provide that each of the purchaser and the supplier (client and contractor) should maintain the insurances listed in the schedule for the relevant period. It is open for the Schedule presumably, to be amended to provide for project insurance.

M4i Consultation Draft

This model form contract embraces the concept of single project insurance. Clause 15 provides that the client (or customer) takes out a project all risks works policy and third liability policy and a project professional indemnity policy requiring such policies to cover all parties as named insureds and for subrogation rights to be waived. Interestingly, this model form contract provides for the potential for insurers to become partners to the Model Multi-Party Partnering Contract although it is not immediately apparent that any insurers would take up this offer. It will be interesting to see how often this option is taken up by insurers.

Prime contracts

Single project insurance may also be taken out on prime contracts – although most of the Regional Prime Contracts which include capital works and long term estate management services will only benefit from single project insurance where there are significant core work projects being carried out. It is, however, an option within the generic Prime Contract templates.

JCT Major Project Form (MPF) 2003 Edition

Clause 27 sets out the provisions relating to the insurance requirements of the new MPF 2003. Clause 27.2 allows the employer to request a copy of the policy documents save in relation to professional indemnity insurance. It is clear that the professional indemnity policy document should be excluded from this requirement.

The time limit for providing evidence of insurance is short at "7 days" of request. It is, however, likely that amendments to this clause will be negotiable. Clause 27.3 makes provision for the costs of any failure to obtain such insurance to be reimbursable or deductible as a debt. This is not unusual.

Some comfort is available to the contractor by virtue of clause 27.5. This clause effectively prevents insurance claims from wiping out amounts due to be paid to the contractor in accordance with the contract subject, of course, to indemnities and excesses payable by the claimant party (clause 25 and clause 27.6).

The issue of terrorism is also addressed in the MPF 2003 in clause 27.8. This new provision places the risk of any additional works to complete the project as a result of terrorism firmly with the employer, who is better placed to manage it. Such extra works would be regarded as a "change" under the contract.

ADJUDICATION AND THE INSURER

Adjudication under the Act and Scheme

Although this chapter does not merit an in-depth analysis of the adjudication process and its relationship with insurers it is worth for completeness, touching briefly on the issue of professional indemnity insurance and adjudication.

As is well known to those who practice in the construction industry, adjudication whilst interim in nature (parties being able to finally determine disputes by litigation or arbitration) is a method of resolving construction/disputes quickly and economically. Adjudication has been recognised by statute as a right to which parties to most construction contracts can resort, if such contracts were entered into after 1 May 1998.

We now have in force the Scheme for Construction Contracts 1998 (the "Scheme") which comes into operation as a default mechanism under the Housing Grants, Construction and Regeneration Act 1996 (the "Act"). Although the Act impacts on many aspects of construction law the statutory rights conferred by this legislation will have a potentially large impact on professional design teams within the construction industry and the insurers who provide them with Professional Indemnity cover ("PI cover").

Part II, s. 104(2) of the Act sets out that:

"References in this part to a construction contract include an agreement (a) to do architectural, design or surveying work or, (b) to provide advice on building, engineering, interior or exterior decoration or the laying out of landscape in relation to construction operations."

Consultants are then, clearly caught under the Act (recently confirmed in the Scottish case of *Gillies Ramsay Diamond* v. *PJW Enterprises Ltd* [2003] BLR 48) and as such will find that they are not only becoming the subject of adjudication but will also be able to seek adjudication. It is unfortunately true of many professionals and design contractors that their greatest attribute from either the point of view of an employer or design and build contractor is the availability of PI cover.

As the adjudicator is to reach a decision within 28 days of the referral of the dispute (unless time is extended by agreement between the parties), the Scheme provides a fairly quick access for the claimant to what may amount to be a considerable fund of money, namely the PI policy. Of course, insurers are now attempting to qualify their policy documents by making it clear that an insured should provide them with detailed documentation in support the claims at the outset of an adjudication if cover is to be given.

If we briefly consider a scenario based upon JCT 1998 with Contractor's Design for an office project, we may see the insurers problem. The project is at the halfway stage, but the programme is slipping due to problems with component fit, ground conditions and the pricing. The contractor is losing money though liquidated damages which become payable on delay, and realises that it has a useful opportunity to obtain ready cashflow, if an adjudication is commenced against his novated consultants.

The insurance monies of the consultant are likely to be regarded as a ready source of funds for the contractor during the currency of the contract, and will not depend on all the parties continuing to trade until the outcome of a lengthy trial.

The problem for the insurer is the possibility that when a contractor with liquidity problems is able to recover sums from his consultants within little more than a month and then ceases to trade. The money is lost if the company was a mere shell, or without parent company guarantees that would indemnify losses as a result of the contractor's default. An insurer will not be able to push to the follow up arbitration or litigation, as the company no longer exists. The insurer's right of subrogation, that is the right to step into the shoes of the insured party to fight the case, is to all intents and purposes redundant.

The consultant may be in a number of unpleasant situations from this point. The claim may fall within the consultant's own agreed upon excess (namely, the agreed amount that the insured will pay from the insured's own resources) which many firms inflate so as to reduce their premiums. This sum which is derived from the insured's own funds will be called upon first when a claim is made, with the consequential result that the insured may have to pay out on 3, 4 or 5 adjudications at once.

The courts have been willing to consider a stay in the execution of an adjudicator's decision in these circumstances. In *Rainford House Ltd (in administrative receivership)* v. *Cadogan Ltd* [2001] BLR 416; [2001] NPC 39), His Honour Judge Seymour QC said that it was not the policy of the Act to transfer the risk of insolvency as between the parties to a construction contract. Where the party seeking to enforce an adjudicator's award was insolvent, it was inappropriate to grant summary judgment in favour of that party without also granting a stay of execution to the defendant. However, granting a stay of execution is not a step that the courts will take lightly. The paying party will have to provide compelling and un-contradicted evidence of the risk that the other party will not be in a position to pay in the event that a court subsequently disagrees with the adjudicator's decision (*Total M & E Services Ltd* v. *ABB Building Technologies Ltd* [2002] EWHC 248; (2002) 87 Con LR 154).

Quantum of excess

The quantum of excess for professional indemnity cover will vary from company to company dependent upon the value of projects, but £50,000 is not unusual and £100,000 plus can be paid out by major consultancies. It is worth noting that most PI policies operate on an "each and every claim" basis which means that the sum assured will be available to meet any number of claims made during the currency of the policy. Hence, a number of claims could be active at the same time, leading to the above scenario being repeated on a number of projects, which could prove very costly to the insured party.

The reserves required to be set aside for paying for adjudications while arbitration or litigation are sought could be crippling. A listed company may have to consider some radical approaches to accounting while large cash sums are paid out after a 28-day process.

It is conceded that the above scenarios are in fact the "worst case" type; However, the insurance industry will need to consider the issue of adjudication and introduce standard mechanisms to enable their legal team to respond with a well-prepared case.

How to respond to an adjudication

When an insured party receives a reference to adjudication, the party's broker/insurer should be informed as soon as practicably possible, which, given the time scale for a response is wholly reasonable.

Some firms of insurer are now offering, through their panel of solicitors, telephone helplines which the insured may call as soon as a reference is received or if one of the contracting parties suggests that adjudication may be about to ensue. Assuming that the contract is one to which the Scheme actually applies, the legal team will be eager to establish exactly what form of contract is used, whether the Scheme or some other procedure prevails and the nature of the dispute.

With all the relevant information at the insured's disposal during the initial contact, the insured will assist the defence team in preparing research cases and arranging initial meetings with experts from the agreed panel.

Insurers are keen to ensure that all parties involved work together effectively under this new procedure which is aimed very much at ensuring cashflow down the line.

How will insurers respond to adjudication?

Traditionally, professional indemnity insurers control the defence of claims, with power to prolong or settle them. Undoubtedly, the cost, tedium and delay inherent in litigation and arbitration are a major part of the insurer's armoury. Will adjudication affect the behaviour of insurers by encouraging earlier, more realistic settlements?

The answer to this question appears to be yes, in light of several recent landmark judicial decisions considering the adjudication provisions under the Act. The decision of Mr Justice Dyson in *Macob Civil Engineering* v. *Morrison Construction Ltd* [1999] 3 BLR 93 confirms that a disputed decision of an adjudicator is binding and effective until the dispute is resolved. In *Levolux AT Ltd* v. *Ferson Contractors Ltd* [2003] EWCA Civ 11, the Court of Appeal held that where there is a conflict between the obligation to pay the amount stated in an adjudicator's decision and the contractual terms between the parties, the obligation to pay takes precedence over the conflicting contractual terms. The culmination of these and other decisions leave no doubt that the courts are keen to support adjudication as an effective means of interim dispute resolution by ensuring enforcement of an adjudicator's decision. The extremely limited grounds upon which a court is willing to interfere with an adjudicator's decision relate to excesses of jurisdiction (*Dahl-Jensen* v. *Bouygues UK Ltd* (1999) CILL 1566; (2000) 70 Con LR 41) and breaches of natural justice (*Discain Project Services Ltd* v. *Opecprime Development Ltd* (2001), unreported). A court will consider granting a stay of execution of an adjudicator's decision in the circumstances described on page 233.

These decisions demonstrate the court's keenness to support the adjudication process. It is yet to be seen how the insurance market will react.

REVIEWING THE IMPACT OF 11 SEPTEMBER 2001, TWO YEARS ON

The terrorist events in the USA of 11 September 2001 have dramatically rocked the insurance world, producing the biggest insurance loss in history, estimated at around $70 billion. The total capital of the world's (non-life) insurance is in excess of $100 billion. Swiss Re have estimated that insured property and business interruption losses worth $19 billion were caused.

In the immediate aftermath, the Government was forced to intervene in the insurance markets to provide cover for the aviation industry in order to keep planes flying. The TROIKA scheme offered third-party war and terrorism insurance for liabilities greater than $50 million, to plug the gap left by cancelled cover from insurance companies.

This type of government intervention is not unprecedented or unusual to the construction and property industries. The Pool Re referred to on pages 225–227, above, was another scheme put in place by government action in 1993 to provide reinsurance for terrorism cover in respect of commercial buildings.

Statutory developments

The UK Government moved swiftly to pass the Anti-Terrorism, Crime and Security Act 2001 following September 11.

The Act provides for a range of new security measures and powers, but the definitions of terrorist action under the Reinsurance (Acts of Terrorism) Act 1993 and the Terrorism Act 2000, s. 1(2), will prove to have had a more significant impact in relation to insurance of building or construction projects. The Terrorism Act 2000 defines a terrorist act as

"the use or threat of action
  • where the use or threat involves serious violence against a person, serious damage to property, endangers a person's life, creates a serious risk to health and safety or is designed seriously to interfere with or disrupt an electronic system; or

- is designed to influence government or to intimidate the public; or
- is made to advance a political, religious or ideological cause."

The legislation has impacted on the building insurance industry in defining what "terrorism cover" will include. As discussed on pages 225–227, above, insurers now tend to adopt this wider definition of what constitutes an "act of terrorism".

Taken together, the 1993 Act can be viewed as focused on activities directed towards the overthrow of influence of Government, whilst the more recent Terrorism Act 2000 extends to cover violence for political, religious or ideological ends, aimed at either the overthrow of influence of Government, or simply to intimidate the public.

Given the widespread use of standard form contracts in the construction industry, it is notable that the JCT in its Guidance Notes to Amendment 3: 2001 (issued January 2001) have made clear that 'Terrorism' for projects on the UK mainland has the narrow definition given in the Reinsurance (Acts of Terrorism) Act 1993 rather than the wider meaning set out in the Terrorism Act 2000.

Hardening markets

Even before September 11, the insurance market had begun to harden; two years on, insurers are passing the burden on to their customers. Smaller contractors are now facing ruin as premiums multiply to freakish levels. Different sources during the course of 2002 estimated these levels as being anywhere between 300% (National Specialist Contractors Council) and 500% (see *Building*, 9 August 2002, p. 19).

The other problem is that these hiked premiums are buying less and less cover. It is common for contractors to be required to obtain cover for "each and every" event. This means that the limit of the indemnity applies to each claim, regardless of how many there are. This is, however, becoming difficult to achieve. Many insurers will now offer only aggregate cover, which caps the amount of money that can be claimed in a given year.

These factors will inevitably increase the cost of carrying out building projects. Risks formerly covered by insurance will have to be priced into the contract. Already, those involved in planning projects are having to revise their expectations of the level of insurance cover available, and if the contract has been signed, it is possible that one of the parties will be unable to fulfil their obligations with regards to the nature and extent of insurance cover required. This is particularly apparent for the more unusual covers such as fitness for purpose which is discussed on page 221, above. It remains to be seen how the insurance market will deal with this growing problem.

CHAPTER 11

RESOLUTION OF DISPUTES

Linda Grayson[1] and Diana Harvey[2]

INTRODUCTION

It is inescapable that even the soundest of relationships generate disputes, and it is essential that this is recognised by the participants to partnering arrangements. Partnering, however well intentioned, does not guarantee the elimination of disputes and it is prudent for participants to provide for their emergence. There are a number of root causes that generate construction disputes. These include insufficiently defined roles, responsibilities and expectations, lack of communication about problems, unrealistic time/cost/quality targets, unfair or unclear risk allocation and uncontrollable external events. Running alongside all these factors is perhaps the most important issue of cost overruns, which above all other factors tends to produce an adversarial approach. The first section of this chapter will consider how disputes that arise in the course of the project might be dealt with so as to preserve the partnering relationship. The second section will look at the issues that complicate dispute resolution in partnering arrangements.

The contractual points of reference in these sections will be PPC 2000, the ECC Partnering Option X12, the Be Collaborative Contract (BCC), the Movement for Innovation Virtual Company Model Form (M4i) and the JCT Partnering Charter. An overview of the structure of all of these contracts, charters and drafts has appeared earlier in chapter 8 of this book.

DISPUTE MANAGEMENT

Construction contracts tend to be highly specialised and comprehensive documents. They are unlike many commercial contracts since they govern a continuing relationship rather than an instantaneous transaction. Conflict occurs partly as a direct result of bringing together a variety of specialists, all of who bring their own agenda to the process. This is a natural consequence of specialisation. A dispute can arise at any stage of the contract and its resolution

1. Solicitor, Construction, Engineering & Projects, Hammonds.
2. Solicitor, Construction, Engineering & Projects, Hammonds.

can be time consuming, expensive and frequently acrimonious, even where the need to preserve good long term working relationships is paramount. Whilst partnering arrangements are calculated to minimise disputes, it is essential that these arrangements include an appropriate dispute resolution process that is also capable of identifying disputes at an early stage. (This highlights the drawback of a charter where the substantive dispute resolution procedures may be in the various underlying contracts, each being between just two of the project partners.) Indeed, it might be observed that a clear indication that the partnering arrangement is functioning effectively is the manner in which disputes are managed so as to enable the continuation of the project. Conflict itself cannot be avoided. The question is whether that conflict can be contained and managed so as not to cause disruption. There are three distinct points in a project, which are critical to the effective management of the causes of conflict and their resolution. These are the identification and allocation of risk at the outset, the establishment of an early warning system for problems that are looming, and the resolution of disputes that have actually crystallised and therefore pose a real threat to the project.

Risk allocation

The root cause of many claims and disputes under traditional construction contracts is the inappropriate allocation of risk or the lack of clarity as to where any given risk actually lies. The clear and unequivocal placing of risk on one party or the other is consistent with the suggestions made for the drafting of post-"Housing Grants" Act contracts, partnering or otherwise. However, it is important to recognise that, unlike objectives such as "zero defects" (clause 4.2, PPC 2000), a risk management system will not eliminate risk. Instead, the rationale for such a system is to anticipate the foreseeable risks to the project, assign these to the party best able to deal with them and to establish a collective means of tackling the unforeseen risks that come to fruition in the course of the project. Dispute management in partnering therefore is as much to do with getting the premise of a project right as it is about tackling issues maturely when they arise.

The multi-party approach of partnering means that the client has to deal with only one integrated contract rather than five or six separate ones. This substantially reduces the risk of gaps or overlaps between the different roles and creates duties of care between all team members, for example between the architect and contractor, and even between the services consultant and services specialist. What is needed is a fair balance of risk and reward between the parties. These parties need to rely on each other and a multi-party contract should mean that they do not pass all their problems up the chain to the client if they can be resolved between the parties direct.

Looking at the risk management regimes within the available partnering forms:

- *PPC 2000* (clause 18) calls upon the partnering team members to analyse and manage risks, which includes identifying likely risks and the associated costs, the elimination or reduction of risks and their costs, insuring risks wherever affordable and appropriate and the allocation of risk according to which one or more partnering team members are most able to manage such risks. Subject to the particular risk allocation arrangements agreed between the partnering team members, the constructor is responsible for managing all risks associated with the project from the date of the commencement agreement. There are a number of specific grounds, which entitle the contractor to an extension of time, the final one being "any other event" that has been agreed between the partnering team members and noted in the commencement agreement. This reflects the necessity for a workable risk management system to be project specific.
- *The M4i* makes reference to the preparation of risk matrices and the management of risk, but no issues of principle to which the project team should have regard appear in the draft.
- Both the *ECC Option* and the *JCT Charter* broadly leave the issue of risk to the underlying contracts. The ECC Option anticipates that it will form part of the "Partnering Information". In the ECC core clauses (clause 60.1), the employer specifically takes the risk of the physical conditions within the site which an experienced contractor would have, at the outset, considered to have had such a small chance of occurring that it would have been unreasonable for him to have allowed for them, and adverse weather conditions the occurrence of which is sufficiently infrequent by reference to a weather measurement within a given timescale.
- In the *BCC*, risk management (clause 4) is a two-stage process. First, there is to be an initial risk assessment the objective of which is to identify potential risks, assess the probability of these risks occurring, arrive at a financial estimate of the likely consequences of each risk occurring, and an allocation of those risks to the purchaser, supplier or another project participant. This exercise is likely to be the responsibility of the supplier, who, in any event will be obliged to provide "all reasonable assistance" in this process. These risks will be recorded in a "Risk Register", for which there is an ongoing updating obligation including the recording of new risks and action taken to manage previously identified risks.

  Alongside the risk register, is the preparation of the "Risk Allocation Schedule", which will set out the identified project-specific risks. A particular feature of this schedule is the degree of specificity in the allocation exercise, so that the cost and time consequences of a particular risk is apportioned by agreement between the supplier and the purchaser on a percentage basis. The schedule will record the amount calculated to represent the potential financial consequence of the specific risk, and the supplier's percentage allocation of that amount will be included in the supplier's target cost or contract sum. In the event that the anticipated risk does not materialise, the supplier will nonetheless retain the share of the risk allocation included in the target cost or contract sum. If the risk *does* materialise, but the costs incurred by the supplier in dealing with it are *less* than the share of the risk allocation included in the target cost or contract sum, the supplier will not be entitled to any additional payment. If the risk materialises, and the costs incurred by the supplier in dealing with it *exceed* the share of the risk allocation included in the target cost or lump sum price, the excess will be shared between the purchaser and the supplier in the proportions indicated in the schedule. To illustrate this:

Adverse ground conditions risk allowance:	£100,000
Risk allocation:	
Purchaser:	50%
Supplier	50%
Amount included in target cost/contract sum:	£50,000

Therefore, in this example, the supplier will not be able to apply for additional payment until he has spent more than the sum of £50,000. Once this level is reached, the excess will be shared in the agreed proportions. Accordingly, if the cost of dealing with the adverse ground conditions is £150,000, the supplier will be entitled to apply for an additional £25,000.

It is interesting to note that the advice contained within the guidance notes advocates the obtaining of legal assistance before the schedule is completed. It appears that an exercise devised to eliminate disputes upon the occurrence of an anticipated risk may itself create disputes in circumstances where the risk description set out in the schedule fails precisely to express what has been agreed.

Alongside risk directly associated with the running of the project, a major risk is posed by the possibility of insolvency of any of the parties involved in the project. In the context of partnering once the control of one of the partners transfers to an administrative receiver, that partner's capacity to partake in the collaborative process is fatally undermined by a competing agenda under which the administrative receiver's primary duty is to the holder of the charge under which he was appointed. The Enterprise Act 2002 introduced a system of administrators who are no longer answerable solely to a secured creditor, and as an officer of the court, their principal objective will now be to rescue the company as a going concern. The administrator will therefore be empowered to do anything necessary or expedient so as to effectively manage the affairs and business of the company. Nevertheless, the administrator's prime concern remains the collective creditors as opposed to the interests of the project, and it is questionable whether he would be bound by, say, any confidentiality clause regarding the flow of information as between the partners on the status of the project. It may be observed that this in turn calls into question what more is expected of a fully participating partnering team member who also has its own company interests to preserve. PPC 2000 recognises the dilemma created by insolvency and provides that this will result in the immediate automatic termination of that partner's involvement under the partnering contract. The ECC and JCT underlying contracts, the BCC and M4i leave the remaining partners parties with the option to terminate in these circumstances.

Early warning signs of a dispute

One of the key developments under partnering is the contractually structured early discussion process. This obliges the parties to bring issues to the surface when a problem is first anticipated or encountered rather than to leave it to develop into a major problem which tends to cause both parties' positions to become entrenched and the problem to become more difficult to solve.

Warning signs may not be significant taken in isolation but observed over a period, a pattern emerges which gives rise to concerns. Amongst the more obvious signs are a downturn in working relationships exemplified by a tail-off in information flow, missed milestone/critical path dates, claims of one partner's interference in the other's work. Whilst these examples are not exhaustive, the accumulation of these or similar warning signs should place project team members on alert.

One of the mechanisms that facilitates the early recognition of a potential dispute, and therefore makes dispute avoidance more efficient, is the establishment of clear benchmarks for performance, and mechanisms operable on failure to achieve such benchmarks. By setting out clear benchmarks within the contract, the parties are better able to allow the machinery of the contract to start working when performance falls below the agreed benchmark. In this way, problems are more likely to be addressed swiftly and effectively rather than left to fester. (For a discussion on the use of key performance indicators and quality management generally, see chapter 8.)

Several of the available partnering forms make provision for an "early warning" system.

- In PPC 2000 all partnering team members have a duty to notify the other partners as soon as a member is aware of any matter that might adversely affect the project (clause 3.7). This includes problems in a partnering team member's own performance or any differences with any one or more of the other partnering team members. That notification is to include proposals for the management of the particular problem. In practice this early warning system works by the client representative convening a meeting of the core group (discussed further below) within five working days from the date of any such notification.

- Whilst not expressed in terms of an "early warning system, the BCC calls upon the purchaser and supplier to notify each other of any anticipated dispute so that it can be avoided by negotiation between them (clause 7.27). In addition, the parties are to specifically inform each other when they first become aware of the occurrence of a risk identified in the risk allocation schedule.
- The principle of early warning appears in the ECC Option (clause X12.3(3)), with the core conditions in the underlying contract requiring the parties to give early warning of matters that will affect cost, time or impair the performance of the works in use. This will be followed with an "early warning meeting" to manage the problem.
- In line with the approach taken on risk allocation, the M4i (clause 9) alludes to an early warning system for "delays, cost overruns, potential defects and the like", leaving this to be elaborated upon if considered appropriate by the project team members.
- The system is not expressly referred to in the JCT Charter.

Could the requirement to provide this early warning be construed as a condition precedent to recovery of compensation where a partner has failed to give an early warning of a matter within his knowledge and that matter has crystallised so as to affect the project? If so, this would no doubt prove an effective inducement to robust management of problems at an early stage. Certainly, in PPC 2000, clause 18 (which sets out the grounds upon which the contractor can apply for an extension of time) expressly provides that the contractor can claim for a delay caused by the failure of the client or any consultant to meet any agreed time limit provided that the constructor has given an early warning not less than five working days before the expiry of the agreed time limit. Equally, clause 63.4 of the core clauses of the ECC core conditions, provides that if the contractor fails to give the requisite early warning and a compensation event does arise, then the contractor's compensation is assessed as if he had given an early warning. This means that the contractor may have to bear any additional costs, which result from an early warning not being given.

However, the courts have been reluctant to construe a term as a condition precedent unless this has been expressed in the clearest of terms. In *London Borough of Merton* v. *Stanley Hugh Leach* (1985) 32 BLR 51, in which the contractor had an obligation under clause 23 of the JCT 1963 edition to "forthwith give written notice of... delay" upon the fact of delay becoming reasonably apparent", it was held that failure to give that notice was not a condition precedent to the consideration of the claim by the architect. An architect cannot ignore events that are known to him. This case was recently endorsed in *Sindall Ltd* v. *Solland & Others* (2002) 80 Con LR 152, in which it was held that a person in the position of contract administrator had always to consider whether there were any factors known to him, which might justify an extension of time. It is, however, worth noting that, at least in the case of the ECC form, the sanctions arising from the failure to give an early warning notice may seek to restrict recovery as opposed to preclude recovery per se. Whether such an assessment is practical in the overall exercise of ascertaining delay or loss and expense remains to be seen.

Dispute resolution

What is the procedure for the resolution of issues that escape the net provided by either the initial risk allocation exercise or the early warning system? Before looking at the various models available for dispute resolution, it should be noted that parties to any contracts which fall within the scope of the Housing Grants, Construction and Regeneration Act 1996 (the Act) are at liberty to refer a matter to adjudication at any time. The following discussion is predicated on the basis that the concept of partnering will predispose the team members to look at more informal routes in the first instance.

Set out below is an overview of the dispute resolution procedures, which appear in the contracts and charters that have been looked at in this chapter (the techniques incorporated in these schemes will be discussed in more detail below):

- *PPC 2000* (clause 27) provides for a structured approach to problem solving and dispute resolution, with the intention of keeping problems and disputes under the control of partnering team members. After the partnering team members have been given notice of a dispute or difference, the first step in the process is referral to the "problem solving hierarchy" that has been devised for that project. Thereafter the dispute will be referred to the core group (whose composition and functions have been described in chapter 8) who are to make constructive proposals so as to arrive at an agreed solution. If the core group fails to achieve a solution, the contract provides for conciliation (under the ACA procedure), mediation or some other from of alternative dispute resolution that can be facilitated by the partnering adviser (who – if appointed – assists in the solving of problems and disputes (clause 5.6)). Running alongside this is the option from the outset to submit the matter to adjudication. The final step is litigation or arbitration.
- The *ECC Partnering Option* provides that a dispute or difference between partners who do not have a contract between them is resolved by the core group. If the core group is unable to resolve the issue, then it is resolved under the procedure of the partners' own contracts, either directly or indirectly with the client. The partnering option does not include direct remedies between non-contracting partners to recover losses suffered by one of them caused by a failure of the other. These remedies remain available in each partners' own contract, but it is suggested that their existence will encourage the parties to compromise any differences that arise.
- The *BCC* adopts the model of negotiation between senior executives as the first level of dispute resolution (clause 7.28). Negotiation can then be

followed by mediation. Where either the purchaser or supplier is a member of the project team, the project team members are to be kept informed of progress in the resolution of the dispute, or otherwise, and can make recommendations for settlement, to which the purchaser and supplier are to pay "serious consideration". Ultimate resolution is by litigation.

- The *M4i* begins with referral to the virtual company board and ends with litigation (clause 33). Unlike the other contracts, it is expressly provided that the partners are to continue to work on the project pending resolution of the dispute. In that interim period, the client will have the decision-making authority in relation to any matter in dispute, to be carried out in consultation with the partners that are not involved in the dispute (clause 34).
- Dispute resolution is not dealt with in the JCT Charter.

The problem-solving hierarchy

The technique common to most of the partnering arrangements is the problem solving hierarchy, whereby individuals within the partnering team members are given a limited period of time to resolve any problem with their opposite numbers in the other partnering team members. If they fail to do so, then the problem is automatically passed up the line to the next most senior named individuals in each organisation. This automatic elevation process prevents individuals from "leap-frogging" or going over someone's head, thereby exacerbating the tensions between those partnering team members caught up in the dispute. It also minimises the disruption caused to the productivity of those individuals at the "working" level thereby allowing the project to make progress.

The further advantage of referral to higher management is that it should enable the dispute to be resolved swiftly as a managerial process rather than with the greater degree of formality, that comes when a process is more clearly labelled as dispute resolution, namely a referral to mediation or adjudication. Whilst it is perhaps preferable that the level of management selected should be sufficiently distant from the substance of the conflict to be unhindered in their decision-making by any emotional involvement, it is essential that they should have authority to determine the issues in question. Managers can be pre-selected before a dispute arises, which has the merit of facilitating the speed of response. However, it may be more appropriate to devise internal systems for the nomination of appropriate managers as and when they are required so as to retain the flexibility to appoint the best suited manager for the particular dispute and to guard against non-availability.

Alternative dispute resolution: mediation and conciliation

Under the umbrella of "alternative dispute resolution", mediation or nonbinding conciliation provides a forum that mirrors the essential element of co-operation that should be fostered when fusing the original relationship within the partnering deal. Mediation/non-binding conciliation techniques, which encourage the parties to examine their interests in a broader context than that of the dispute itself, are highly compatible with the philosophy of partnering. The advantages of mediation/conciliation are well documented and these include confidentiality, speed, comparative minimal exposure to costs, a process which is within the parties' control, imaginative solutions, the encouragement of dialogue and the greater potential for the preservation of the business relationship.

Alternative dispute resolution techniques are not only gaining in credibility but are being positively promoted by the courts as the first step in the dispute resolution process. In *Susan Jane Dunnett* v. *Railtrack plc* [2002] 2 All ER 850, although denying the claimant's application, the Court of Appeal held that it would be inappropriate to order the claimant to pay her costs, given the defendants refusal to consider mediation. A successful party will not however be deprived of its costs where it is reasonable to refuse to participate in mediation because there is no prospect that this will accomplish the desired outcome (*Société Internationale de Telecommunications Aeronautiques SCA* v. *Wyatt Co (UK) Ltd and Others* (2002), unreported).

A form of contractual resolution is the dispute review board, used in the Prime Contracting initiative, described earlier in Chapter 8. These boards have been used in a number of major projects, such as the construction of both the Channel Tunnel and the new Hong Kong Airport and are now required by the World Bank in any bank-financed construction project having a cost of more than US$50m. Under this procedure a board, usually consisting of three members, is created at the start of the project. One member of the board is appointed by the client and a second by the lead contractor. The third member is then selected either by the other two board members or by mutual agreement between the client and the contractor. This form of nomination might present a difficulty in multiparty partnering arrangements, which do not identify one of the partners as having overall responsibility to the client. The board is generally empowered to examine all disputes and to make recommendations to the parties concerning settlement. If the parties to a dispute act on a recommendation, it becomes binding. If however, they are dissatisfied, they may proceed to arbitration or litigation.

In projects that can justify the costs of retaining a dispute resolution board through the life of the works, this provides an effective means of settling disputes whilst permitting a continuation of the project. Further advantages are that because the parties designate the board at the time they sign the contract and before any specific conflict arises, their acceptance by the parties is assured and they approach their task with a high degree of legitimacy. Also, as the board members are kept informed of the contract status throughout its progress, this is likely to result in a better understanding of the specific issue in dispute when the board is called upon to facilitate negotiations. The board may also have gained an insight into the underlying motivations of the parties, and can therefore identify more options for resolution. They might also have the technical expertise that can assist the resolution of most disputes that may arise in the course of the project.

However, if the core working groups set up within the partnering arrangements are working effectively, is there a place for mediation? In other words, will a referral to mediation or conciliation merely repeat that which has already been discussed at length and therefore simply delay the effective resolution of the dispute by a tribunal with the power to impose a resolution on the parties? If mediation cannot add to the previous deliberations of the parties, then going down this route will also add to the costs of the process. However, the distinguishing feature of mediation, conciliation and dispute resolution boards is independence from any of the parties involved in the dispute and therefore the capacity to remain unfettered by the political/emotional agendas of the parties. In the example of dispute resolution boards, the value of this has to be set against the costs involved of retaining the board through the life of the project and how these are to be allocated between the partners. Equally, whilst mediation is an important tool in the resolution of disputes generated in project partnering, it has a particular application to strategic partnering where the objective is a long-term relationship. It is the essence of mediation that it seeks to assist the parties in resolving their differences in the context of their relationship and interests as a whole rather than by narrow reference to the rights and wrongs of the dispute itself.

ISSUES IN PARTNERING DISPUTES

Having set out the strategies that the partnering forms have incorporated to minimise the occurrence of disputes and the means of containing budding disputes, the following section will look at some of the practical problems confronting dispute resolution in this context.

Formal dispute resolution mechanisms

Adjudication

If a partnering relationship is contractual, it may constitute a "construction contract" for the purposes of the Act. If so, it must conform to the adjudication provisions contained in the Act, otherwise the Act's own provisions for adjudication contained in the Scheme for Construction Contracts will apply. The main feature of the process which affects dispute resolution strategies in the context of partnering arrangements is that any party is entitled to refer a dispute to adjudication at any time – a statutory right that cannot be modified by contract. Adjudication is generally recognised as calculated to deliver a swift and cheap decision, usually adopting an informal methodology and intended to provide an interim resolution of the dispute with a dissatisfied party being entitled to revisit the issue by arbitration or court proceedings. It is commonly accepted that a degree of accuracy maybe sacrificed on the altar of speed and cost effectiveness. It is often perceived as rough and ready rather than precise in its outcome, but sufficient to put broadly the right sum of money in the right pocket pending a more thorough and final determination of the issues. In the interim, it allows everyone to get back to work. A huge number of disputes have gone to adjudication and a huge number have been solved at adjudication. However, it is these very characteristics of adjudication that has led to the criticism that it has been used for disputes that could have been solved by more effective communication between the parties. So whilst the project in relative terms is "kept moving", disputes have been formalised; and formalised disputes have a habit of destroying relationships, which is the very antithesis of partnering.

Other criticisms include:

- As a fundamental issue of principle there is a tension between the expectation that the parties will collaborate in the agreed dispute resolution strategy and the statutory right to submit disputes at any stage to adjudication. This statutory right clearly enables any party to circumvent the contractual dispute management process, which has been designed in the interests of preserving the overall partnering relationship. As a result of having made adjudication a non-excludable statutory right, there is now an interesting anomaly in the approach to alternative dispute resolution. If, in any other context, the parties are taking active steps towards litigation, both pre and post the issue of formal proceedings, the courts are actively promoting the use of ADR. This is not simply given lip service by the courts, but is backed up by cost sanctions where a party has unreasonably refused to engage in ADR mechanisms such as mediation. Ironically, in partnering arrangements where many of the dispute resolution strategies specifically direct the parties to negotiation and mediation so as to avoid formal proceedings, any party can as of right ignore those provisions by a referral to adjudication – a step which cannot but seriously undermine the partnering arrangement and precipitate the parties down the road to a formal dispute.
- A further area of tension relates to the question of whether one party's resort to adjudication in the absence of any regard to the problem solving hierarchy, places that party in contractual breach of the undertakings of co-operation and the like. Ordinarily it might be difficult to draw any other conclusion where a party to a partnering arrangement has refused to co-operate by engaging in any negotiation and/or mediation. Against the background of the Act, this interpretation is, it is submitted, unlikely as the courts would be reluctant to conclude that a party can be said to have acted in bad faith by recourse to a statutory right so as to place that

party in breach of contract. However, the necessary endorsement of a party's recourse to adjudication ahead of an agreed dispute resolution mechanism means that the contract is being construed in a manner that does not reflect the parties' original intentions of co-operative dealings.

- A final criticism is that the very nature of adjudication makes it inappropriate for some disputes. In this context, one partner's dissatisfaction with the extent of another partner's collaborative efforts, does not seem to be immediately accessible to determination by an adjudicator, who could be called upon to determine matters of principle, with as yet no guidance from the courts. Whilst the courts are reluctant to put any issue beyond the scope of adjudication, (see for example the case of *Gillies Ramsay Diamond* v. *PJW Enterprises Ltd* [2003] BLR 48, which left issues of professional negligence firmly within an adjudicator's jurisdiction), it will be interesting to see whether the practical difficulties prompted by "conceptual" disputes in the partnering framework finally pose a challenge that stretches the usefulness of adjudication.

Arbitration

Section 46 of the Arbitration Act 1996 represents an important development. For the first time under English law, the arbitral tribunal may be given the power to decide disputes not only in accordance with the governing law but also, if the parties agree, "in accordance with such other considerations as are agreed by them or determined by the Tribunal". In essence, this means that the tribunal does not have to strictly adhere to the principles of the law governing the contract, but can adopt a broader approach. It should be emphasised that the tribunal cannot unilaterally decide to follow this route – it must be authorised to do so by the parties. In a partnering dispute the parties can therefore agree that the tribunal should decide issues relating to, for example, the extent to which a non-binding charter can or cannot affect the existing obligations in the underlying contracts. There are two ways of viewing this provision:

- This should be approached with caution. Depending upon the expertise of the tribunal, it may be asked to decide upon issues of principle for which there is currently no precedent. If the tribunal makes an award for which there is no jurisprudence, given the limited rights of appeal under the Arbitration Act 1996, it is unlikely that the parties will have any recourse against the award.

- Alternatively, this provision could be viewed as providing an innovative approach to dispute resolution to correspond with the general trend in the industry that is seeking to move away from the traditional adversarial stance. Section 46 could be interpreted as enabling the parties to write their own dispute resolution mechanism, consistent with the principles expressed in the partnering arrangement. The tribunal would then decide the dispute in line with the expectations of the parties. However, the overarching statutory right to adjudication, as discussed above has seriously undermined the potential for the Arbitration Act to perform in this way.

Conceptual issues

Liability

The allocation of liability in the event that a project goes wrong is one which is generally at the forefront of the parties' minds at the outset. It is critical that there is an assessment of the extent of one's potential exposure to liability, both in respect of the client and the corresponding liability between the parties involved in the delivery of the project. The issue of contribution is particularly relevant in the context of partnering, where a criticism levelled against collaborative working is that it blurs the lines of responsibility between the partners. This section will look first at how the industry forms deal with the issue of liability as between the partners and will then consider the legal issues arising from this.

The allocation of liability in the industry forms

The express provisions relating to liability are:
- Clause 22 of PPC 2000 provides that in all the partners' activities relating to the design, supply, construction and completion of the project, they are to use reasonable skill and care and are to owe each other such duties of care as are stated in the project partnering agreement. In the project partnering agreement, these duties of care can be amended by reference to a series of the following alternatives:
  - The contractor accepting full liability to the client for the design and construction of the project such that it is fit for its intended purpose as described in the project brief. This is without prejudice to the duty of care owed by each of the partners (other than the client) to the contractor in respect of their respective contribution to the design and construction of the project.
  - The parties can limit their responsibility for loss suffered by any other partnering team member to that proportion of the other partnering team member's loss or damage "as it would be just and equitable to require that partnering team member to pay having regard to the extent of that partnering team member's responsibility for such loss and damage".
  - The responsibility of the partnering team members for loss and damage suffered by the client and for which any one or more partnering team members (other than the client) are responsible shall be in pre-

determined proportions "irrespective of the extent of each partnering team member's actual contribution to the cause of that loss or damage".

- According to the guidance notes to the ECC Option, it does not provide direct remedies between non-contracting partners to recover losses suffered by one of them caused by a failure of the other. These remedies are to remain in each partner's own contract but the hope is expressed that the existence of these remedies will encourage the parties to compromise any differences that arise.

- Clause 1 of the M4i provides that no liability is to attach to any of the partners in respect of matters discussed prior to the contract being signed. From that point onwards, a "no blame culture" set out in clause 5 restricts the capacity of the partners to make claims against each other for any matter arising out if the contract except in defined circumstances. These include where a partner has acted in bad faith. Clause 6 provides that there is to be no liability in respect of loss of profit, loss of use, loss of contract or loss of production. Clause 37 states that the liability of the partners to each other is several and not joint or joint and several.

- In the BCC, the contract conditions act as the underlying contract to the project protocol, which is drawn up on a project specific basis. Accordingly the contract conditions govern liability as between the supplier and the purchaser. Clauses 7.3 and 7.4 provide that the supplier and purchaser will be responsible to the other for the direct costs, losses and expenses incurred as a result of a breach by the relevant party. Under clause 7.5, the supplier's aggregate liability under the contract may be limited to a specified sum.

Liability as between the partners

Unless the partnering arrangement is a multi-party structure, with express contractual rights of contribution, the project partners will be concerned as to their position vis-à-vis the other project partners in circumstances where, for example, the end design is a collaborative effort. The potential for the blurring of responsibility between the partners can be illustrated by an example from PPC 2000. Clause 8.2 provides:

"…each design team member shall contribute those aspects of the design of the project that fall within its role, expertise and responsibilities as stated in the partnering documents. The design team shall work together and individually in the development of an integrated design, supply and construction process for the Project…"

The difficulties presented by this type of working will be exacerbated by changes in the members of the partnering team, with new parties being allowed to join the original team, either as replacements or additional members.

Therefore the issue raised in these circumstances is if A (the client) successfully pursues B for damages in connection with a design error on B's part, then, can B look to recover some or all of the damages that it has had to pay to A by a claim for a contribution from C, his partnering team member whom B believes to have contributed to the damage caused to A?

The circumstances in which party B can claim contribution from C is governed by the Civil Liability (Contribution) Act 1978. Section 1 provides that "any person liable in respect of any damage suffered by another person may recover contribution from any other person liable in respect of the same damage (whether jointly with him or otherwise)". Where the conditions of section 1 have been satisfied, what may be due by way of contribution is assessed in accordance with s. 2(1) of the 1978 Act. This provides that the extent of the contribution is such as is "just and equitable" having regard to the extent of that person's responsibility for the damage in question." This terminology is adopted as one of the PPC 2000 options for allocation of liability discussed above on pages 249–250.

Section 1 therefore contains two prerequisites to C being compelled to make a contribution to B, namely:

• C must also be *liable* to A in respect of the damage which is the subject of A's claim against B, and
• C's breach must have contributed to the *same* damage as that for which B has been found liable to A.

Both limbs of s. 1 of the 1978 Act have been the subject of recent House of Lords guidance as how these are to be interpreted.

Looking first at liability, this was considered by the House of Lords in *Co-operative Retail Services Ltd* v. *Taylor Young Partnership Ltd and Others* [2002] 1 WLR 1419. In this case the defendants were architects and engineers. The works in respect of which the defendants were engaged were badly damaged by fire and the defendants were sued for negligence by the developer. The defendants denied negligence but sought a contribution from the contractor and subcontractor on the grounds that they also caused the fire. However, the contractor and the subcontractor were co-insured with the developer under a joint-names policy taken out to cover losses, including fire damage. On the basis of the 1978 Act, the House of Lords decided that the defendants were not entitled to a contribution from the contractor or the subcontractor. The relevant clauses in the JCT contract under which the contractor was employed, excluded any liability on the part of the contractor to the developer for losses covered by the joint-names policy. These contract clauses were reproduced in the subcontract, so that the subcontractor could not be held liable to the developer under a warranty given to the developer. It therefore followed that since neither the contractor nor the subcontractor could be held liable to the developer for the damage that occurred, the defendants could not make a claim against them for contribution.

Assuming that B can establish that C has a direct liability to A, the next proviso within the 1978 Act is that the party against whom a contribution is sought must be liable for the same damage. What therefore constitutes the "same damage"? This was considered by the House of Lords in *Royal Brompton Hospital National Health Service Trust* v. *Watkins Gray International (UK)* [2002] 1 WLR 1397. The case concerned the carrying out of major building works to the hospital. The contract overran by 43 weeks for which the architects certified an extension of time. Consequently, the employer had to pay more than £2.3m to the contractor. The employer referred the matter to arbitration to recover this sum and a similar sum by way of liquidated damages, on the basis that the extension of time should not have been granted. As the contractor was able to rely on the architect's extension of time certificate, the employer's position in the arbitration was seriously undermined and it therefore settled the arbitration with the contractor for a much lower sum. The employer then sued the architects, alleging that their negligent certification had led to it being at a disadvantage in seeking to recover its money by way of arbitration. The architects claimed contribution from the contractor.

Endorsing the conclusion reached by the Court of Appeal, the House of Lords held that the architects could not claim contribution, because the architects and the contractor's assumed liability to the employer was not liability in respect of the same damage. The contractor was potentially liable for damages for delay. The architects were potentially liable for the impairment of the employer's prospects of success in the arbitration. It was emphasised by their lordships that s. 1 of the 1978 Act refers to "damage" not "damages". The phrase "the same damage" was not to be widened so as to mean substantially or materially similar damage.

Finally, supposing C has already reached a settlement with A, who then pursues B for a shortfall in A's loss that was not covered by the settlement, does the fact of that settlement preclude a claim for contribution by B on the basis that C is no longer liable to A? From a combination of two cases, *Heaton* v. *AXA* [2002] 2 WLR 1081 and *Cape & Dalgleish* v. *Fitzgerald* (2002), unreported, it appears that C can only be protected from a contribution claim by B, if the settlement agreement between A and C clearly covers all loss. In other words, it must say that there is no further loss for A to pursue or that A has agreed not to pursue any third parties for un-recovered loss. Correspondingly, A can only continue against other parties if such continuing claims are not precluded by the language of the settlement.

Collaborative working – a breeding ground for new sources of disputes?

The substantive provisions of many of the available partnering forms seek to address the issues that are likely to cause disputes, so that for example, the partners will agree project specific quality targets thereby facilitating a "team understanding" of goals and objectives. However, what might serve to undermine these initiatives is that the substantive terms have been set within an overall framework that is apparently fraught with uncertainty. Chapter 7 has already examined the concept of good faith and how this conflicts with fundamental principles of English contract law, albeit that other jurisdictions have made inroads into the recognition of this principle. Aside from good faith, the terminology used in many of the partnering arrangements necessarily calls into question what is meant by "a spirit of mutual trust and co-operation" (the ECC Option). What is entailed in a commitment to "trust, fairness, dedication to common goals and an understanding of each other's expectations and values" (clause 4.1(i), PPC 2000)? What is the loss that flows from a failure to collaborate and how would this be measured?

From the perspective of a general debate on the development of English contract law, these are reasonable questions. However, in the context of the actual examples of partnering contracts and charters now available, the criticism that partnering terminology is too vague is to suggest that the collaborative obligations exist in a vacuum without reference as to how these obligations are worked out in practice. A tangible example of where co-operation can be translated into a measurable activity, is the obligation relating to the exchange of information.

Within the available partnering forms, the obligations relating to the provision of information include:

- In PPC 2000 clause 3.1 provides that the partnering team members are to work together and individually "to achieve transparent and co-operative exchange of information in all matters relating to the Project and to organise and integrate their activities as a collaborative team".
- The Be Collaborative Contract provides, in clause 3.1, that the supplier is to provide to the purchaser and other members of the project team, all information in its possession regarding performance of the services, which the purchaser or any other member of the project team reasonably considers relevant to the delivery of the project.
- Under the M4i, the project team leader is to ensure that information is exchanged in a timely and co-ordinated manner within the project team (clause 14).
- Under the ECC Option, partner A may ask partner B to provide information needed for partner A's work and partner B is to provide it (clause X12(2)). In addition any partner may give "advice, information and opinion" to the other partners and the core group about that partners work scope, that is to be given "openly and objectively" (clause X12(8)).
- Under the "commercial" sub-heading within the JCT non-binding Charter, the team's objective is to "provide transparency and certainty of information".

These clauses provide a practical context in which a co-operative exchange of information may be understood, and as such, seem reasonably clear. A more difficult question is the identification of the loss that would flow from a failure to co-operate and how that loss should be measured. As and when this issue arises, the outcome is likely to depend on the facts of each case. Although this exercise may be complicated, it is premature to draw the conclusion that this renders these provisions unworkable.

Non-binding charters

There is a particular issue in relation to partnering arrangements that express these undertakings in non-binding charters, such as that produced by the JCT. The BCC provides for the partners to draw up a "project protocol", which will set out the parties' joint aspirations and "how they are going to work together to achieve these aspirations". Clause 1.6 of the Be Collaborative Construction Terms provides that "The provisions of the project protocol will not create any contractual obligation and any failure to adhere to its terms will not of itself constitute a breach of this Contract".

These charters and protocols present the prospect of their being used as a tool by which to interpret the substantive provisions of the underlying contract. This seems to have been the approach of Judge Humphrey LLoyd in *Birse Construction Ltd* v. *St Davids Ltd* [1999] 4 BLR 194. (The facts of this case and extracts from the judgment are set out in Chapter 7.) This is also consistent with the general trend by the courts towards a broader view of contract interpretation, acknowledging the significance of the commercial context within which the contract has been created. A charter or protocol, which runs concurrently alongside the underlying contract, provides that commercial context. In these circumstances, the contractual doctrines of estoppel and waiver may affect the extent to which the parties are able to strictly rely upon the terms of the underlying contract.

The significance of waiver and estoppel is acknowledged in the JCT Charter. The practice note accompanying the Charter cites an extract from *Birse* and comments that

"The partnering charter does not change the terms of the underlying contract but may well affect the way the Courts will exercise their discretion or more particularly how the participants exercise their discretion. Consequently, a partnering charter may become material, albeit not entirely woven into the contract."

The practice note raises the issue of how waiver of legal rights might affect professional indemnity insurance and says further that

"Action such as waiver also creates uncertainty, which is no problem whilst the parties are prepared to resolve their own differences, but can be a major difficulty if a dispute emerges that needs resolution in arbitration or the courts."

Insurance

Of the different available forms, that which goes the furthest towards "putting the lid" on disputes is the M4i. As described above, the circumstances in which one partner can claim against another are limited. Additionally, the exclusion of liability as between the partners for various traditional heads of claim such as loss of profit provides little incentive for the parties to take an issue forward as a formal dispute given the limited scope for financial recovery. The insurance provisions support this "no blame" approach. The guidance notes for the M4i explain: "The Professional Indemnity cover should respond regardless of negligence or fault. Excesses will be borne by the Project unless the expenditure exceeds any agreed cap in which case they will be shared between the partners in the proportions set out in clauses 18 and 20." These clauses set out the agreed proportions in which rewards and liabilities are to be apportioned. However, the difficulty posed by the M4i is whether it will be possible to procure insurance cover on these terms. The policies to be taken out by the client are to cover "all interested parties as named insureds" including the client, the partners, suppliers and works contractors. This will therefore necessarily exclude provision for the subrogation of rights for the insurer to recover monies paid out given that all the parties who would have contributed to the loss are covered under the same policy of insurance.

It will be interesting to observe the extent that this contract is adopted in the partnering contracts of the future and particularly the take up of its approach to professional indemnity insurance.

CONCLUSION

This chapter has provided an overview of the various methods of dispute resolution currently provided in the published forms and has attempted briefly to consider some of the issues which will need to be addressed in resolving partnering disputes, such as the interpretation of collaborative working and the allocation of liability amongst the partners. It does not provide an exhaustive commentary of the benefits of less formalised means of resolving disputes since such a debate is not restricted to the resolution of partnering disputes in the construction industry but has a more general application in the context of dispute management generally.

Further areas where we might anticipate activity in the future will be guidance from the courts on some of the issues that arise by the nature of the parties' collaborative obligations undertaken in a partnering arrangements such as the extent to which loss can be measured following a party's alleged failure to work collaboratively and the approach that should be taken to the doctrines of estoppel and waiver referred to briefly under *Non-binding charters*, above. It will be interesting to observe how the law encompasses the challenges that will be presented by one of the industry's recommended procurement routes.

As discussed above, partnering arrangements of themselves seek to ensure that there is an early evaluation of a potential dispute and that if the dispute crystallises that it is dealt with by way of a hierarchical dispute resolution process without the need to resort to more formal proceedings. Leaving aside the potential for formalisation of a dispute through the statutory right to refer a dispute under a construction contract to adjudication at any time, the dispute resolution mechanisms in partnering arrangements focus on the management of the dispute and its resolution prior to the point where each side's position becomes entrenched. Whilst effective partnering techniques can minimise disputes, at the end of the day a partnering contract survives not only by tackling issues early but also by the relationships, and behaviour, of the parties involved. The success of any dispute resolution process in a partnering contract will ultimately depend on the spirit in which it is conducted. If the relationship between the parties is strong enough there is no reason why a dispute (and its subsequent resolution) should damage the underlying partnering arrangement.

INDEX